The Western Crisis

Peter J. Sandys

Table of Contents

Copyright

The Western Crisis
Copyright © 2025 Peter J. Sandys
(Defiance Press & Publishing, LLC)

ISBN-13: (Paperback) 978-1-963102-80-2
ISBN-13: (eBook) 978-1-963102-79-6

Published by Defiance Press & Publishing, LLC
Bulk orders of this book may be obtained by contacting Defiance Press & Publishing, LLC. www.defiancepress.com.
Defiance Press & Publishing, LLC
281-581-9300
info@defiancepress.com

To Emily, Eva, Robb, and Matthew

The only rational purpose of life is self-development —
the realization, advancement, and fulfillment of oneself —
and the understanding that the secret of happiness is
composure. Since nothing is more dangerous than the truth,
communicating recognized or perceived facts exclusively is
not only risky but also reckless. Merely knowing the truth
without possessing intelligence is no guarantee of a favorable
outcome.

Preface

I was born in Central Europe two years after the end of World War II. In the early 1970s, I fled communism by escaping to the West, specifically Italy, and applied for asylum in the United States. It was a challenging and dangerous odyssey, but had you asked me before, I would have said I would do it again enthusiastically for the price of free speech, personal freedom, and to escape from communism — the worst form of socialism — forever. Unfortunately, communist ideology is alive and well in the Western world today.

I never thought I would encounter the same mentality, ideology, and propaganda in the West by the time I retired, from which I once had fled: arrogant favoritism; reversed discrimination instead of merit-based achievement; political correctness instead of freedom of opinion; indoctrination and "influencing" instead of freedom of thought in education; and feigned justice instead of genuine fairness. Did I have the wrong map?

To think freely and speak without fear used to be worth everything — including facing death. My only wish was to raise my child in a land that would not oppress her for daring to speak out. To my horror, even the people's right to freedom of speech is in grave danger today.

It is ironic, discouraging, and very frightening that as I reached retirement age after struggling, studying, and working in the West for many decades, I should feel intimidated to express my ideas, convictions, and experiences. Indeed, by design, I should feel threatened to speak and write freely to voice my beliefs if they do not align with the officially approved ideology and political dogma.

My life has been almost evenly divided between Central and Eastern Europe (before the collapse of the leftist totalitarian system), the United States, and Western Europe. As a high school student, I had to be ideologically, politically, and socially docile and obedient even to be considered for university acceptance. As an engineering student, I had to "push the line," i.e., commit to serving the system or be bullied, threatened, and punished by my professor of Marxist philosophy in such a menacing way that I am still reluctant to engage in serious discussions with my left-leaning peers.

The ideological-political experience gained at the University of California and a Jesuit-run university in Los Angeles was somewhat different but not significantly better. While there, I first recognized the similarities between the Christian church and its modern-day replacement, socialism. I could not fully conform ideologically, politically, and culturally or feel free to express my cautiously traditional and guardedly bourgeois opinion in a liberal-democratic America either. Nevertheless, I was aware of the emigrant's fate: the foreign land does not become his homeland — instead, his homeland becomes foreign.

Moreover, I could hardly cope any better in Western Europe. The last third of my life has been spent in Austria and Germany, and, not unexpectedly, I quickly discovered a dormant but overpowering feeling of fear and coercion regarding what one says if one holds "non-progressive" beliefs in European society. Left-leaning citizens are outspoken, threatening, intimidating, passively aggressive, and rude because they see traditional, "conservative" opinions as personally offensive and a menace to their socialist worldview of being a victim.

I am a naturalized U.S. citizen retired in Germany, a happenstance that occurred due to the ironic circumstances of my life. Indeed, I do not arrogantly tout my innate national-conservative and "illiberal" values or my instinctive love of individualism, self-help, and personal responsibility in a country where most natives believe in their already enlightened and progressive conditions — and I have learned that the natives are "always right."

The liberal-democratic Western world's policy has been "provocative containment" of the fast-developing non-Western world ever since the First Cold War. The implicit enemy is any country that does not subscribe to the left-radical, pseudo-democratic, fake-capitalist, multicultural, socially engineered, and monopolistic one-world ideology of the West. Such a "rogue state" would be politically, economically, or militarily provoked, intimidated, embargoed, sanctioned, boycotted, and excluded from the deceptively called "community of nations." Meanwhile, the "lucky societies" of the righteous, freedom-loving, liberal-democratic, and morally infallible West, fighting for human rights, equality, social justice, and more, are de facto lost, confused, and disoriented, in addition to being split and divided. But our noble opinion makers keep telling us that the West must contain all illiberal, national-conservative, "no-good" democracies. According to these thought influencers, all Chinese provocations — such as those concerning Taiwan, the East China Sea, the South China Sea (why are they even called "China Seas" if they belong to other countries?), the New Silk Road, and the Indian border clashes — and Russian aggression in Ukraine and Syria, threats against the Baltic States, or the construction of the Nord Stream 2 pipeline, demonstrate the hostile intent of these two main adversaries.

"We," on the other hand, must show the world our superior values, humanity, and culture while our fair and always unbiased media gallantly defend free speech and opinion, human rights, and social justice — always in other countries, of course, never at home. However, the West should not expect a democratic China because if it became a liberal democracy, Chinese society would collapse. That is precisely why the West is trying hard to push the country in that direction. The West has never understood the meaning of "integrating socialism with local conditions" in non-Western lands — meaning national independence.

For the U.S., the right strategy concerning China should begin at home: Washington must support a genuinely knowledge-building education sector, protect U.S. intellectual property from espionage and theft, and regain the admiration, respect, and friendship of people worldwide — an uphill battle against hypocrisy. So long as the U.S. addresses its real problems at home and holds tight to its practical instead of idealistic, missionary, or hypocritical values, i.e., the culture of deceit, it can manage China's rise. But if it cannot do that, China will certainly not constitute America's most significant problem.

Our righteous and infallible leaders are always in the process of clearing the road for the next "war of liberation" to defend Western values, fairness, the rule of law, and social justice. The planes are on the runways and aircraft carriers are in position, though the people must still be turned around — like in WWI and WWII — so expect some more "unprovoked attacks."

With the Western "allies" fighting another hopeless and reckless war for their typical values in Afghanistan for more than a decade now (longer than in World War II but without a victory in sight), the Taliban controls more of the country than the United States and its NATO allies combined. What are the alleged terrorists, jihadists, and radical Islamists fighting for? What are the goals of al-Qaeda, Boko Haram, and the Taliban? They all want foreign troops, the alien Western culture, and its infidel faith out of their lands, and they all seek the overthrow of regimes that collaborate with the West. All wish to establish their systems that comply with the Prophet's commands. That is what they are recruiting for, killing for, and dying for. We hate their terror tactics and deplore their aims, but they know their goals at home, in their own countries. Do we know what we want in ours? Do we know what we are doing to our land and people?

The Founding Fathers' America died in the Civil War. The unraveling of its mutation, a country without a nation, began at least a hundred years ago. The dissolving process started accelerating about sixty years ago but was first openly, directly, and honestly discussed merely four years ago. None too soon, to be sure, but likely in vain.

The U.S. is no longer a constitutional state ruled by law. Black Lives Matter wants to see blood, and the government will give it to them to keep the country calm. I think that many white citizens — reluctantly, to be sure — would eventually leave the country, as many colonists did during and after the American Revolution. However, where would they go? There is no sane place to have a new home in the Western world today.

I would phrase it this way: there is no national consensus on the nature of the current events that define the United States of America. This lack of consensus is, arguably, modern America's greatest failure as a non-nation. It is true; the U.S. has long managed to get through this flaw. Her civic narrative, i.e., the arrogance of ignorance, has proven powerful but false, attractive but Disney-like, popular but hypocritical, missionary but idealistic. A self-declared free people struggle to extend their imaginary liberties to those who do not yet enjoy them, a union offering everyone equal rights and a fair shot — first based on Christian principles and ending in secular socialism. A contradictory past had once betrayed itself in a Civil War, and American society has not recovered to this day. The unanswered question is whether there is a way out.

With lawlessness, chaos, terror, anarchy, disorderly conduct, destruction, looting, and more in the cities of America and the West, where is the law? Where is the state? Where are the "law enforcement agencies"? Of course, they are all busy sanctioning other countries. These are all signs of a degenerate, decaying, and life-weary society suffering from self-inflicted damage.

The "System" gave, and the "System" has not taken it away — yet. What is the point of complaining if the "System" makes all this possible? Change the "System" (good luck) or those who created or maintain it (if you can). Oh yes, I forgot, it is too late now; we must live with it. Oh, well then. It reminds me of the "real" Hollywood, where people want to hear fake stories of the "truth" or real stories about lies. In any case, it pays.

Modern liberalism is a euphemism for *freedom simulators*; democracy is a euphemism for *camouflaged entrapment*; and liberal democracy is a euphemism for *subversive deceit*. Living in a Western socialist dictatorship called liberal democracy is where injustice becomes law, and resistance becomes a right. And what are liberalism and socialism if not secularized Christianity?

Anti-American, leftist intellectuals have led the Western world for decades — with some rare exceptions. They are globalist ideologists spreading their messianic messages in an ever-changing mélange of various shades of democracy, socialism, liberalism, and conservatism. The leftist political parties have gained the support of the Western intellectual "elites," who merely perform the intermediary role of disseminating "progressive" ideas. This intellectual class of globalists consists of more groups and professions than journalists, teachers, ministers, lecturers, publicists, radio and television commentators, writers, cartoonists, or artists — it also includes political and business leaders. They all are masters of the technique of expressing and conveying ideas but are usually amateurs as far as the essence of what they say is concerned. However, that does not seem to be a problem — their handlers know better.

A Western, left-liberal, and woke civilization hides behind "democracy," "equality," and righteous ideology, while non-Western, non-liberal, and national-conservative nation-states promote independence and traditional moral values. It is an ideological and cultural conflict, not simply "democracy vs. autocracy."

Not $1.9 trillion or even $19 trillion can change the dying culture of a decaying, lawless, and life-weary society — such materialistic, ephemeral energy shots are like morphine "curing" terminal cancer. The desperate struggle of a globalist-imperialist civilization hiding behind "democracy," "equality," and left-liberal ideology against national-conservative nations defending their independence and traditional moral values will last until the winner's declaration of victory is generally acknowledged. Until then, the media will be spewing out their falsehoods full-time.

From the Western perspective, there are no enemies on the left — China is a particular case since it has always been an unsolvable enigma for the West. The enemy is always on the right. And because reality contradicts this central tenet of liberal ideology, it cannot ever be conceded — only deliberately confused.

I am unhappy with the endless and increasingly religious climate babble, fantasies about the energy transition, worship of electric cars, and alarming stories about doomsday scenarios from COVID-19 to conflagrations to weather disasters. I cannot stand the people who shout this into microphones and cameras or print it in newspapers every day, and I suffer from seeing how they have turned science into a tool of politics.

I am tired of abused adolescent children telling me what to be ashamed of and what to regret. I am disgusted by the notion that I am to blame for everything and everyone, but above all, as a white man of European origin, for the whole world's past, present, and future misery.

I am annoyed by racial, religious, national, gender, sexual, or linguistic minorities who shamelessly exploit their well-established minority rights with constant media support and want to dictate what I can and cannot do and say.

I resent it when misguided people mess up even the languages I speak and think they must teach me how to write and speak in a politically acceptable, woke, or mainstream way.

I am appalled by how uneducated individuals, who have done nothing except carry someone else's briefcase, believe they can govern a country.

I can no longer bear it when, under the pretext of a "diverse society," law and security disappear, and when you come out of a train station or subway station in the evening and must navigate heaps of dirt, filth, homeless people, drug addicts, and thieves while passing walls covered in graffiti and scrawl.

I want the people in my country to be valued and supported, regardless of gender, color, religion, or origin. They produce the wealth of society with their knowledge, experience, diligent, productive, and value-adding work: the employees of companies, the artisans, the freelancers, and the committed and socially active entrepreneurs of small and medium-sized businesses. I expect our children's teachers, doctors and nurses, workers, and farmers to receive the recognition, appreciation, and support they deserve daily. I want the young, impetuous, and idealistic to let off steam within the clear-cut boundaries of their legal space but also to bow to their parents and grandparents, the elderly and experienced, because they are the creators of their wealth, freedom, and future.

If one can believe the mainstream media and elite educators, I am a reactionary, a grump, a curmudgeon, an out-of-date, dyed-in-the-wool fuddy-duddy, and more: I am also privileged, racist, bigoted, misogynistic, homophobic, transphobic, and just about everything-phobic. I am also a snob, a white supremacist, and just a plain nasty specimen of humanity. Yes, I am a man who marches to a different drum; I look at facts, not propaganda, and assess truth according to a higher standard than yesterday's trends and tomorrow's fashions. I, an engineer, even question the assumptions of science and the trickery of technology.

In other words, I push against the pillars of modern techno-political power structures. I resent the unthinking reliance on technology and refuse to "follow the science." Instead, I call for simplicity and prefer a life centered on ideas about a more humane economy based on home and family rather than the office and the marketplace. I endorse a retreat from the non-stop lies of the public mass media and entertainment industries and encourage picking up reading, writing, and learning an instrument instead. But I also reject the idiocy of modern conservatism with its marriage to unrestrained consumerism and internationalism.

Men lost their health when they lost meaningful work on the land, costing them their freedom and independence. Today, they settle for "fitness" and "wellness." However, the gym culture produces only fake masculinity — all muscles and fragile machismo. I call for rugged individuals like Teddy Roosevelt, who loved the great outdoors and the fresh air. I am against the deranged modern world in which we find ourselves. We depend on mortgages, jobs, gym memberships, Netflix, and social media.

My traditionalism may inspire others to get married, have many kids, choose country living, thrive, build a better future, and raise hearty children who know how to survive in the wasteland of modernity.

I promote a responsible, merit-based aristocracy instead of a mob-driven, politically correct system that smartly serves the unknown and invisible rulers, for such is the current order disguised as "democracy." Its policies and practices promote a mob mentality and lead to the takeover of the United States — if not the entire Western world — politically, socially, culturally, and intellectually, compelled by ideologically and politically correct propaganda. Every country gets the politicians it deserves; after all, it elected them democratically. As ye sow, so shall ye reap — especially if ye refuse to pluck out the weeds.

Only a fool or a pretender believes that we can or should learn nothing from our elders. We must see history as the science of the past, allowing us to learn from humanity's collective experience over many centuries. The great works of the classics are magnificent expressions of that collective inheritance, which reveals the truth of the *permanent things* and the truth about us reflected in those *permanent things*. Reading the classics, studying history, and remembering our traditions liberate us from the prejudices of the fads and mindsets of our time and connect us with the bedrock realities of what it is to be fully human.

History and tradition allow us to evaluate the present from the perspective of the distant past. Today is always grounded in yesterday because the preceding culture influences it — this rootedness makes life part of a *continuum of culture*. Any contemporary culture that tries to ignore the past is fatally flawed by embracing the shallow and superficial. In refusing the life-giving roots of tradition, such a culture will wither and die within a few years because fashions are always coming and going — and mostly going. A healthy culture, rooted in the perennial aspects of humanity, has a shelf life measured in centuries, not months or a few years.

Humanity does not develop linearly, reaching a peak in the end. We are imperfect creatures, and there will never be paradisiacal conditions. We must appreciate the institutions and norms that history has created for us with which we can live and work. Therefore, we should not condescendingly judge or condemn historical figures, such as Napoleon Bonaparte, for whatever they did or did not do from a distance of hundreds of years. Yes, Napoleon marched to Moscow, only to lose hundreds of thousands of men, his crown, glory, and esteem, but he was undoubtedly one of history's most outstanding political and military leaders. Napoleon also left a wide-ranging and powerful impact on the modern world and brought liberal reforms to the Netherlands, Switzerland, Italy, and Germany. He implemented liberal policies in France and throughout Western Europe. Napoleon championed, consolidated, codified, and geographically extended the Napoleonic Code, as well as the ideas of meritocracy, equality before the law, religious toleration, modern secular education, property rights, and sound finances. A rational and efficient local administration, the termination of the bloody revolution, the abolition of feudalism, the encouragement of science and the arts, and the most significant codification of laws since the fall of the Roman Empire were just a few of the achievements of the man who never recoiled from assuming responsibility for his actions.

Contemporary Western liberal democracy neither assigns responsibility to its leaders nor holds them accountable for their actions — instead, it merely spinelessly criticizes the past vanguard. Of course, not all sovereigns are great leaders, but all great leaders rule sovereignly.

Violence is inherent in man. The use of force in international relations has been present in all epochs, civilizations, and geographic spaces. It remains indifferent to the drivel of "democratic peace" theorists.

However, the left-liberal "just war theory," combining abstract principles with political prudence, will inevitably, if not deliberately, lead to confusion and disorientation. A supposedly "just war" is directed by "universal" missionary ideals, but it can only naively be thought of as mediated by practical considerations.

For a country such as the U.S., unhappily dedicated to abstract truth, "theoretically just causes" cannot inevitably call for military intervention. The United States is neither a mere abstraction nor has it been a nation for a long time now, if ever. The U.S. has borders, interests, and conflicts with others in a fallen world.

But how could American statecraft reconcile the mistaken commitment to missionary universalism with the temporal conditions in which the country finds itself? By intellectualizing the "just war theory" and politicizing moral obligations according to left-liberal globalists as opposed to illiberal nationalists? Because the Locke-Wilson-Bush path directly led to the "everlasting foreign wars" with all their "just causes," color revolutions, nation-building, prevention of human rights violations, etc. — without the understanding and consent of the American people. And what can these "just causes" for foreign wars show for the cost paid and the sacrifice suffered?

A prudent foreign policy based on objective national interest, instead of lacking a shared conception, would sound very good. However, modern liberals, leftist sympathizers, and progressive intellectuals are not known for their deep humility. Indeed, they have repeatedly exhibited a total lack of restraint, caution, or foresight in foreign policy, among many other areas. They have commandeered the U.S. to run on the same tracks, with the same missionary zeal, and in the same direction the Soviet train passed a few decades ago. The question is whether America can still find a switch to avoid hitting a hard, non-theoretical stop at the end. The hurled and heavy millstone flies, but who knows where it will land or whom it will strike?

Being incapable or unwilling to understand and accept other people's views, cultures, traditions, and experiences will lead one to consider them "thugs" or worse. Moreover, this unfortunate attitude fosters rabid hatred and makes one a tool of blind propaganda — in the name of "human rights," of course. It is such a waste.

As a "morale officer for dissenters," I ask myself what I hope to accomplish by writing about ideas the Left would either ignore or demonize. My answer is to enlighten and encourage those who would otherwise consider the Left's teachings indisputable and inevitable. It is not to deny that the Left currently wields enormous political and cultural power, and leftist dominance has become so intense that many see no need to debate conservative viewpoints or respond to conservative arguments. Instead, the Left often seeks to fire or ban the people presenting traditional ideas by declaring them a form of "hate," thus marking them as dangerous to even know about, much less advocate.

There is no more obvious example that leftist ideology is neither irrefutable nor inevitable than Viktor Orbán's Hungary today. Under Mr. Orbán, Hungary has managed to increase its birth rate, secure its borders, stop the flow of propaganda advocating homosexuality and gender fluidity, and counteract the influence of billionaire George Soros, the activist instigator and principal agitator for a borderless West. Mr. Orbán believes that his most important task is preserving his country and its people, and the above actions improve Hungary's chance of remaining Hungarian.

The thought that Mr. Orbán's Hungarian success might help build a new American Right focused on preserving the U.S. and its people rather than a set of abstract propositions is more than a bevy of neocons and fellow travelers can bear. They repeatedly assert that Hungary is not a free country because Hungarians fear publicly expressing their views. They claim that Mr. Orbán has destroyed media, crushed academic freedom, and created the most anti-Semitic country in Europe. They even allege that American conservatives who see anything Hungarian worth emulating are "anti-American." They keep repeating that Mr. Orbán is the "ultimate twenty-first-century dictator" and a "fake Christian."

Most of these allegations are blazingly senseless, desperate, and false. Any country willing to listen to the creators of these accusations is already in or will soon be in a deficient condition, as indeed America has been since it heeded their advice, and from which plight it may never recover.

But it is worth noting that the modern pseudo-conservatives, modern Republicans, and neoliberals have been content to whine ineffectually about leftist control of the academy and the media for many years. The problem has only worsened during decades of grumbling and moaning. Mr. Orbán has wrested control of much of the media and some of the academy from the Left, and it is precisely his success in defying and challenging the Left that angers the left-liberal, socialist, neoliberal, and neoconservative intellectuals, not the state control of the media or the academy.

One faces consequences for not supporting the ruling Western ideology or for disagreeing with radical leftists. These repercussions occur at colleges, universities, mainstream media outlets, and other public or government institutions serving as mouthpieces of the ruling Left across the Western world. That is the real pandemic — the indoctrination they are spreading.

The ruling elites and their minions regularly look the other way when non-progressives suffer marginalization. The establishment claims to support diversity, but it rejects the diversity of thought.

However, they will never silence, intimidate, or ridicule me — I have come far, fought hard, and experienced too much to surrender.

Peter J. Sandys
Memmingen, Germany
Winter 2021

Chapter 1

The Decline of the Western World

"Western civilization" and related terms such as "the West" are increasingly present in public debate and discourse. The eruption of demonstrations, violence, protests, and civil disorder in the United States and other Western countries has caused some, including myself, to claim that we see the fast-approaching end of "the West." Nevertheless, "the West" lacks a precise definition of Western civilization.

Before turning to more upbeat descriptions of "Western civilization," some common misconceptions about "the West" must be addressed, and I will categorize them as misconceptions from the Left and misunderstandings from the Right.

Thinkers, writers, activists, and journalists of the political and cultural Left often characterize "the West" as a civilization perpetuating a series of injustices. In other words, its evils define Western society, and the concept itself denotes a racist colonial undertaking to subdue, change, enslave, eradicate, or genocidally erase different cultures. To these leftist intellectuals, to "civilize" is a verb that divorces people from the values of their community and indoctrinates them into another's — but isn't that like the current globalist efforts vis-à-vis the "illiberal" nation-states? Historical rhetoric judges the "civilized" Westerner as superior to the dehumanized "savages," "beasts," "primitives," and "barbarians" of the term's late 18th–19th-century everyday use.

According to this framework, the West manifests and preserves economic injustice (feudalism, capitalism, unemployment), social injustice (patriarchy and racism), sexual injustice (repression of LGBTQ people and patriarchy again), and religious injustice (Christianity). I could characterize this position as defining the West by every negative cultural and political feature of the Eurasian continent's Western parts. In short, Western civilization is both oppressive and repressive.

Conversely, the West's distorted picture comes from some corners of the political and cultural Right defining the West in idealistic and ideological terms. These right-wing dreamers have a white, Anglo-Teutonic understanding of Western culture and often admire philosophers such as Herbert Spencer, Nietzsche, or Heidegger, as well as composers like Richard Wagner. The West possesses a sense of the beautiful, aesthetic, cultivated, and refined, as seen in grand castles, elegant monarchs, dramatic scenes depicted in paintings of European glory, and magnificent opera overtures (opera usually gets put in the corner of the Right).

However, one could argue that the West is an aesthetic for both the Right and the Left. For the Left, the West represents a history of past and present oppression, embodied in the Ugly. Leftists delight in tearing down the West as associated with anything they dislike. For the Right, the West embodies a sense of already lost grandeur, illustrated in the fading Beauty. They praise the West for anything they appreciate. Therefore, both sides utilize the West for their political agendas.

The concept of "the West" is multifaceted and often misunderstood. It is not a monolithic entity but a complex interplay of various cultures, histories, and ideologies. The notion of a brutal, ever-oppressive, inhuman, patriarchal, and unjust West, as portrayed by leftist social justice warriors, is a fiction in their minds. Indeed, the West has perpetrated grave injustices, and Western civilization may have been patriarchal — along with every other culture and society in history. However, to suggest that oppression and injustice are primary markers of Western civilization is reductionistic and simplistic.

Similarly, the view of Europe as a grand and glorious white monarchical Christian civilization — with knights in shining armor riding through picturesque pastures to meet the approaching barbarian hordes — all to the soundtrack of Wagner's *Rienzi* or *Tannhäuser* overture — is a romanticized view. However, the civilization that emerged after the fifth century in Western Europe was the site of humanity's many great triumphs, such as the Renaissance, the Enlightenment, and the Industrial Revolution. There is something truly inspiring about the dynamics and cultural achievements of Western civilization over the past two millennia.

Neither of the two unadulterated "Wests" has existed: the purely and brutally oppressive or the purely paleo-Greek, knightly-Christian West. An unhealthy aesthetic nostalgia, characterized by a romanticized and idealized view of the past, has driven both sides' interpretations. This nostalgia often overlooks or downplays the complexities and contradictions of Western civilization, leading to a distorted understanding of its history and culture. It is crucial to approach the study of the West without ideological bias to truly understand its complexities.

Can we conceive of a Western civilization without ideological terms or romantic aesthetic nostalgia? How can we frame it in depoliticized and realistic terms? Should we consider the religion-inspired dynamism and spiritual vitality provided by the Christian Church, or the Greek emphasis on philosophy and reason while highlighting human achievement for excellence? How about the medieval Christianity that suppressed the human spirit until the Renaissance and Enlightenment finally brought humanism to triumph over the irrational? That perspective could even be labeled "rationalist," emphasizing human reason as a shaper of Western culture and identity.

Perhaps in the synthesis of "Ego" and "Soul," the Ego represents the individualistic drive for self-expression and achievement, while the Soul symbolizes a sense of transcendence and divine order, which together form the essence of Western civilization. The West is the civilization that incorporates and encourages the innate drive to create meaning for ourselves and transcend our limits.

Does Western civilization rely on the triad of Greek, Hebraic-Christian, and Roman sources?

The synthesis of these roots, ideas, and themes is evident in the West, which is marked less by what it positively asserts to the world and more by its stance toward outside influences. Of course, its method of incorporating external elements can define the West; for example, the Romans' openness to the external influences of Greek and Christian sources, such as the adoption of Greek philosophy and Christian ethics. Its "Romans" characterize the West, using content from beyond its people, culture, and time that is internally transmitted and assimilated. Another way of summarizing this is that the West is notable for its interest in "otherness."

In any case, the challenge of pinning down a conception of Western civilization is a distinctly Western dilemma, and a precise solution will remain eternally elusive. The importance of Christianity is clear, especially if we consider the inclusion of the Hebraic civilization from which it emerged. Despite the shortcomings of the rationalist framework, Greek human reason is significant for understanding the West. A third inescapable aspect is "Roman character," since the West's traditional disposition is essentially Roman in its willingness to be at least partially open to and engage, within limits, with influences beyond its ethnonational cultural borders. Unfortunately, the current trajectory of Western society and civilization, marked by philosophical, ideological, and political polarization, sharply diverges from the Roman — and directly toward the Judeo-Greek inclination.

Christianity, a religion that transcends ethnic and cultural boundaries, has significantly shaped the Western mindset toward "otherness." It is not an imperialist force but a supra-cultural system of beliefs that has historically sought to be spread, adopted, and adapted into existing cultures. The historical record demonstrates its transformative power, underscoring its profound societal influence.

This path to cultural influence is evident in how Western civilization perceives its culture spreading to other places. Accordingly, Western culture is, by definition, neither monolithic nor imperialist but something that can be accepted and integrated into different contexts. Non-Western countries, e.g., Japan, South Korea, and Taiwan, do not need to become culturally Western to be influenced by Western culture. In short, the Western disposition is open to exchange and renewal. But the exchange can go both ways. The Western mind and culture are ready to welcome influences from the outside and can accept other ideas being adopted and adapted.

Intellectual curiosity and openness to the unfamiliar and the "other" characterize the Western mindset. This description does not imply blind acceptance of all encountered ideas but rather a willingness to consider them thought-provoking and potentially enriching for Western formation. This historical approach to culture has yielded the rich intellectual and cultural diversity that the Western world cherishes today.

Every society wants to survive in the world and, simultaneously, seeks partnership in the human order. In other words, human communities seek an organized way to live in reality. People seek an objective order; the struggle to find it is their struggle for truth. As societies advance toward the truth, replacing one another over time, each one exceeds itself and becomes a partner in the joint endeavor of humanity to live in the given order. Faith in this given order is a marker of the West and allows Western civilization to reach across its boundaries in search of truth. This confidence assures the West that it is one of many civilizations with access to the human condition and experience. The wisdom of Western civilization is the knowledge that human understanding is free from constraints of our own time and place. Therefore, we can seek the truth because it is out there; we can reach out and find it because there is an order and a reality somewhere beyond us.

Other distinctive features of Western civilization include the eminence of human nature and the importance of the human condition in Western philosophical and cultural works. Of course, different cultures also ask questions about the human predicament, but demonstrably, the West's probing led to Athens and Jerusalem.

Western civilization marks a particular approach to the human condition. The problematization of human nature, emphasizing the human predicament, is approached from two perspectives in the West: Greek rationalism and Christian mystery — or the viewpoints of the "Ego" and "Soul."

The "Greek approach," a philosophical tradition of ancient Greece, and the Hebrew Bible, a different method acknowledging the depths of despair and the crisis of the human condition, are significant in shaping the Western path to understanding the human condition. The former emphasizes self-understanding, resilience, and action, while the latter recognizes the mystery surrounding and permeating reality. Understanding these approaches is crucial to our analysis.

The struggle between different approaches to reality is fundamental to the Western path to the human condition. It refers to the tension between the "revealed" and the "knowable." The "revealed" represents what is known or understood, while the "knowable" refers to what can be known or understood. This tension suggests that what we can see or understand is not the final answer, and what we can rationally define is not the conclusion. Instead, practical and accessible reality, shrouded in mystery and darkness, marks the Western examination of human life.

The set of conceptual features that provide a framework for assessing what belongs to the West includes elements such as democracy, individualism, and the rule of law. This framework prevents unnecessary dogmatism and allows for a nuanced understanding of Western civilization, which, while remaining problematic, can be renewed through careful reflection.

Revitalizing Western civilization's Christian, Greek, and Roman roots is crucial, but I propose that integrating outside sources, particularly elements of Russian and Asian cultures, could be key to its renewal. Retrieving these sources and examining the texts and ideas that shaped the Western imagination could strengthen the ailing culture of the West, offering a hopeful path forward.

The Western view of the human condition is both revealed and mysterious. It suggests that human nature does not change, yet the world around us does. This view implies that discovering new sources of Western culture should be an exercise in helping the West face an ever-changing world by adapting its understanding of human nature to these changes.

During the bad old days of the Cold War, the threat of nuclear conflict engulfing the world in an apocalyptic inferno was ever-present, with atomic arsenals on a hair trigger. This period of intense ideological and political tension profoundly impacted the Western path to understanding the human condition, shaping its perceptions of power, conflict, and the potential for global catastrophe.

The Convergence Theory was one of the most intriguing ideas about alternatives to species committing suicide over opposing ideologies and values — socialism versus liberal democracy and capitalism — complemented by differing interpretations of freedom and equality. This theory, which drew in some of the brightest minds in the West and East, including the Soviet nuclear physicist turned human rights dissident Andrei Sakharov (TIME Essay, 1970), suggested that societies generally become more similar as they develop economically. In the context of the Cold War, it offered some hope for a more peaceful and cooperative future between East and West, potentially influencing the Western path to understanding the human condition.

According to Convergence Theory, societies generally become more similar as they develop economically. That may seem simplistic, but in the context of the Cold War, it offered some hope. While Cold Warriors were preoccupied with the differences between killing and being killed for something, convergence theorists noted that East and West, communism and liberal democracy, were not so different at all. Both camps, the opposite poles, featured urban societies with hydrocarbon-based industries and significant bureaucracy, although the nature of those bureaucratic systems depended on which side of the Iron Curtain one was on. Although both sides claimed to uphold Enlightenment values, they could not agree on what that meant. The two blocs embraced industry, technology, expertise, and propaganda — and believed in "progress."

Ultimately, the convergence theorists of those days presumed that the two hostile systems would evolve enough to become more similar and compatible. Consequently, they would recognize their commonalities and seek to resolve their remaining differences amicably.

However, before they could prove the validity of this hypothesis, the Soviet Union first retreated from the Cold War and shortly afterward abolished itself. Ironically, some of the ideas that had influenced the policies of Soviet reform, such as those inspired by Convergence Theory, unintentionally triggered the communist collapse. This unexpected turn of events had a pervasive impact on the Western path to the human condition, reshaping its understanding of power, ideology, and the potential for radical political change.

At that time, convergence was a distant dream; the situation had diverged to the extreme: The West was thriving while the East was withering away. China, as usual, was disregarded or condemned. In its Hegelian interpretation, history spoke to those who rushed to conclusions. The West's model of liberal democracy, propelled by the controlled capitalism of a managerial society, not only emerged victorious but was deemed the only path to the future for all.

Moral and Cultural Decline

Today, a third of a century later, the world under Western management has not been a resounding success. Democracy, once thought to be the heart of modern Western civilization, is in a precarious state, threatened by rampant economic inequality, state ineffectiveness, the disillusionment of many, the myopia of globalizing oligarchies enriched and empowered as never before, and the corresponding rise of national conservatism and populism. Contrary to expectations, global international relations suffer less from breaking the rules than from their total absence. Regulations and laws only hold when consistently followed and applied to everyone equally. However, we do not live in that kind of world but in one where there seems to be only one reliable standard: rules are made for geopolitical and ideological opponents, while friends, often those in power, can do pretty much what they want without significant consequences.

We live in a Western world that may be dying — or, more precisely, committing a drawn-out suicide. Presumably, the powerful and wealthy will always find ways to navigate the authoritarian politics that come with self-made emergencies.

In any case, the first post-Cold War order has failed miserably, mainly in the hands of a temporarily elevated yet long-lasting, manipulative but complacent, globalist yet introspective West. This clearly shows that the current Western approach, still influential, arrogant, and firmly entrenched in the perceived but fictitious victory of the Cold War, is not sustainable for managing the world peacefully. This book calls for a change in the Western approach that we cannot afford to ignore.

It was sheer ignorance to misunderstand the collapse of Soviet Bolshevism as proof of the viability of the West's left-liberal democracy. From where we are today, it almost appears as if, with a slight but historically insignificant delay, the ideologies of the Cold War East and Cold War West, once considered starkly different, are, after all, converging. If only in failure, this convergence suggests a shared inability to effectively address societal and political challenges.

Western civilization has sunk to a depth where the restatement of the obvious is considered heresy. We must engage in critical reflection and reevaluate our traditional disposition, which is essentially Roman in its willingness to be at least partially open and engage with influences within limits beyond its ethnonational and cultural borders. The current societal and civilizational problems may arise from the recent Western course that points sharply away from the Romans and directly toward the Judeo-Greek predilection.

The diagnosis of self-deception is particularly apt regarding the Right in Europe and the U.S., which persist in asserting that our world, while imperfect, is one where the West remains dominant and capable of self-reinvention. However, the reality is starkly different. The rise of China as an economic powerhouse, the increasing influence of non-Western cultures in global affairs, and the erosion of Western values within our societies are all clear signs of the decline of the Western world. Conservative institutions, advocacy groups, think tanks, and proponents of civic nationalism, in their denial of these facts, advocate for legislative and bureaucratic solutions to cultural and civilizational challenges. To them, any suggestion that Western power and hypocrisy mask underlying decay and vulnerability seems like paleo-reactionary propaganda and unpatriotic defeatism.

For over a century, there have been warnings about the peril of Western civilization from philosophers, political scientists, theologians, and others — mainly disbelievers in "progress" and the improvability of man. These are not just idle speculations, but credible insights backed by a wealth of evidence. All those questioners — at least since Oswald Spengler published his *Decline of the West* in 1918 — have used a massive amount of evidence to point out that ours are abnormal times, characterized by the breakdown of moral norms and civilizational standards throughout the entire Western world (Spengler, 2021). The malaise is magnified in our own time by the metastatic growth of self-hatred throughout the West.

Over the past decades, the crisis of the American sociopolitical system has not just matured, but has reached a boiling point, with increasingly frequent manifestations of acute dysfunctionality. This process is not just a trend but a dangerous spiral, demonstrated primarily in the legitimization of violence, the perversion of the "democratic process," the imposition and acceptance of crude forms of censorship, and the criminalization of words, thoughts, and actions deemed unacceptable by the ruling establishment and its cohorts in the media, Big Tech, the academic world, and Hollywood.

There is a palpable sense that the current state of affairs will eventually result in a significant and lasting rearrangement of the world's geopolitical map. This shift has already occurred along the western rimland of Eurasia, with the European Union morphing from a potential actor in its own right into an American bridgehead composed of nominally sovereign countries stripped of substantial decision-making powers. The globalists are preparing a ghastly new order.

Much of Europe is not just changing; it is being transformed politically, culturally, and demographically into a sad caricature of its former self, and its southern maritime border is as open as the U.S. border with Mexico. Europe's "secular hierocracy" is not just focused; it is obsessed with reforming and reshaping its subjects' conscience to accept multiracial, multicultural, multigender, and anti-national self-annihilation as a set of beliefs, attitudes, and mandatory policies.

Consequently, the Old Continent is increasingly populated by non-natives, foreigners, and illegal aliens physically residing in Berlin, Toulon, Naples, or Leeds, but spiritually in Anatolia, Punjab, East Africa, or the Maghreb. First, they are often desperate to get to Europe, but once they arrive, settle there, and start receiving social benefits, they seek to reproduce the cultural environments of their unpleasant native lands in their new home. Scornful of the hosts' culture-war pursuits of "tolerance" and "diversity," their disdain remains unappeased by servile concessions.

Today's "United Europe" is far from the reasonably decent community of nations that existed before 1914. The European Union (EU) does not create social and civilizational commonalities except through the wholesale denial of authentically European standards and values. The result is a dreary, lifeless, disingenuous culture of manipulative "anti-discriminationism," genderism, and anti-Christian veneration of Otherness.

Even after Brexit, the controllers of the EU machinery have not given up on their Superstate Project; they seek to obliterate the identities, cultures, traditions, histories, and uniqueness of European nations. They see national elections as a nuisance that throws reactionary-sovereignist spanners into their works, such as imposing mandatory Muslim immigrant quotas on each member country. Their obsessions, which merely two generations ago would have been deemed eccentric, bizarre, or mad, now dominate the Western mainstream.

The Western intellectual elite has abandoned the promotion of lasting civilizational values and allowed short-term political preferences to distort its understanding of the academic vocation. In the 1920s, intellectuals discarded their regard for traditional philosophical and scholarly ideals, venerating particularisms and moral relativism instead. The new professional-managerial elites — lawyers, media commentators, influencers, academic experts, think-tank analysts, financial planners, etc. — have become detached from the organic growth and evolution of communities. They exist in an abstract world of manipulating information inputs and figures, generating a unique, strongly ideological form of political discourse. Their secularism, moral and cultural relativism, and rejection of any sense of attachment to the broader community highlight their disconnect.

The leaders of major corporations harbor a vision of a world without nations, where they can operate without being accountable to any country or society. They actively work against national sovereignty, meticulously dismantling it piece by piece, following the Gramscian theme. This corporate-driven globalism should raise alarm bells everywhere.

In the same spirit, Bill Clinton's one-time Deputy Secretary of State, Strobe Talbott, famously declared shortly after leaving office that the United States would not exist "in its current form" in the 21st century because even the concept of nationhood would become obsolete (Talbott, *America Abroad: The Birth of the Global Nation*, 1992). Mr. Talbott declared in 1992 and repeated in his 2008 book, *The Great Experiment*, that in the 21st century, "nationhood as we know it will be obsolete; all states will recognize a single, global authority," and "all countries are social arrangements, accommodations to changing circumstances. No matter how permanent and even sacred they may seem at any one time, they are all artificial and temporary" (Talbott, The Great Experiment, 2008).

The members of the Western elite class have no loyalty to any country or nation. They seek to mold deracinated and brainwashed masses into a postmodern socio-technological system regulated by themselves. Their plan rests on the dictum that lands do not belong to those people whose ancestors have inhabited and developed them for generations; they belong to all who happen to be within their boundaries at any given moment. "Enlightened and progressive persons" must not feel obligated to any group except for allegedly underprivileged minorities.

Accordingly, these elite members of Western society actively promote self-destruction, encourage the self-hate of Caucasians, and demonize all white male heterosexuals. They seek and work toward the final blending of races, genders, and the burgeoning collection of sexual preferences into a pliable and undeterminable mélange ruled by Dr. Talbott's Single Global Authority.

The American Founding Fathers overthrew the colonial government for offenses far less severe than these. Nevertheless, I am neither a reactionary nor do I believe a reversal may happen at this late stage. The model for renewal requires a catastrophic event: a rapidly spreading global crisis combining a financial meltdown and a truly deadly pandemic. The predictable failure of the left-liberal system and its regime to manage such a calamity would force the pliable mélange of people to reconsider their lives and beliefs.

The first victim would have to be the notion of "progress." The changeover from the insidious idea of the "right side of history," which implies that societal progress is linear and inevitable, to upholding tradition, identity, and culture — from the obsessive "becoming" back to "being" — is the critical change for Western renewal. Such renewal will restore the typical "nuclear" family as the primary survival unit. Amid collapsing political structures, lost faith in politics, and economic struggles, it will also reject the current ideological obsessions of the Western rulers as absurd. People bonded by blood, memory, culture, and tradition will regroup to stay alive. In this respect, ongoing treachery and moral corruption within organized Christianity will present an additional challenge, with infiltrators among the elite class occupying very high ecclesiastic positions.

When contemplating the political theory of resistance, it is essential to stress the chasm between the ruling elites' promise of freedom *from* things, acts, behaviors, policies, and rules (haters, police violence, offensive speech, white privilege, phobias, patriarchy, racism, discrimination, etc.) and the other kind of liberty, the one that upholds freedom *for* things that make life worth living. This scheme may offer a consensual platform for various traditions, which must hang together now, or they will hang separately later.

As everyday Americans confront the wanton brutality of their regime, they should not succumb to despair. History has shown that nothing is inevitable — artificial or evil ideologies and regimes are transient. Real people, with their capacity for feelings and reasoning, know who they are. Their struggle against the so-called elites in power is fair, legitimate, and moral, even if the outcome is uncertain. In the midst of this, real Westerners can and should cling to beauty, truth, and faith, finding solace and strength in these values.

Culture War Threatening Western Power

The current Western worldview, which has gradually reverted to the familiar "rules-based international order" embraced by the intellectual elite of the Great Powers pre-1914, must be comprehended within its historical backdrop. This perspective, which posited that diplomacy was too intricate, the global economy too intertwined, technology too advanced, and the balance of power too well-calibrated to permit a prolonged, devastating war, was tragically mistaken then. Those who persist with the contemporary iteration of that worldview are equally misguided today.

The new order established following World War II discarded the idea of war as a legitimate extension of politics and national policy. Instead, politicians and the media referred to military conflicts as "police actions" or "counterterrorism operations." Traditionally, there are two paths in international relations: diplomacy and war. Usually, diplomacy has been the favored route; once it fails, war becomes the only alternative. For most of human history, that option was acceptable as a reasonable, practical, and legitimate means of attaining national objectives.

However, this perception began to shift after the horrors of World War I, the devastation of World War II, and the subsequent establishment of the United Nations. Furthermore, due to the post-WWII order and the West's triumph in the Cold War, the establishment now perceives foreign policy — where it believes the "experts" can account for and plan for every possible outcome — as a means to ensure the inevitability of liberal democracy's dominance. Although this perspective creates the illusion of control over something inherently uncontrollable, in practical terms, it has been disproven by the rise of China, the persistence of authoritarianism in Eastern Europe, Asia, and Africa, and the utter failure of nation-building in almost every corner of the globe.

In theory, the Western perspective does not align with human nature. It is challenging to fully map out interactions among individuals, let alone among nations with complex histories, socioeconomic pressures, unpredictable politics, and diverse cultures. Therefore, international relations inherently involve speculation that does not fit into the current model of "scientific certainty," a concept that needs to be reevaluated in the context of international relations and its limitations.

Instead of dismissing Russia's annexation of Crimea as an aberration, it is crucial to recognize it as a calculated move by a strategic power. Whether it is Vladimir Putin, Donald Trump, Viktor Orbán, Jair Bolsonaro, Recep Erdoğan, Kim Jong Un, Alexander Lukashenko, or Bashar al-Assad, attributing their actions to mental instability is a simplistic and misguided approach. It is a disservice to their strategic thinking and the complex geopolitical dynamics they navigate.

"He is just sick" or "he is simply crazy" vindicates the popular Western understanding of the ruling order and sidesteps the possibility that those leaders are rational actors taking logical steps to achieve their goals. The American political establishment retreated into similar modes of thought when Donald Trump won the White House. For the political leadership, there was no logical reason why Trump and his voters would stampede the establishment's order — they were simply crazy.

The leaders mentioned above may be adversarial to the West in their policies and actions, but they are not unintelligent. Countries as large, powerful, and rich in resources as Russia, China, Brazil, or Turkey are almost impossible to isolate or subdue.
And it is foolhardy to expect antagonists of the liberal-democratic West to play by the rules that the West created for its own benefit.

China will not comply with World Trade Organization (WTO) rules that threaten to weaken its regime or worry about copyright laws preventing it from overtaking Western technology. China and Russia have refused to conform to rules set by their adversaries and have drawn a few red lines for the West in Ukraine, Taiwan, and the South China Sea — among many others. The Western-designed international order expected the Chinese Communist Party to "play by the rules" when China joined the World Trade Organization. Instead, it has slyly engaged in industrial espionage on a massive scale and succeeded in decimating American industry with the tacit connivance of American Big Business. The World Health Organization (WHO) expected China to be straightforward about the origins of the coronavirus. Instead, China put up roadblocks to a serious investigation and used the WHO as its mouthpiece to deflect any blame for causing the pandemic.

The fact that those actions were "unthinkable" to Western policy analysts shows that their current view is fundamentally flawed. The rivals of the West have no compunction about disregarding rules they find troublesome — and why would they? The contenders will continue to flaunt those rules — unless the West is willing to use military power or wage mutually devastating economic warfare — hoping that one day, most of the world will find American political, cultural, and military control more toxic than Chinese economic influence. And that is a distinct possibility. "Culture wars" are in vogue in the Western world today, but the political powers do not acknowledge the danger from the forces of division, critical race theory (CRT), and Islamism, and they ignore the possibility that only civil war can and will end the growing chaos.

In Central Europe, Hungary has already approved a bill giving nongovernmental, semiprivate foundations control of the nation's higher education sector. Hungary and Poland have outlawed gender studies and are now consolidating national-conservative ideological foundations in the academy, which they have correctly identified as the most subversive section of society.

At this dangerous moment in history, the more liberal democracy doubles down on promoting CRT, DEI (diversity, equity, and inclusion), gender ideology, feminism, and other divisive left-linked ideologies, the more it will alienate those national-conservative countries that pursue far more robust, distinct, and homogeneous polities.

Throughout the Anglosphere, the entrenched idea exists that the younger people are, the further to the left they will be — and, therefore, they should be allowed to vote to consolidate a leftist political hegemony. Specific social science theories originating from the United States fuel a self-loathing existential crisis within the Western world. There is a battle to wage against the subversive, anti-national, and left-leaning intellectuals produced by American universities.

In Poland, nationalists have organized militias to guard statues, monuments, and churches, primarily against abortion advocates and criminals.

In Hungary, the state has approved a law defining a family unit headed by a man and a woman and has started paying couples to have more children, resulting in a slight increase in birth rates.

In Britain, the government has recently mandated free speech in universities at the risk of significant fines and defunding, authorized laws to counter woke museums and to deal with controversial art and statue removers, and legislated harsher punishment with ten-year jail terms for participating in mobs and desecrating statues and museums.

Consolidating Europe under American hegemony once brought a net benefit to U.S. influence worldwide. However, that influence and respect have been lost through repeated attempts to impose an American culture war on others. History teaches us that alliances always take a long time to build but only days to end — along with the ultimate loss of influence.

Diana, Princess of Wales, was a symbol of dysfunctional modern Western society. A poor little rich kid, she looked beautiful, but adultery and divorce marred her childhood. Her education was flimsy, her religion superficial, her inner life nonexistent, and her emotions unstable. She was a lost lamb in the wilderness, vulnerable to the mass media and establishment wolves. Then, her marriage and family crumbled under infidelity and treachery. With little meaning in her life, she kept wandering into empty, meaningless relationships until the final wreck.

Small wonder there was such an outpouring of grief at her death. Many in the population identified with her — including the "intellectuals." Their lives, too, were awash with affluence soiled by broken dreams, broken homes, broken marriages, and broken hearts. As victims of a barren, materialist culture, they were not only weeping for the poor little princess; they were crying for themselves.

Administrative-Remedial Regime

Soft totalitarianism, a stark contrast to the proclaimed freedom, emerges in Western countries that boast of being the freest and most democratic. In the developed and wealthy societies of North America, Western Europe, Australia, and New Zealand, a system has taken root, often called the "administrative-remedial regime." This stark dichotomy between the rhetoric and the reality is a cause for disillusionment.

Countries such as Germany, France, Canada, and the Netherlands today may exemplify such an administrative-remedial regime, one that is socially radical but favorable to corporate capitalism, with discernible plutocratic aspects to the modern-day Western world.

The administrative-remedial regime has emerged from the relatively new structures of social, political, and cultural control. It can be viewed as objectively anti-democratic, creating a "democratic deficit" and exerting power, up to a point, in a "soft" manner. This development includes promoting consumerism and pop culture, shaping social and political reality through news, politicized entertainment, mass education, and judicializing political questions.

The widespread presence of these structures in society throws long-standing classic understandings of government, politics, and democratic self-governance into question. For example, the right to freedom of speech — one of the assumed bedrocks of democracy — is no longer valued or regarded highly, even in theory, when it opposes the imperative of being "politically correct."

Western countries no longer understand democracy as a vehicle for choosing between political persuasions. They present the concept of democracy as a universal system of particular ideological, cultural, and, for them, Western values that must be upheld and imposed on everyone in society and the world — the word "democratic" is now used with the implied meaning of being socially left-leaning.

These tendentious social and legal instruments have so deeply permeated the Western fabric that they can easily filter out, remove, or disempower any challenge to the regime. The government is further fortified through pseudo-polemics between an official Left and Right, excluding any earnest public debate. Elections may bring different political parties and candidates into office, but the administrative-remedial regime persists.

East-Central European countries like Poland and Hungary have thus far avoided this fate. The result of Communist Party rule is that Eastern Europe became somewhat "frozen in time" and was, therefore, able to escape the radical social dynamics that overtook the liberal-democratic Western world, where members of the ruling class give orders without having to obey any superior and control society's wealth and privileges.

To paraphrase James Burnham, I consider the incumbent ruling class the "managerial elite," a group that characterizes the 20th and 21st centuries. Only that group has the technical capabilities to manage the vast manufacturing, consumer, financial, media, educational, electoral, and governmental organizations that typify the modern world (Burnham, 1941). Those at the top are a class united not by material conditions but by ideology. They think alike and move effortlessly between the public and private spheres.

The Western world already had two elite classes, the feudal and the bourgeois. Both ruled in their own interests, just like the ruling elites today, but they also had an ethic of service, i.e., a sense of *noblesse oblige* that made them beneficial to society. They wanted stability — so their position could be passed on to their descendants — and relied on religion and culture to retain their influence. Importantly, local and independent functions persisted in most people's lives throughout the reign of the old elite classes. Understanding natural law and natural rights were the moral and ethical concepts that constrained these earlier privileged classes, who could not consolidate power in their hands as the modern-day managers did.

Today's ruling elites have total power over society but none of the virtues that restrained the previous governing classes. Unlike the other elites who ruled primarily through force, the modern establishment relies mainly on deception, such as manipulation and fraud, to maintain and expand its reach, not constrained by national borders. The current ruling class relies on controlling public discourse through the "soft" suppression of dissent and a pseudo-moral quasi-religious belief that modern technology and propagandistic education will, in the future, bring relief to all human ailments for the masses. This fiendishly idealistic faith requires the cultivation of a replaceable populace attuned to rootless hedonism without any significant private or local life. The utopian future it promises is just a gimmick to maneuver the people into prolonging the hegemony of their rulers. It also demands ideological homogenization to the lowest common denominator, termed "democratic consensus."

But there are signs from different quarters that this hegemony is weakening — manipulation has its limits.

Therefore, the regime must constantly find new justifications for its continued existence and expansion. It is incapable of stability and relies on further deceptions — chimeric concepts such as "white privilege" and "global democracy." It seeks to use "minorities" as foot soldiers for middle-class Americans, instilling in them a constant sense of victimhood and violent resentment. In a phenomenon Samuel Francis called "anarcho-tyranny," the institutions of law and order are progressively callous and ruthless toward the law-abiding but easy and forgiving toward the lawbreakers.

The narratives currently used by the ruling elite to justify their rule are:

1. Security against health emergencies,

2. Protection of the population from disasters related to global warming,

3. Enforcement of "social justice" according to Critical Race and Gender Theories,

4. Protection of "our democracy" from the small governments of "fascists."

The last two narratives represent two aspects of the same situation: to reward political allies and crush opponents.

However, modern Western rulers have proven unable to cope with realities like Russia and China, which they cannot successfully handle with empty declarations of moral superiority. Their regime is forcing the adoption of increasingly overtly repressive measures as internal and external instability mounts, showing the iron fist under the velvet glove every time it lashes out at the "deplorables."

It is frightening to see how the regime works to dispossess those who oppose it and what may lie ahead in the turbulent waters of these dark times.

End of the Traditional Family

By the 1930s, the family institution, once a pillar of societal order, had crumbled. This decline, rooted in the modern world's rejection of the concept of natural order, had profound implications. As patriarchy deteriorated and the acceptance of any natural supremacy vanished, the family, the community, and the nation fell into disarray. For instance, the breakdown of the traditional family structure led to an increase in single-parent households, which in turn led to a rise in juvenile delinquency. The world, once again, was plunged into a state of chaos, a stark reminder of the importance of the family institution in maintaining societal stability.

The end of American pioneering — a period of exploration of new territories — was settlement, which implied the establishment of families and communities. The transient, by contrast, was in continuous motion, crisscrossing the countryside without any purpose, direction, or time limit because, in the America of the Great Depression, there was no longer a place to go.

Lacking a proper setting, the qualities essential to the endurance and success of the pioneering American spirit, such as strength, independence, tenacity, and resilience, had grown decadent and pernicious. The pioneering American spirit, characterized by these qualities, was a driving force in establishing and maintaining the family institution. And precisely that gave Big Business its ruthless drive, the gangster a cruel authenticity, and the vagabond a vicarious feeling of power, readily making them tools of those who possess real power. In essential respects, these people all became victims of capitalism. Their ambition, self-reliance, and stubborn determination had been virtues on the frontier, but with the advent of the industrial age, these old virtues became new vices due to the terrible power placed in the hands of machines. The pioneering settlers' moral degeneration began when they recognized the opportunity to make money quickly and in abundance. With modern life considerably quickening due to the endless striving and remorseless ambition of the twentieth-century pioneer, it was no surprise that American society began to fragment, and Western civilization succumbed to the throes of dictatorship.

Tyrannical regimes denied transcendent authority and embraced an abstract power that originated within history — a power that made man the final judge of man. The resulting political and social arrangements doomed human beings either to blind submissiveness or to sectarian conflict. The outcome of the human will was no longer restrained by the rule of natural law; this dispensation promoted the "truth" that all power emanated from man, i.e., a flawed domain.

The only viable alternative to despotism lay in the revival of a polity founded on the togetherness of families. No monolithic, totalitarian state could subjugate a collection of families living on the land — the family was and still is the source of the traditional and conservative state. For that reason, socialists, whether fascists or communists, opposed the family and sought to dismantle it. Whether family, church, or aristocracy, no corporate body could intervene between the government and the individual, who had to constantly feel his weakness, vulnerability, and dependence. The modern totalitarian state seeks to control every aspect of life, whether public or private. Nothing, in theory, is beyond its purview, and every means, including mass execution, starvation, war, or epidemic, is considered germane to realizing its ends.

The familial hierarchy replicated the structure of creation, with the patriarch — the male head of the family — responsible for the welfare of his wife, children, property, and household dependents. There was little in the family order that resembled democracy or equality. As the ruler of people, flocks, and herds, the patriarch was committed to caring for and protecting those under him. Family and household were thus more spiritual than material interests and considerations. Just as money could not replace land as the source of wealth, neither the businessman, financier, manufacturer, nor politician could substitute for the patriarch of old. The role of the patriarch in the family institution was crucial, as it provided a sense of order and stability.

The family structure was a pillar of legitimate authority and discipline at the heart of societal order. However, with the advent of industrialization and urbanization in the late 19th and early 20th centuries, these foundations began to crumble. The shift from agrarian to industrial economies, coupled with the rise of individualism and the erosion of traditional religious beliefs, led to a breakdown of the traditional family structure. Individual family members, much like citizens of a state, were prone to pursue their personal interests to the detriment of the common good. As patriarchy waned and the acceptance of any form of authority diminished, the family and, by extension, the community and the nation fell into disarray, leading to a world in chaos.

Before the Civil War, thinkers of the American South, both secular and religious, decried the violence inherent in the classic patriarchy of the ancient world. The representation of the patriarchal family was once Christian patriarchy, at least in the Western world. Each planter was a Patriarch — his position compelled him to be the ruler of his household. From early youth, his children and servants looked up to him as the head, and obedience and subordination became essential elements of education. Domestic relations became the most prized, and each family recognized its duty, with its members feeling responsible for discharging their share. The state was regarded only as the ultimate head in external relations, while all internal responsibilities, such as support, education, and the relative duties of individuals, were left to domestic regulation. This fact underscores the profound sense of responsibility and duty the traditional family instilled in its members, a quality that commands respect and admiration.

I wholeheartedly endorse the virtues of such inequality, which, in my view, are inescapable as they are inherent in human nature. A family, much like any business organization, is never a democracy. In the American South, these unequal relations did not breed a vicious competition among individuals, leading to a war of all against all based on the survival of the fittest. Instead, they fostered a stable, joint undertaking where husbands, wives, children, kin, and slaves each played their part in the household and were, in turn, sustained by it according to their various needs and capacities. The members willingly set aside their personal interests in service of the family, for it was this service that nurtured shared love and life, creating a profound sense of security and order.

For these reasons, I deeply mourn the loss of the traditional family, a social unit that defined the essence of the American South. The traditional family, with its diverse blood ties, embodied love, particularly through the presence of children. Today, the modern family is a mere facade, an empty shell devoid of significance, from which intimacy, affection, and love have fled, leaving behind a lingering scent of selfishness, greed, and enmity. This dissolution has had a profound impact on the fabric of our society.

The patriarchal family was not a tool designed to reduce and subjugate women. Family life requires discipline, restraint, and sacrifice from all members. The father also had to take on a heavy responsibility and submit his personal feelings to the interests of the family tradition. Moreover, the family's spiritual dimensions, accompanying the rise of Christianity, transformed the meaning of womanhood, revering the ideal figures of virgin and mother, a testament to the homage that women garnered in a healthy society. A commanding matriarchal presence also permeated the Western image of the family — the domestic order, i.e., all matters involving the home and family depended on women. They gave birth to the next generation, were the bearers of culture and tradition, the origin and conduit of manners and memory, and allured men into virtue and civilization. They managed the family as the power behind the scenes and safeguarded the purity of the blood. Women were placed in a role above the brute nature of men, setting limits for both genders. Romantically, women were elevated to the "divine" and put on a pedestal. With women at their center, families were vital elements of any community. Order in the family and the household signified structure, control, and peace in the state and the nation.

Family discipline also tempered human nature and maintained appropriate relations between the sexes. Regulating sexual activity and ensuring the bearing and rearing of children to preserve social coherence and human identity were the two cardinal purposes of the family. The stability of society rested on the institution of marriage. The sexual and other restraints of marriage opposed the dangerous volatility of feeling, which prompted men to emphasize desire at the expense of duty — adultery, like war, endangered social peace. The family was the one thing that lasted, and to accomplish that, it required men to temper their instincts and serve a social and cultural purpose. Capitulating entirely to nature rendered men worse than the beasts whose biological urges and impulses they shared, and such a complete surrender to instinct reduced them to degradation and ruin.

Culture is not innate, spontaneous, or automatic; it arises from the free moral choices humans make and for which they assume responsibility. There is no doubt that the institution of the family inevitably creates a vital tension that is both creative and painful. Although a source of decorum, the familial obligations all members had to perform were also sources of apprehension, misery, and sometimes grief. Attempts to evade such constrictions in the name of personal liberation brought even more oppressive and harmful consequences. Culture and civilization advance only through unremitting moral effort. The complete freedom from restraint once thought to characterize savage life is a romantic myth. It is the fundamental error of modern hedonism to assume that man can abandon all moral effort, throw off every constraint and spiritual discipline, and still preserve all cultural achievements. Sexual promiscuity, i.e., lust, is a misapplied and destructive expression of power, the antipode of love. The lustful man uses, abuses, and then discards the object of his desire, devouring everything he craves and giving nothing of himself in return, while mutual lust deceives and corrupts both partners, leading to apathy, aloofness, and misery.

Only the conventional standards and inhibitions of the family can restrict the unchecked power of lust. The demands of the Christian patriarchal family ensured that humans would not be left unprotected against raw instinct and limitless will. When social and economic conditions favored men without families — men on the move or tramping along the roads without direction and nowhere to go — it was a clear indication that the fabric of civilized social order was beginning to unravel. The preservation of cultural forms, such as the patriarchal family, despite its onerous preconditions, was crucial to prevent society from descending into decadence and, worse, depravity. The disregard for marriage and family institutions not only jeopardizes civilization but also risks the loss of countless individual souls, underlining the importance of these traditional values.

Since time immemorial, marriage and family have provided the essential bond between men and women and bridged the vast chasm between the sexes. The union of husband and wife extends to children, kin, and the community, standardizing benefaction and responsibility while channeling sexual desire away from all that is hurtful and harmful. Marriage demands that men and women subordinate personal desires and sacrifice personal freedoms not for each other, but for the common good of both and their offspring. Thus, two become one, and "I" becomes "we." The spiritual aspects of marriage and family far exceed the significance of material conditions. Members pledge their possessions and property to one another within the family and promise themselves. The eclipse of the family portended disaster, meaning that, from then on, individuals stood alone before the world in a struggle of naked power that was sure to consume them. They would cave in to the most sinful and destructive aspects of human nature or succumb to despair so complete and unrelenting that they would lose faith in themselves.

Being no expert, I can only glimpse, in embryonic form, the pathologies that currently infect the family. By the 1930s, the home had ceased to be the center of social activity, instead becoming a boarding house for vagabonds, wayfarers, and itinerants who rarely shared a meal, often remaining strangers to one another. The state increasingly replaced parents in raising, supervising, and educating children and bypassed the family in supporting and caring for the poor, infirm, and elderly. Family life's moral checks and restraints had loosened, allowing "the forces of dissolution" to operate without hindrance. Marriage would soon forfeit all attractions for the young, pleasure-loving, poor, and ambitious. Society assigned the energy of youth to contraceptive love, and only when men and women became prosperous and middle-aged would some of them think seriously about settling down to rear a strictly limited family. A half-century later, the situation was perhaps worse than anyone could have anticipated: not only had men and women delayed or refrained from marriage, but illegitimacy, cohabitation, and divorce placed the traditional Christian family in danger of extinction. Still, the problems that the modern family experiences are more symptoms than causes; the real problem is alienation, i.e., lack of love. By the end of the twentieth century, love, incarnated in the lasting union of a man and a woman in holy matrimony, was no longer a precious ideal — it had become an existential necessity.

In my way of life, I reaffirm the patriarchal order of the universe without challenging it and embody a piety toward nature integral to the human tradition. On the one hand, I see the triumph of mind over nature as a kind of progress, for I have no wish for humanity to remain backward, mired in primitive superstition and fear. Yet, on the other hand, I consider the application of mind to the stubborn and impenetrable aspects of the cosmos perilous if men go too far, as they always do, and become forgetful of their character. Hence, there is a need for a deferential outlook to suppress the untrammeled reason and will characteristic of modernity.

I consider discipline essential, but one cannot lead through fear alone — rather, it must be through experience instead — transforming fear into respect and love. Unqualified fear is a questionable and precarious form of authority. A good leader does not need to punish or reward his subordinates — only to command them, for they will revere him, subordinate their wills to his, and entrust him with their lives.

Among the most grievous consequences of the family ceasing to exist is that individual members come to indulge their private whims and desires. In this process, they abandon all measures and restraints and submit to their appetites and compulsions. They assert their wills, gratify their egos, and sacrifice all they love and the nature entrusted to their care. Bewildered, weakened in body, mind, and spirit, and thereby diminished, the men and women stumble mindlessly through their dark predicament, each facing their struggles and sacrifices.

All human relations are associated with power and are fraught with tension that can sometimes become difficult. But what is genuinely significant are the personal experiences, struggles, and memories and what they portend for the future of the younger generations and the traditional social order. The children, innocent bystanders, witness the vicious contest of wills between their father and mother. These circumstances can lead them to wreck their lives with alcohol, drugs, and crime. They will wander through life as bewildered souls, perpetual children, at once jealous of their lost innocence and evading the knowledge that accompanies maturity. They inherit only confusion and tumult, discerning but unable to explain their perplexity. The errors, transgressions, sins, and the merits, loves, and virtues of the past can befoul the lives of the next generations.

Radical Feminism and Gender Ideology

If I want to be honest, I have to say that all politically correct (PC) brainwashing shrouded in sensitizing do-gooder manners is harmful and should, therefore, be repressed. Radical feminism, uncritical glorification of multiculturalism, homosexual propaganda, anti-life abortion movements, or gender ideology all stem from the same tree; their dissemination follows the same choreography and takes society on the same slippery road of "acceptance" and "embracing," on which there is no stopping. And this slippery slope works not only vertically but also horizontally. I mean that not only does one "sensitization cause" stem from another, e.g., from radical, anti-male feminism to homosexual propaganda and then further on to gender ideology, but the brainwashing process also spreads geographically, gradually from West to East.

A few years ago, perhaps even last year, Eastern Europeans were amazed to read stories from America or Western Europe about gender-neutral washrooms or so-called drag queens "teaching" preschoolers about transgenderism. Incredulous, they found the demolition of statues symbolizing the former rule of "white, heterosexual men" and the relabeling of institutions and public spaces named after them as the opium of the declining West. Strangely, almost in disbelief, they received news from Western university campuses with "safe spaces" created for young people with different "freshly thought-out" identities and groups with "snowflake-like vulnerabilities." These sensitive and endangered beings could not suffer any mental or emotional harm. Of course, the curriculum, paintings, works of art, and books are renamed or rewritten. But, just in case, the students will receive a proper "trigger warning" first so that the allegedly misleading and outdated "binary gender coding," "patriarchal structures of rule," and possibly imprints of "white superiority" that may appear here and there from the past do not violate the spirituality and mental balance of these sensitive groups.

However, the theories of sensitizing brainwashing, which divide society into groups according to predetermined specifications and then proclaim and promise continuous liberation for those groups, know no bounds in the strict and figurative sense of the word either. After many ideological antecedents, numerous famous books have already been demanded to be removed from the obligatory readings recommended for primary school children — due to the depiction of female figures. According to the explanation, the female figures in these works are based on stereotypical gender roles, and the men (husbands, fathers) depicted next to or above them are symbols of heteronormativity.

In the meantime, organizations such as Rainbow Families are campaigning not just for the acceptance and understanding of homosexual individuals, not only for them to be able to live in legally recognized relationships, but also to allow homosexual couples and the children they adopt to form the same type of family as heterosexuals. Many people on both the right and left liberal sides argue that reactions to the subject should not be overestimated since these are merely marginal, insignificant manifestations at the social level. Others agree with the issue, asking, for example, who would be harmed by the gay lobby that launched the campaign to make the concept of family more open and inclusive?

The problem is twofold, but it stems from one root. On the one hand, especially in light of Western examples, it is evident that in the case of gender ideology and homosexual propaganda, the story is no longer about "accepting each other." Instead, it is about well-thought-out advertising, i.e., a propaganda campaign that seeks to elevate the abnormal to the level of normality, make the main rule out of the exception, and define it as the moral guide of social behavior.

The need to pay attention to such communication actions, which at first seemed like little shouting from the sidelines, cannot be better exemplified than by the writing of a gay couple that has since become dominant and was published in book form in 1987. In America, the "cultivation" of the homosexual subculture was already in full swing, but Marshall Kirk and Hunter Madsen went much further in their 1987 article, "The Overhauling of Straight America," followed by the book *After the Ball: How America Will Conquer Its Fear and Hatred of Gays in the '90s* (Kirk & Madsen, 1989).

They outlined the following scenario to go beyond "mere acceptance":

1. Talk about homosexuality as much as possible and as loudly as possible.
2. Portray homosexuals not as aggressive challengers but as victims.

3. Provide proponents of homosexuality with a defensible cause.

4. Homosexuals need to look like good people.

5. Make critics of homosexuality look terrible.

6. Take financial and moral responsibility.

In the context of the fifth point, the authors state that in the late stage of the campaign, "when gay ads are already commonplace," they must "settle accounts with the remaining opponents." How? "To be honest: they must be slandered." There were examples of similar, extreme advice decades ago: the radical French feminist Simone de Beauvoir, who openly supported pedophilia, said that "women will not be liberated until they are liberated from their children" — so then, abolish the family (Beauvoir, The Second Sex, 1953) (Beauvoir, The Ethics of Ambiguity, 1976).

It is, of course, difficult to resolve the peculiar contradiction that while "progress" proclaims the obsolescence and rejection of marriage and the (traditional) family, it is precisely these institutions that must open to homosexuals or those practicing polyamory ("multi-love"). However, the most embarrassing but unsurprising case is the attempt to create a rule from the exception: a generally accepted and mandatory norm developed from exceptional circumstances.

The fundamental difference between conservative and socialist-left-liberal perceptions is that the latter does not accept that the world has a natural, inherent, innate, and intrinsic order but believes that everything (the totality of all) is a purely artificially manufactured construction, the product of the ruling power structures. And if they have been mere constructions of society, they can also be deconstructed, dismantled, and reshaped. Therefore, "progressive" people also believe in social engineering concerning "gender roles." This view holds that natural, biological gender has secondary or negligible importance, and people — by creating and experiencing their own gender — should identify as they see fit. Thus, if the "gender role" is forced or "learned," therefore not natural, it can also be changed and transformed; then everything else based on these "gender roles" can be changed too: male-female relationships, family, sexuality, and gender. Accordingly, radical feminists, led by Simone de Beauvoir, among others, denied that a woman must or should be a woman (and a man should be a man); homosexual propaganda would extend the notion of a "not inclusive enough" family, and gender ideology would go beyond the "binary gender matrix."

However, the slippery slope is not in vain — it is slick. Suppose we say that gender identity is a matter of individual choice. In that case, all forms of discrimination based on sexual orientation are prohibited; there is no such thing as "normal" and "abnormal," everyone is equal, and "a family is a family." Then who and on what basis will set moral limits for a pedophile abusing young children who cannot yet express themselves? Because the "influencers" becoming crazy about the sensitization marketed as new conformity will surely not.

A strange madness has spread across the world: the biggest haters demand unconditional love for themselves. The very ones who love "everyone" but have never done any personal good for anyone have just required this great "love" from others. They are the ones who say a mother should see the polluter in her child, the oppressor in her son, and the pathetic cis heterosexual in her daughter.

According to their logic, we should call "love" what the Nazis felt about the Jews, the gypsies, or the gays. Because the lion loves the antelope, the fox loves the hen, the divorced husband loves the ex-wife, and the ex-wife loves the new woman. We should love everyone who is unlike us, thinks differently, feels differently from us, or believes other things. We should only hate those like ourselves because it is a transparent, exclusionary feeling. To love is a pleasant feeling; it does not consume a person's energy; on the contrary, it increases it. If we love our fellow human beings, we can gain a lot of extra energy from it. Unfortunately, the reverse is also true: if we lose energy by "loving" someone, we are deceiving ourselves — we are just labeling a burden as love.

Regrettably, "hate" does not do the exact opposite: if it is a burden to hate someone, we usually do not disguise our love with it but instead release a small portion of the poison that consumes us. Typically, in a tiring and self-destructive way, we hate someone who possesses something notably missing in ourselves. The ugly hates the beautiful, the fool hates the genius, the imperfect hates the perfect, the unhappy hates the happy, the sad hates the cheerful, and the unfortunate hates the lucky — but it is all based on faith. The only thing worse is when "perfect people," who think of themselves as beautiful, intelligent, happy, and sweet-smelling, hate the world and all the living and dead in it because they feel lousy despite being very fortunate.

Unfortunately, universal human stupidity escapes all scientific scrutiny; anything can make our friends and neighbors miserable, even those things that bring happiness and contentment to others. The world of politics is a particularly painful cauldron of human stupidity. For decades, we have observed with amazement and incomprehension how a nasty and hateful consciousness industry has developed to educate and condition society to hate normality — and hate miraculously found its audience.

It is with great amusement that one can watch, for example, the warfare on the extreme radical left taking place between those who profess to be transgender and those who profess to be feminists. Men who are hated by feminists for their masculinity and who, of course, know more about the social construct of women — since all gender stereotypes are merely a consequence of social violence, i.e., patriarchy — also want to claim the extra rights feminist women have won for transgender women.

Every extremist movement instantly becomes a prisoner of its own extremists, and the struggle against patriarchy almost instantly became a struggle against gender identities, fought just as successfully against women as against men. The first step, without exception, for all such world-saving ideas is to hate someone as a starting point. In the ultra-left media, there is constant moaning by the victorious radical feminists that they are judged based on the extreme trans movement. Yet feminism acted like any other identity disorder: first, it wanted to masculinize women, then feminize men. However, they did not mean a surgical solution; they just wanted to eradicate biological differences through psychological means.

According to feminists, a man is not worthy of becoming a woman, but women are entitled to all the masculine qualities and everything else that is beneficial to them from patriarchy. Yes, they still call the system patriarchy because, as long as there is a dissatisfied woman and a satisfied man, the feminists will not calm down. Feminism is like communism; the "enemy" is at fault for its inoperability. Women are much unhappier today than they were a hundred years ago, and it is the fault of men, who are also much worse off than before. But the latter does not matter — they do not yet have it bad enough.

Feminism, which defines women as an oppressed group superior to men, is just as insane as any other aggressive nonsense concerning gender ideology. Feminism has led to an unprecedented decline in femininity while reflecting virtually nothing about the economic and social changes of the past 100 years, other than some modernization of the "vulgar Marxist" verbiage. Already 20 years ago, feminists significantly influenced Western societies, forcing their agendas into social policy without any meaningful rival.

However, they could introduce only the insatiable dreams of foolish women, identity politics, and the revenge of offended females into big politics — not ordinary women's feelings, desires, and expectations.

As a result, Western society is more anti-female than ever if we consider women as human beings wanting to live in a family and have children. Gender ideology has become unique over the past few years and strangely includes critical race theory and intersectionality today. Gender ideology is the culmination of feminism and a companion to "human rights" but does not acknowledge women. Gender ideology considers white women merely auxiliary to world-oppressing white men, especially if they dare to reproduce.

All "isms" created after 1968 are meant to designate hate destinations solely; they have added nothing else to human thinking. Anyone in this world of madness loves no one else — only demands that their hatred of the world and other people be called love and that they be loved for "loving" everyone so much.

Anxiety through Moral Collapse

The rulers of the Western world want us to lose our belief in ourselves. As the transgender lobby inspires us to doubt our biological sex, the BLM-inspired "wokeists" embolden us to question our decency by suggesting we are unconsciously biased and racist. As tech billionaires persuade us to doubt our ability to navigate the world and make life choices without artificial intelligence, the COVID-19 "delusionists" incite us to question our health and ability to look after ourselves without their products. Even the climate change industry drives us to trust them to know how to tackle the threat of global warming rather than to address the population explosion in Third World countries. All good liars understand that the best lies carry a kernel of truth; that is why their lies and hypocrisies are so effective. Yes, a tiny minority are genuinely transgender; there is indeed some racism in our society; in some circumstances, artificial intelligence can help guide human judgment. Yes, COVID-19 is dangerous to some people, but it is preventable; therefore, experimental pharmaceutical intervention may be appropriate for them, and the world might be getting warmer.

The rulers want to create a culture of dependency on a progressive technocratic elite that relentlessly entices, bullies, and tricks people into seeing themselves and their fellow humans not as mortal and, therefore, flawed sources of wisdom, joy, and inspiration but rather as threats to each other individually and to all of us collectively. It is a dehumanizing attempt — the denial of biological sex is just the first chapter of a nasty transhumanist novel.

Like all revolutions inflamed by a collectivist ideology, the Western rulers' story will not be sustainable either — its flame will be extinguished by its contradictions sooner or later. Unless they succeed in altering the nature of humanity itself, in what Aldous Huxley called the "final revolution," which is "a pharmacological method of making people love their servitude, and producing dictatorship without tears, so to speak, producing a kind of painless concentration camp for entire societies, so that people will, in fact, have their liberties taken away from them but will rather enjoy it because they will be distracted from any desire to rebel by propaganda or brainwashing, or brainwashing enhanced by pharmacological methods" (Aldous Huxley, Tavistock Group, California Medical School, 1961).

"None are more hopelessly enslaved than those who falsely believe they are free." Goethe wrote these words nearly 200 years ago, but they are more relevant in our time than in his. Most people assume they live in a free society simply because they believe that tyranny would be overt and obvious and that all would recognize it. But could it be that technology, drugs, mainstream media, pornography, the entertainment industry, the education industry, and countless other diversions have created a citizenry too distracted or otherwise rendered incapable of noticing the chains and irons that bind them?

When Huxley wrote *Brave New World* in 1931, he did not regard the dystopian world depicted in the book as an imminent threat (Huxley, Brave New World, 2004). However, a significant shift occurred in his perspective after World War II, the expansion of totalitarianism, and the significant advancements in science and technology. In the future, Huxley stated, ruling elites would learn that it is possible to control a populace not only by using explicit force but also with the more clandestine method of inundating the masses with an endless supply of intriguing and enjoyable diversions. This shift in perspective should make us realize the gravity of the societal control issue.

"In *1984*," Huxley explains, "the lust for power is satisfied by inflicting pain; in *Brave New World*, by inflicting a hardly less humiliating pleasure" (Huxley, Brave New World Revisited, 2006). This stark contrast should prompt us to consider the subtlety of control in *Brave New World*.

The parallels between *Brave New World* and modern societies are apparent. In *Brave New World Revisited* (1958), Huxley examined how social engineers in the future could persuade their subjects to take drugs "that will make them think, feel, and behave in the ways [they] find desirable." He concluded: "In all probability, it will be enough merely to make the pills available."

Today, the opioid crisis has spread across the Western world. The feasibility of gratifying sexual impulses online has led many to become pornography addicts. Smartphones and other technologies provide mindless and pleasurable distractions that consume most people's attention for most of the day. It is uncertain to what extent these sedating, soothing, and relaxing diversions are intentionally pushed upon us or to what degree they are market responses to consumer demand. But the reality is that a distracted, preoccupied, and dumbed-down population lacks the mental resources to resist their enslavement.

Presuming that people trade their liberty for comfort, pleasure, and security — as they always do — the type of social conditioning Huxley warned about will only become more refined, sophisticated, and effective as technologies advance and more insight accumulates regarding predicting and controlling human behavior. Most people will not resist this manipulation, and their pleasure-induced cooperation will even increase.

Assuming current trends continue, humanity may soon divide into two groups: those, the majority, who welcome their pleasurable servitude, and those, the minority, who resist it in order to preserve their liberty and humanity. As the writer, orator, and former slave Frederick Douglass noted long before Huxley's *Brave New World*, when a slave becomes a contented slave, he has effectively abandoned all that makes him human. "I have found that, to make a contented slave," wrote Douglass, "it is necessary to make a thoughtless one…He must be able to detect no inconsistencies in slavery; he must be made to feel that slavery is right; he can be brought to that only when he ceases to be a man" (Douglass, 2016).

In the minds of the postmodern Western world's ruling elites, nations shaped by Christianity belong to an alien and sinister tradition. By contrast, many Western Christians — especially American conservatives — see Christianity as a morally, ethically, and traditionally sound stronghold against a West gone mad with self-destructive wokedom and the progressivist leanings among their senior prelates.

Unfortunately, separated into different factions, conservatives are helpless in the fight against the cancer of the postmodern world, whether it be against the Left, i.e., the socialist replacement religion, or the pseudo-progressive, treacherously collaborating quasi-Right, e.g., the modern Christian Church.

Resisting the forces of liberal-democratic totalitarianism will exact a high price, as witnessed in the persecution of those parents who refuse to let the schools brainwash their children with LGBTQ ideology. The Western (Christian) experience inextricably links persecution and martyrdom. But in this century, it will be the turn of traditional conservatives to experience maltreatment in earnest. As the liberal terror intensifies, it will become necessary for all conservatives, regardless of tradition or denomination, to define what is acceptable and what is not in the curious connection between church and state, especially concerning a state that pursues evil policies and a state-subsidized church that is willing to collaborate with it, i.e., be bought out by it.

For traditional conservatives, Christians, and all decent and moral citizens of the Western world, it is necessary to say "no" to and outright reject the absolutization of not only state authority but also democracy, liberalism, or any other ideological perfectionism. Institutions and laws should be accepted as authoritative and imperative only as they seek to uphold the "good" and confine the "evil." If legal opposition is impossible, as in the case of children's ideological and moral indoctrination, then all conscientious people must turn to civil disobedience. If the state's authority forces them to commit sinful and spiritually harmful actions, they have the right and duty to deny obedience to that state. They must continue to attest their beliefs openly when persecution begins.

The West's ongoing moral collapse is truly Spenglerian. After the disastrous European civil wars (1914–1945), the flowers of evil bloomed during the 1960s, a decade that proved to be a hotbed of bad ideas, including the U.S. involvement in the Vietnam War. The spirit of civilizational self-denial and deconstruction swept across the Western world, combining Michel Foucault and the Frankfurt School. It generated an obsessive need to celebrate the "Other" and an even more bizarre obsession with race, gender, and sexual orientation — a form of madness that spread to both sides of the Atlantic.

We are witnessing the beginning of the mature phase of the West's decline: the totalitarianism of the Davos elite. The system produces a vast amount of information processed through the media, embedding itself in a pseudo-reality where words and concepts acquire new meanings, e.g., inclusion, tolerance, etc. Strict nominalism dominates empiricism; the reality of experience must not prevent the development of an ideological view that produces its own reality. The recipients of the commanding politically correct messages either submit to the manipulation or are declared deviant. In this way, democracy has become — indeed, it has always been — a manipulative process, i.e., camouflaged entrapment, based on a predetermined, ideologically esteemed outcome. Culture ceases to be an integrated system of belief, knowledge, and behavior; instead, it becomes superfluous as a mechanism for maintaining social dynamism and inclusion — a product to consume, not experience.

If someone is "in," i.e., belongs to the majority but does not strive for the truth, then the power of the majority is being abused. On the other hand, if that person knows and supports the facts but cannot influence the majority, how will they act in the interest of that truth? Therefore, the task is to connect the majority and the truth, which is challenging but possible. Politics is mandated to protect human dignity, the family, the nation, culture, and civilization, which is the critical challenge of politics in democratic societies.

Political power creates joint action through the political process, elections, the constitution, or otherwise. However, leaders cannot achieve collective action solely by political means; they should develop it spiritually, ideologically, or both. It is the task of the Church to establish joint efforts through spiritual leadership, while politicians do so by political means, and these two sides should connect. For that reason, if religious leaders and even Christian politicians do not accept and practice the separation of Church and State in the suicidal West, they would have to mount a rather hopeless rearguard action today. To the detriment of traditional

Western society, the Christian Church spiritually and Christian democracy politically have already lost the credibility they once enjoyed. Sadly, only the socialists, the flagbearers of the replacement religion for the progressive left-liberals, remain to fill the ever-increasing spiritual-ideological-political void and join the leftist managerial elites.

Secularism has replaced Christianity as the basis of Western identity. The Left — masquerading as a liberal democracy — rejects the notion of a European or American social, geographic, and cultural space guarded against physical and spiritual penetration. Europe and North America are now on the path to a historically unprecedented demographic and cultural self-dissolution. From Africa, Asia, and Latin America, this gives the impression that the Western world is on a downtrend. This picture shows that Europe and North America are posh estates with vulnerable, elderly, and wealthy tenants occupying them; the fancy mansions have broken locks and no security guards. Without non-leftist and realistic beliefs, moral values, and genuine virtue, the result will be death for the natives.

The elite class is at the root of the West's fatal weaknesses, including both the primary causes — loss of courage, leadership, and virtue — and several secondary ones, such as open borders encouraging illegal migration, actively inviting cultural invasions, financing non-native (i.e., non-European) childbirth, and the cult of "diversity" and "tolerance." These concerns go hand in hand with the demonization and criminalization of any dissent, the enforcement of Draconian laws against language deemed politically incorrect "hate speech" by ideologically biased institutions, and drastic surveillance measures against the "unsuitable," e.g., the democratically elected and sole opposition party AfD in Germany.

The culture of death manifested in the cult of deviation has produced bitter results, but effective opposition is still possible, as the examples of Hungary and Poland show. Otherwise, by the end of this century, no "Europeans" will be left as members of nations sharing the same language, culture, history, and ancestry and inhabiting the lands named after them. At the same time, to complete the irony, Western Europe's decadent, retrograde, and moribund nations are told that demographic change is a boon, enriching their societies and making them excitingly diverse.

The postmodern West rests on the fiction that there is no Truth, no Goodness, no Beauty; everything is relative, and therefore, everything is permitted; that man can rely on his own objectivist ambition and subjective reasoning to solve all the issues of his existence and find an eschatological shortcut to the end of history — a worldly one, following John Lennon's formula: without heaven and hell, a world without nations and religion, in which everyone lives just for today, where life is mere existence.

Conservatives must unite to resist the vision of a left-wing, liberal-democratic Nirvana based on the same ideological premises that fueled previous idealistic, totalitarian, materialist schemes from Robespierre, Marx, and Lenin to Hitler, Mao, and Pol Pot.

There is hope because there is Truth.

Christian Democracy's Failure and Surrender

The parting ways on March 20, 2021, between the Hungarian ruling political party, Fidesz, and the European People's Party (EPP) should be excruciating for Christian Democrats. The EPP, a transnational organization founded by primarily Christian-democratic parties in 1976, is a European political institution composed of political parties with Christian-democratic, conservative, and liberal-conservative members. After all, the idea of a united, someday free, and explicitly Christian Europe standing between the Soviet Union and the United States suffering from the post-Vietnam blues was alluring at the time.

The EPP's exclusion of Fidesz is a rejection of much more than merely Prime Minister Viktor Orbán's persona. It is the seal on the EPP's forsaking of its heritage or any meaningful allegiance to Christianity or democracy. Fidesz's real offense was its adherence to both.

The upsurge of infanticide, euthanasia, and gender confusion engulfing the liberal democracies in the past five decades was neither initiated nor sanctioned by the majority of the formerly Christian world. It was mainly imposed by judicial and occasionally legislative fiat — and various churches' responses ranged from flaccid disapproval to avid acceptance. Nevertheless, the "termination" of the unborn, elderly, and infirm on the one hand, while "about-facing" on marriage, gender, and sexuality on the other, can never be anything other than sins. Never can a sane person be content with a State that tolerates such things and actively promotes them as equal to or better than the things established by nature.

With the repeated approval of the Hungarian electorate, Fidesz committed the unforgivable — it attempted to adhere to the original tenets of Christian Democracy regarding social issues. Worse, it has clipped the judiciary's wings, which in modern times is used to exercise absolute control over "democratic" countries and their "democratic elections." The court has been the primary agency imposing those evils promoted by the Western elites.

It is easy to understand why all this would scandalize the EPP leadership. Despite the EPP literature's alluring references to Europe's Christian background, beliefs, culture, and character, the leadership has not attempted to implement any Christian principles and values in EU legislation or in bureaucratic or administrative decisions. Just the contrary: the leaders condemn those who do. Nothing is so horrifying as someone else living up to the beliefs that one claims to hold, thereby exposing one's hypocrisy.

To understand how far mainstream Christian Democracy and the principal Christian Churches have fallen, one must grasp where they came from and how they got here.

The interwar period of the 20th century saw the birth of many ideologies in response to socialism, communism, Bolshevism, hyperinflation, and the economic collapse of the post-WWI period. The fertile mix of political, social, cultural, and economic ideas attracted many devout Catholics and Protestants alike (such as Stauffenberg and Jünger) around the "Conservative Revolution" in Germany; it also appealed to various neo-pagans and other "interesting types." One deep desire united them all: a yearning for a new order to embody the best European traditions and bring them into the modern world. But what would that new order look like? How would one make it function? And what about socialism, fascism, communism, national socialism, and the other new cognate ideologies popping up everywhere and claiming to be able to accomplish the longed-for synthesis of old and new?

Pope Pius XI would condemn the errors within the Italian and German movements, "errors" that inevitably revealed their left-wing origins and practices. It was no coincidence that Benito Mussolini was named after Benito Juarez, President of Mexico, and started his political life as a socialist (Powell, 2012). World War II and its horrors presented Christianity with a terrible dilemma. Those who believed in collaboration with the Axis Powers, based on their principles, found themselves politically and morally (and often physically) destroyed by the war's end — regardless of how much they had tried to apply those principles wherever and whenever they could. However, those whose interpretation of the same ideals led them into the resistance — even side by side with their old enemies, the liberals and communists — very often survived, offering a glimmer of hope in the darkest times. After 1945, they faced a new dilemma once predicted by the *Paneuropa* founder Richard von Coudenhove-Kalergi after World War I (Coudenhove-Kalergi, 2019).

As the Iron Curtain descended across the continent, the survival of Free Europe hinged on the semi-occupation by and goodwill of the United States. America, with its classical liberal principles, found itself in a complex relationship with the European conservative Christian Right. The remaining

Christian politicians had to navigate this new situation, understanding that there could be no thought of monarchical restoration. However, the principles of subsidiarity and solidarity, along with the embrace of liberal democracy, remained in the script. A "confessionally neutral state nevertheless illumined by Gospel values" would be ideal, as envisioned by Pope Benedict XVI — a vision that seemed to be embodied in Eisenhower's America.

Christian democracy took shape in the immediate aftermath of the war and endured until recently. The integrity, sincerity, and piety of its originators, including Konrad Adenauer, Maurice Schuman, Alcide De Gasperi, Pope Pius XII, and Pope John XXIII, are beyond doubt. The birth of modern Christian Democracy was intricately linked to these men and their association, which eventually evolved into the European Union. This association was not just an economic and political alliance but a shared vision of a united Europe guided by Christian principles and a commitment to peace and solidarity.

To be sure, it was a beautiful dream, conceived by romantic idealists escaping from their history, symbolized to its founders by the Crown of Charlemagne — and to a great degree embraced by the two "Austrian Paneuropean" figures, Richard Coudenhove-Kalergi and Otto von Habsburg. These two individuals played significant roles in the early development of the European Union. For the "Archduke of Austria," the European Union seemed a way to achieve his House's enduring vision and lasting desire: a great European Christian Commonwealth, a new Christendom — a peaceful paradise on the ruins of the past. To that vision of the phoenix, the "Archduke" remained faithful to the end while, fortuitously, following the same phoenix, German, French, Italian, and other European interests and dreams also coincided.

Yet, the foundations on which the Fathers of Christian Democracy and the European Union built their vision were not without flaws. The United States, once a beacon of moral consensus and social accord, was showing signs of faltering. The same anti-Christian "leftist modernity" that had given rise to socialism, communism, fascism, and national socialism was now emerging from Christian Democracy's liberal and social democratic partners in Europe.

Within seven decades, three main catalysts, each of which significantly impacted the trajectory of the European Union, radically transformed the Christian-Democratic scene from its bright beginning to its current colorless state.

The first catalyst was the Catholic Church's post-Vatican II self-immolation, which debilitated it. Rather than actively "guiding" the nations through moral leadership, its hierarchy settled for merely "accompanying" them — hence the flaccidity earlier noted and witnessed, as exemplified by the Church's order to the persecuted underground followers in China to submit to their Communist overlords' "patriotic church."

The second catalyst was the surrender in various ways and at different times to the "68 Generation." This group of privileged or perpetually self-pitying children had the unusual experience of aging without maturing — a uniquely left-liberal intellectual occurrence. Nevertheless, they acquired the reins of power in government, church, and culture and have spent their time attempting to destroy that inheritance in favor of obscure visions, e.g., the Green movement.

The third catalyst, ironically, was the collapse of the Soviet Union. Lacking the need to play "Masters of the Free World" any longer, the fossilized "new generation" of Christian-Democratic leaders, who hold on to power, have gone astray and become ever more dictatorial, betraying their hapless but still loyal followers and imposing upon them pseudo-changes to chase.

Against that hideous strength of the Left, partially created by their own treacherous incompetence, Europe's Christian Democrats are ultimately faced with the same painful choice today that their forebears confronted in 1939: collaboration or resistance. The Hungarian national-conservative and Christian-Democratic Fidesz party's exit from the EPP reflects their chosen path.

Unfortunately for the Western world, the EPP has backed an ultimately losing horse: collaboration. It is a surrender to leftism, socialism, and globalism. As the fall of Afghanistan graphically illustrates, however compelling the Christian Democrats may be in manipulating and outmaneuvering divided, if not incompetent, domestic opponents, they are sadly surpassed when it comes to determined outsiders who possess a religion of their own. Whether the future threat is Islamic (external or internal), Chinese, or Russian — that the last must appear among their foes speaks to the Western leadership's diplomatic, political, and strategic ineptitude — they shall certainly be more than the present Western masters (with the modern Christian

Democrats in or out of government making no difference) can handle. At that point, the people will cry out for alternative leadership, which will finally emerge and no doubt be readily accepted.

Therein lies the rub. During the Conservative Revolution in Germany, many shades, colors, and bodies of thought existed among the alternatives that Western leaders, ruling leftists, and intellectual elites preferred to lump together as the "Far Right." To be sure, there are also neo-Nazis and neo-pagans among them, straight out of any Antifa's worst nightmare. There are believers in blood and soil, populists and nationalists, conservatives and nativists, pragmatists and idealists, exploiters and followers who shall know, when the time comes, how to mobilize the fear and resentment of countless Americans, Europeans, and perhaps other Westerners. All those people — long tired of being laughed at, poked fun at, and seeing their most cherished beliefs spat upon by political leaders (including Christian Democratic ones) who are incompetent, arrogant, and treacherous in their defiance of a real threat — will be ready to embrace the alternatives. And what might come from following a dark road to an uncharted destination with an angry mass is frightening even to contemplate.

Encouragingly, a more rational leadership is beginning to emerge in Hungary and other parts of Central Europe. These leaders are revisiting the principles of Christian Democracy and adapting them to the modern context. The influence of this non-collaborating opposition is significant and on the rise. However, if the situation were to become unstable enough to allow the ascent of the groups that the current leftist rulers dread the most, the initial resistance to the forces of darkness might still be hesitant, given the ignorance and ideological bias that the current system has instilled in the population.

For those who dare to dissent, the ultimate reward is the relentless pursuit of truth. And if history has taught us anything over the past five centuries, it is that determined minorities shape it.

Chapter 2

It is the day after Christmas and a perfect day here in Memmingen, Germany — to think. It occurred to me that several staggering 19th-century "ideologies" and "discoveries" were just plain inventions or scams perpetrated to make the perpetrators rich, famous, and all-powerful.

First, Marxism was one of the most evil ideologies ever, alleging to explain all of human history as a class struggle. Its initial document, "The Communist Manifesto," is a brilliantly written, even exciting, short pamphlet that makes readers feel they have learned an enormous secret that explains everything. It can further make readers believe that if they act upon its theses and the world is taken by its understanding, humanity will live in a golden age, i.e., communism, forever (Marx & Engels, The Communist Manifesto, 2014).

In reality, all that was based on nothing else but a lengthy analysis of its author's hatred, jealousy, and resentment of his wealthy relations. Karl Marx's genius did not lead to a new golden age — an old golden age never existed either — but to the worst dictatorships: those of Lenin, Stalin, Mao Zedong, Pol Pot, et al. More than a hundred million people died in the service of trying to make Marxism work — and it still never did. Instead, it led to mass murder, imprisonment, starvation, poverty, and whole nations becoming miserable and insane. Think of Mao's "Great Leap Forward," Stalin's gulags, Kim's North Korea, the Shining Path communist movement in Peru, or Pol Pot's "Khmer

Rouge," and you have the idea. That glorious ideology was just a stratagem to give absolute dictatorial powers to lunatic murderers.

A variant of socialism was also National Socialism or Nazism, which claimed to be anti-Marxist, and in some ways, it was. But it was just another promise of paradise on earth — if a new system would only give all power to the state. And incidentally, it also led to mass murder and the ghastly spectacle of two uber-monster states, Nazi Germany and the Soviet Union, battling it out to dominate Europe and maybe the world. Luckily, climate and geography led to the defeat of the Nazis, and, as luck would have it, the U.S. got the atomic bomb first, also saving Europe from total communist domination — for a while.

Then there was my other favorite, Darwinism, claiming to explain all plant and animal life by gradual adaptations and mutations that allegedly led mud puddles and amoebas to become Nobel Peace Prize and Academy Award winners — after a while.

But Darwin never had any evidence of how life began. He never provided or proved even one example of one species mutating into another — he had only his assertions. Darwin confronted and challenged the Believers without showing better evidence than Genesis of how life began. Nevertheless, his statue is everywhere, and if anyone questions him, they may be terrorized or worse.

And what will the "Great Ideas" of our century be? Environmentalism? "Diversity"? "Equality," I shudder to think. But why bother? It is a perfect day. As someone who has lived and worked in Europe and the United States for decades, I am well aware of how Western culture and civilization have been commandeered by advocates of leftist ideologies. It is almost impossible to have a critical discussion of Western civilization without being insulted by the pernicious conduct and attitudes of modern fanatics, whether in the form of feminist criticism, critical race theory, Marxist criticism, queer theory, deconstructionism, or any of the other manifestations of the contemporary intellectuals' leftist agenda.

I object to the nihilistic and reinterpreting explanations of modern liberalism, which serve warped designs, and I do not feel comfortable putting subjective and objectionable nonsense into the hands of today's youth. Therefore, I think that tradition-oriented people need an alternative to this poison, and I have written my books from a distinctly tradition-minded but forward-looking perspective.

Remember that "important" is not synonymous with "good." Evil is relevant because we practice or ignore it at our peril, but it is not good. We should also remind ourselves that "culture" is not synonymous with "good." A book, film, or opera could be a significant work of culture while simultaneously being profoundly uncivilized and harmful to everything good, true, beautiful, or valuable. There is an obvious analogy with those other "cultures" appearing in nature. For example, just as it is dangerous for the body to see no difference between penicillin and E. coli, it is hazardous for the soul to recognize no difference between good culture (civilization) and bad culture (barbarism). It is, therefore, essential to remember that cultures can be barbaric. The culture of Nazi Germany, the culture of the Soviet

Union, and the culture of today's institutionalized hedonism are all cruel, uncivilized cultures controlled and dominated by intelligent barbarians. We should never assume something is "good" or civilized merely because it is "sophisticated."

Communism is like a child's story, and being childish is one of that ideology's principal dangers since, often, the romantic notions justifying its incredible cruelties sweep away immature minds. Children usually display a ruthless capacity for inflicting damage, injury, and brutality, and any impartial scrutiny of ideological extremists, whether communist, fascist, or religious, reveals similar tendencies — that is why they are so dangerous. In pursuing the ideal and perfect society, principles and truths can be sacrificed for the "greater good," leaving the common domain of humanity at the mercy of the cause so nobly furthered by its devotees.

The awful books written by highbrow intellectuals lionized among the cultural elites reveal the abject emptiness on which the status of those elites rests. These globalist elitists maintain that those who do not fall in line with the left-liberal, multicultural, and woke ideology of obsequious intellectuals have already succumbed to "the seductive lure of authoritarianism" and label them resentment-filled liars, anti-Semites, fascists, racists, and greedy careerists.

The leftist white intellectuals tend to be privileged individuals with Ivy League educations, coming from wealthy families and holding good, well-paying jobs. They are generally the type of people who enjoy life's advantages by being born into money, power, fame, status, and other privileges. Moreover, they believe their luck signifies they did something to earn it. They also feel that the threat to democracy comes from "illiberal autocrats" like Hungarian Prime Minister Viktor Orbán, who believe that nation-states should be guided fundamentally by their citizens' interests. To the leftist intellectuals and liberal Western elites, just as appalling are those influential political leaders who steadfastly pursue national policies when confronted with vigorous opposition from supranational and international institutions.

While these leftist intellectuals fully recognize the role Marxist revolutionary theory plays in the origin of authoritarianism, they remain silent on contemporary left-wing tyranny. They pay no attention to American cities burning during the riotous sieges conducted by Black Lives Matter and Antifa or to European countries facing unprecedented waves of crime and terrorist violence perpetrated by radicalized foreign nationals. They also ignore how mainstream Western politicians on the left, from the current U.S. president and vice president to the German chancellor, cozy up to left-wing militants.

However, elite liberal intellectuals depend on many causes of these conflicts for their status. They never attempt to examine the tenets of nationalism empirically and fail to even glance at the reasons typically given by national conservatives for their concerns about the future. This includes marital and familial dissolution; cultural decay under the incessant force of consumerist individualism; immigration-driven demographic transformation with the promise of a permanent and ever-growing electoral majority for the Left; elites who have economically sold out the working class for their own bottom lines; and the inexorable leftward skew of every single cultural institution. The globalist intellectual gentry fancies flying high above the "backward" populists and nationalists.

Who Is a Leftist Today?

It is questionable whether the militant "wokeness" culture spilling over from the U.S. to the entire Western world promises more or less freedom. But nobody can dispute the point that the Left connects the struggle for the underprivileged with the defense of individual dignity.

The Left has an obsession with "identity politics," but it is not solely a leftist obsession. Right-wing nationalism and neoconservatism compete with each other in condemning the alleged leftist identity politics, pulling all sorts of anecdotal evidence and hearsay rumors from their pockets. Strangely enough, "leftist identity politics" plays a more critical role in right-wing discourses than in left-wing debates.

It fits this strange panorama that it is unclear what "identity politics" is supposed to be, and no school of thought identifies itself as such. Indeed, some people uphold "wokeness," or "mindfulness and attention to emotional wounds and discrimination of particularly oppressed people," but that is not yet identity politics.

"Identity politics" would have to uphold particular previous identities; indeed, it would have to revolve around the term "identity" itself. On the one hand, it is questionable whether people's political convictions, activities, and self-esteem revolve merely around a natural element of their identity, e.g., skin color, ethnicity, sexual orientation, Jewishness, or being Muslim.

The struggles of the working classes have always been about recognition and respect. Insisting on a specially prioritized identity component is a trap, as we all have patchwork identities. A gay male technician from the French middle class has an identity, but it is not sufficiently traceable by any one of the single identity components of "gay," "male," or "French." In short, thinking about identity falls short if it overestimates individual personality traits.

At the same time, however, both personal and collective identities are a fact, and there has never been a political movement that, in this sense, was not also about "identity politics." It has become popular to point out that the political Left, generally, and socialists in particular, have always centered on the "social question." However, one should recall that the working classes' struggles were not just about job security, pension systems, higher wages, and maximum working hours, such as the eight-hour day — all these movements were, at the same time, struggles for recognition and respect.

Ordinary people wanted to be recognized for their achievements, wanted fairness, and did not want to be treated or commanded from above but wanted their values to be central to their lives. The working classes wanted respect for "their identity," with everything that goes with it, e.g., the pride in hard work, the pride in being able to support one's own family, right up to the cultural styles of the working classes and — after their gradual rise — the lower middle classes. Fish and chips in England and beer gardens in Germany were just as much a part of working-class culture and identity as the fan club at the local football association and local patriotism. What else but identity politics is that?

In short, identity politics, defined too narrowly, leads to a blind alley; identity politics, understood more broadly, is simply a historical fact and a matter of course.

Simultaneously, socialist movements emerged as champions of democracy and human rights, especially in their birthplaces of Germany and Austria, where they had to confront autocratic monarchies and semi-despotism. These movements were built on a foundation of values such as freedom, equality, justice, and solidarity, which extended beyond the "social question." This shared commitment to these values fostered a sense of unity among the diverse groups within the movements.

The socialist movements were also champions of women's emancipation. At the same time, particularly low-status working-class sections had to fight to be part of the movement, such as the Irish in England, the proletariat of Polish descent in Germany, or the "Bohemians" in the Viennese workers' movement. Everywhere, one can see struggles for recognition and the values of a liberal, non-discriminatory society brought forward simultaneously as social concerns. The socialist movements were not monolithic entities but complex, often conflicting alliances. For instance, social democratic women's rights activists were often at odds with workers who held more traditional values. Ethnic divisions within the movements also led to bitter disputes. Even within the socialist and progressive parties, differences of opinion were not just political but also reflected cultural backgrounds. These internal tensions and contradictions were not weaknesses but a testament to the diversity and complexity of the socialist movements.

The Left, e.g., "the social democrats," "the communists," and "the progressives," has also been divided into supporters of "identity politics" or a socio-political orientation toward the masses.

Some believe that all discriminated minorities have a right to a voice and to be "heard." Others contend that "particularly discriminated minorities" have a right to a voice and to be heard, but caution that falling into the trap of fragmentation must always be avoided.

Some view the demands of particularly discriminated minorities with sympathy; others do not hold a completely different opinion but find that the challenge of establishing alliances and majorities should not be overlooked either. Some favor absolute equality for homosexuals and lesbians or respect for both workers on the building site and employees in the office. While others mostly agree with them, there are differences in detail, focus, or choice of words. They all seek respect for the lifetime achievements of factory workers who have toiled on the assembly line and improved legal status for migrant care workers or parcel deliverers.

Allegedly, the leftists have to represent those who, because of their skin color, origin, and the degradation they experience, are constantly treated with disrespect and therefore face a significantly more difficult time, often trapped in status poverty, precariousness, and new proletarianization.

Furthermore, leftists also have to represent the concerns of the autochthonous white working class, who are afraid of their declining status and have a justified feeling that nobody is listening to them or is interested in them anymore. An absurd assumption is the belief that these issues are mutually exclusive. On the contrary, they belong together — a Left that does not unify them is not worth the name. Karl Marx believed it is necessary to overturn all conditions whereby man is a humiliated, enslaved, abandoned, and contemptible being (Marx, A Contribution to the Critique of Hegel's Philosophy of Right — Introduction, 1843). This artful humanism is at the core of the Left's masterful propaganda, to which the Right has not yet found an answer.

The problem is not the marginal differences of opinion but the toxic passion of declaring others enemies because of these differences. Whenever I reflect on the current trajectory of left-liberal democracy, I conclude that its followers are mere "lifestyle leftists" who pay homage to a cult of arrogance and oversensitivity.

The modern, mainly social-democratic Left has moved away from its mission and no longer advocates for people who want to rise economically and socially. On the contrary, these *bon vivant* "lifestyle leftists" look down arrogantly on their former working-class voters, who, not surprisingly, flee in droves to the populist Right. It is not the strength of the Right but the preposterous intolerance of the Left that is the cause of its lessening.

Today's "lifestyle Left" is chasing after the wrong, overrated, and sometimes absurd topics. I relish the "identity politics" of young leftist intellectuals whose obsessive preoccupation with language and gender issues points to the right path to insignificance. Moreover, the "lifestyle Left" has also accepted — in a downright submissive way — the intellectual sovereignty of the Greens, who embody the leftist lifestyle type in its purest form.

The political Left is a wounded, cornered animal that lashes out aggressively out of desperation and weakness, which fits the "lifestyle Left" perfectly.

Socialism — Welfare State, Divorce Revolution, and Limit of the End of History

With the family and sexuality politicized, the Left fooled conservatives and everyone else into becoming their accomplices.

Since the electoral coup in 2020, the United States has been on the path toward having a de facto socialist government. However, it is not the socialism the conservatives had warned against, nor did it come about as expected. Conservatives bear considerable responsibility for what happened because, by misunderstanding and overlooking the dynamics of the Left, they cowardly helped fulfill their own prophecies.

The American people have long prided themselves on being immune or impervious to socialism and avoided creating a European-style welfare state. However, the U.S. elites and their government were not lagging behind Europe. As always, they led the way by taking a different road to socialism: they created a government device that produced its own class of insurgents. Knowing that dogmatic Marxism held little appeal for Americans, the Left enlisted conservatives to the cause of socialism by abandoning the hyperbole of class warfare, appealing instead to a sense of empathy for women and children that benevolent but conservative gallants could not resist.

The American liberal Left erected a different welfare state: not comprehensive social insurance for all, but a "safety net" limited to the poor. By doing so, the leftists defied the purists within their ranks who rejected "welfarism" as a capitalist scheme to co-opt the working class. This "safety-net socialism," operating according to its innovative dynamics, bred its own quasi-proletariat of the marginalized, resentful, and entitled while being led and managed by a vanguard of indoctrinated and radicalized civil servant apparatchiks. At all levels of the system, women performed essential roles.

The welfare machinery devised and executed by pseudo-socialist and progressivist agendas, the New Deal, and particularly the "War on Poverty" social welfare legislation of President Lyndon B. Johnson's Great Society program accomplished what slavery and segregation could not: it destroyed the African-American family and formed a self-perpetuating underclass of single mothers and fatherless children.

The outcome of safety-net socialism was a self-destructive and sociopathic horde of criminals, truants, addicts, and derelicts who went on to demolish their communities and quickly fill the world's most extensive prison system. Overseeing their lives was a cadre of functionaries — again, increasingly female — with self-interest in expanding and perpetuating the devastation.

As this disturbed, neurotic, and troubled population was composed overwhelmingly of "minorities," i.e., non-whites, the rest of American society got used to not caring — this is one ironic element of truth in the worn-out charge of "racism." While the Left feigned compassion for black "oppression," it could not decide if the cause was racism or capitalism — it was neither.

Conservatives could have reaped the enormous political benefit by identifying that the real culprit was the destruction of the family. Instead, their only solution was to enact ever-harsher penalties that further expanded the gulag system and increased resentment from blacks. Then, to help crime victims, conservatives put together an additional bureaucracy, which the gender justice warriors would later hijack for their own purposes, applying political criteria to the "victim" label.

After having surrendered the moral authority to the Left, conservatives had nothing effectively valuable to offer — other than a punishment mentality — when confronted with periodic revolts, race riots, and urban uprisings, e.g., those following the assassination of Dr. Martin Luther King, Jr., the beating of Rodney King, the shooting of Michael Brown in Ferguson, Missouri, and the death of George Floyd.

Some conservative intellectuals conducted investigations during the 1960s and 1970s and issued urgent warnings. However, any comprehensive scrutiny or thorough study ceased when they ran against entrenched political interests on the Left and Right. Then, conservative thinking about welfare eventually atrophied altogether.

Meanwhile, the state continued expanding exponentially in colossal welfare expenditures and expensive bureaucratic industries designed to control and keep the social fallout in check: education, housing, healthcare, social services, law enforcement, and incarceration. An exploding domestic budget became allocated almost entirely to the social ills bred and sustained by welfare.

The result is more insidious than waste because welfare is the people's wealth spent to reduce new supplies to criminals, addicts, dropouts, rioters, and even terrorists. For statists, welfare is the government's great instrument for devising problems for itself to solve.

Complementing all this, the new socio-political ideology of feminism had arrived on the scene, drawing upon socialist and communist ideas while also transforming them. These new ideologues fully understood that minority poverty and hardship were not the effects of racism or capitalism but the consequences of the destruction of the family, which they had exacerbated and exploited — if not created.

While the media smokescreen portrayed feminists as homely women simulating black grievances, the feminist movement was causing an altogether different kind of destruction: it intentionally glorified and helped proliferate the single-mother homes that created the new underclass and stoked its self-destructiveness and rage. "Independence" was supposed to offer more sexual freedom than the affluence, stability, and social conformity gained through marriage and dependence on one man.

The original impetus behind welfare was socialism, and the operatives were radicalized women from the start.

However, women volunteers inspired by a sense of Christian calling and supported financially by their husbands also administered private charity. But welfare speedily replaced them with a new class of paid professional social workers who quickly established a vested interest and personal stake in perpetuating the problems they were supposedly solving, exploiting the youth and ignorance of the poor and unemployed.

Anti-male ideology dovetailed with bureaucratic self-interest to ensure that breadwinning men, who alone could have freed women and children from dependence on the state, stayed away.

Then, to avoid bankruptcy and address the underlying problem, the welfare state quietly turned upside down from distributing charity to collecting revenue. The result was authoritarian machinery: in addition to prisons, a massive system summarily placed millions of law-abiding citizens under correctional supervision. The new phrase to conjure was "child support," through which the deadbeat dad holds a place of particular opprobrium as a selfish fugitive condemned by liberals and conservatives alike.

While it was readily accepted that many young black men were semi-criminals, nobody bothered to understand why. The actual criminal violence was primarily the product of growing up in single-mother homes, as social science demonstrates unequivocally. The welfare system then added criminalization to criminality; the use of welfare payments resulted in the removal of fathers and turned adolescents into criminals. Social workers then used child support laws to criminalize the fathers. Social service agencies transformed their personnel into plainclothes feminist police. The third stage of criminalizing their rivals — the legitimate authority attempting to ensure order amid all this — is now in full swing.

Social workers, judges, lawyers, and others had a substantial pecuniary interest in using children to rationalize their power and earnings while demonizing fathers. The bureaucrats' requirement for fathers to pay to support children they had allegedly "abandoned" had at least superficial appeal.

After creating this self-growing machine to proliferate, entrench, and reinforce the underclass, the next step was to expand the rationale to middle-class society.

The feminists achieved that by engineering the most radical, leftist, and subversive legal innovation ever instituted in Western democracies. It was so diabolical that, at a stroke, it decimated the integrity of the family and the judiciary: it overthrew the common-law system that had safeguarded freedom for centuries. That concept, borrowed from the insurance industry, of "no-fault" justice was used to abolish civilization's most fundamental institution: marriage.

And few even noticed what happened. The U.S. was busy with the Cuban missile crisis, the Kennedy assassination, the Vietnam War, the civil rights movement, rioting, the rise of a militant antiwar movement, and the counterculture from the beginning of the 1960s — and the incipient sexual revolution was adjusting the culture to radical sexual permissiveness, experimentation, and acceptance. Deceptive propaganda promising divorce "by mutual consent" fooled almost everyone about what created involuntary divorce — the abolishment of marriage as a legally enforceable contract. That permitted one spouse to end the marriage unilaterally without giving recognized grounds or accepting responsibility for the consequences vis-à-vis the other spouse or the children. In 1969, California Governor Ronald Reagan signed the first no-fault divorce bill.

Feminists had devised this no-fault sleight of hand in the 1940s and were waiting for an opportunity to unleash it. No-fault divorce was so extreme in revolutionizing family relationships and legal actions that its only precedents occurred during the French and Russian Revolutions — and the governments of those nations later repealed it because of the social chaos it had caused. But it swept the U.S. and the Western world with almost no resistance or discussion.

It took decades to reach the full impact of its logical conclusion: the middle class diminished to conditions comparable to those of the underclass. Feminized functionaries of the welfare state administered middle-class lives and relationships permeated by bitter and entitled single mothers, dysfunctional children, and criminalized fathers.

"No-fault" justice was breathtaking in its nihilism and in the virtually complete control over the individual granted to the state. For the first time under the common-law system, courts could summon innocent people, take control of their private lives, and penalize them for legal actions they took during their personal lives. Courts acquired the power to dissolve marriages without consent or grounds. They could evict people from their homes, confiscate their houses, restrict their movements, seize control of their children, garnish their wages, raid their bank accounts, extract payments for "services" they never requested, take their professional licenses, deny them passports and driving permits, and incarcerate them without trial or record.

Involuntary, unilateral divorce allows for the child-support Gestapo, first devised to persecute poverty-stricken young men, to target productive middle-class wage earners and entrepreneurs with deeper pockets to loot, thus providing an irresistible bribe as an incentive for single mothers-to-be, but also lucrative revenue for state-governmental coffers. Federally funded propagandists at universities and courts smugly declared or decided that these fathers had carelessly abandoned their children when it was easily provable that the children were "judicially kidnapped" through literally "no-fault" of their deceived fathers. The same bankrolled scholars and leftist intellectuals who spread this defamation against citizens without any platform to defend themselves became the darlings of right-wing moralizers lavishly supported by numerous conservative foundations, like the Family Research Council.

The unchecked hysteria swelled throughout the 1990s. Anyone questioning this narrative was ignored, demonized, or sacked — even by conservative institutions. Conservative politicians gleefully joined the witch hunt. The Republican Bush administration carried forward the worst measures initiated by the Democrat Clintons, supported by Republican senators.

Meanwhile, the apparatchiks, judges, lawyers, feminists, and politicians teamed up to erect an American apparatus of unprecedented repression. Federal subsidies for child-support collections make divorced and single-mother homes enormously profitable for state governments, giving them incentives to encourage as much divorce and create as many fatherless children as possible. They achieved this by ratcheting child-support payments to excessive levels, making divorce lucrative for mothers and lethal for fathers, often resulting in inevitable and summary incarceration followed by inescapable homelessness.

This de facto socialist machinery functioned while conservatives fatuously philosophized about families being "building blocks" of society. The result is that generations of children of divorce have grown up hating their fathers and all traditional authority, feeling alienated from the institution of marriage, and seeing civil servants of the state as their providers and protectors. Many feel betrayed, are scared of love, and have no idea how to form healthy, enduring, and sacrificial relationships with the opposite sex or even their own children. Moreover, like their mothers and the ever-helping civil servants, these victims of facilitated divorce feel entitled to the fruits of the state's ever-expanding power. Having been raised on the proceeds and costs of their fathers' enslavement and impoverishment by the child-support system, they have no compunction about enslaving productive taxpayers in two-parent families to provide for their own needs and wants.

All of this even supplied the essential ingredients for the Left's electoral coup in 2020, such as:

- The enraged resentment and violence of black youth and their white middle-class peers and facilitators (similarly nihilistic despite their advantages).

- The shameless manipulation and exploitation of poverty by feminists, like the now-affluent women who started Black Lives Matter.

- The disdain for constitutional procedures and civil liberties manifested in faultfinding "cancel culture."

- The iconoclasm and irreverence that externalized the scorn for once-revered traditions.

Meanwhile, the privileged and complacent conservative leaders stubbornly refuse to listen to the few scholars and journalists who could tell them what is happening.

The perversion of the justice system is the most insidious, abrogating the constitutional protections it is supposed to uphold. Throughout its growth, the welfare/divorce apparatus has improvised mock courts to legitimize unprecedented criminalization and preposterous incarceration. Judicial operators do not merely fail to protect constitutional freedoms — they take the lead in removing them.

Family courts adjudicate no-fault divorce — a grotesque travesty of law: Since every verdict is predetermined and only one outcome is possible, justice never enters divorce cases. The divorce kleptocracy ravages legally irreproachable citizens, using their children as leverage. False accusations of "domestic violence" are arbitrated in assembly-line-like procedures lasting merely a few minutes, where outcomes are predetermined. Similar miscarriages of justice typify "child abuse" accusations. Psychotherapy is applied to rationalize convicting people who committed no crime.

These crooked courts are so "empowering" that the feminists replicate them elsewhere. They used to invent similarly trumped-up rape accusations against black men (reminiscent of lynching) before becoming mainstream in the white middle class. Universities were particularly welcoming of this tactic and quickly organized pseudo-tribunals composed of students, professors, and administrators to conduct show trials against male students accused without evidence in a harmful way. That, in turn, led directly to the #MeToo movement, with more evidence-free and witness-free accusations and trials targeting more prominent political figures like Judge Brett Kavanaugh.

These disciplinary tribunals were a rehearsal for the penalizing zeal seen in and after the electoral scheme against President Donald Trump and his supporters. Kafkaesque travesties developed in the divorce courts provided the *modus operandi*.

Before the election, the radical Left demanded the punishment — using civil or criminal charges — of anyone challenging or interfering with the leftist path to power. This extended to lawyers challenging electoral illegalities or representing Donald Trump; election officials hesitating to certify questionable results; members of Congress trying to use the constitutional process to ensure electoral integrity; members of the media disseminating criticisms of the Left;

105

ordinary citizens supporting Trump or questioning government actions; and, of course, Mr. Trump himself.

What are called "show trials" of political opponents culminated in the commandeering of the presidential impeachment process, turning it into an unconstitutional act of what is known in the legal profession as "attainder," i.e., the legal consequence of a judgment of death or outlawry for treason or felony, involving the loss of all civil rights. The Left's adversaries are not to be debated but "cleansed" and "canceled." Psychotherapy and accusations of mental illness are weaponized for political purposes, including silencing dissident attorneys and becoming routine in divorce proceedings — resembling Soviet practices.

The Left pioneered the techniques used against their enemies in America's divorce system. Today's Left does not discuss or debate but only accuses concerning divorce courts, rape trials, domestic violence, child abuse accusations, #MeToo targets, police using lethal force, or the election aftermath. Dissenters who obstruct the leftist hegemony must be on trial for their supposed crimes.

We may be nearing a historical time of momentous troubles, which will not be without its irony. It has been almost thirty years since the world learned that the "end of history" had arrived. That was the lesson political philosopher Francis Fukuyama taught after Cold War I had ended, and Western values of liberal democracy seemed to reign supreme (Fukuyama, 1992).

The Soviet Union and the Eastern Bloc had fallen without firing a shot (except for Romania), and communist China had opened itself to both the West and capitalism. The world seemed to be almost at the point of agreeing that liberal and capitalist democracy was the best way to organize countries and represented the only path to a new future, heralding lasting peace, prosperity, and progress.

The general consensus seemed to be that the American model — or some reasonably close approximation of it — was the answer to the world's problems. America, the "shining city upon a hill," meant salvation by American example and not by the American sword. Moreover, as former enemies gradually became more like the West, they might even become new friends or, at least, peaceful partners.

Amid all that optimism, there would no longer be a need to advance or spread democracy at gunpoint. With World War I and II now ancient history, Wilsonian calls to "make the world safe for democracy" would no longer be of primary importance to any Western declaration of war.

Indeed, there was a kernel of truth in claiming that the end of history had finally arrived. The West could thank the American Founding Fathers for establishing the documents that assumed joining political and economic freedoms together best ensured both. The framers also believed that people could not have one without the other for more than a short time. While the United States has benefited from that understanding for over two centuries, the entire world, including America's rivals, was suddenly poised to benefit at the "end of history" — heaven on earth was at hand. Countries enjoying the fruits of democracy do not fight against one another; they trade with one another — so they told us.

Let us leap forward three decades. Neither Russia nor China has come close to adopting a commercial republic, liberal democracy, or any version of it. The idea of history reaching its end in 2021 is as distant as it was in 1992. Vladimir Putin's Russia has embraced its traditional conservatism, and Xi Jinping's China is adhering to an alternative model based on controlled economic "openness" under the umbrella of socialism with Chinese characteristics.

China is challenging Francis Fukuyama's assertion. It argues that a nation does not need both economic and political freedoms to succeed and exert influence. It is enough for a country to have elements of the former and none of the latter. Not only was Mr. Fukuyama wrong about China, but it was also beginning to appear that he was wrong about the West. A prosperous China is not becoming more "liberal" or "democratic," but the United States threatens to become more like China.

Today, the United States is poised to leap toward a Chinese-style centralized government and one-party rule. At least, that seems to be what the ruling Democratic Party is prepared to attempt. Donald Trump may be gone for now, but that is not enough for them: they will do much to ensure that there will never be another Trump presidency or any other presidency with Trump-like ideals, mores, and manners. This potential shift in the U.S. political landscape is a cause for concern and should engage our attention.

The most significant players in this political landscape are the "big tech companies." Their power surpasses that of the 19th-century robber barons, and their intentions are far more sinister. We can anticipate a further implementation of surveillance capitalism and "cancel culture," with the entertainment industry, education establishment, and mainstream media all aligning with Big Tech. The mainstream media, in particular, now operates as an arm of the Democratic Party.

The end of history, which was to occur with the end of the first Cold War, has hit a snag. Worse, the "snag" includes a mighty effort to close down the United States — thanks to the Left's clout within the Democratic Party and its auxiliary henchpersons.

All of that portends an approaching time of troubles instead of anything resembling the end of history. After all, a concerted leftist attempt to end the American experiment in limited government, coupled with the stifling of the Bill of Rights and the possible changing or canceling of the U.S. Constitution, will likely provoke a contentious new history. If not, a fresh spate of Fukuyama-like books will predict a very different "end of history."

The shock troops for this effort, such as the BLM movement and Antifa, i.e., anti-fascist, are also in place. With fascism ascending in Europe in the 1930s, they asked Senator Huey Long of Louisiana if fascism would ever reach America. "Sure," he replied, "only we'll call it anti-fascism" (Life Magazine, 1939). What has descended upon the United States is a new 21st-century totalitarian regime, and it is just beginning its reign of terror. The rogue regime, i.e., the Deep State, consists of Big Government, the Big Tech of Big Business, Big Education, and the Big Globalists. Its DNA is inherited directly from radical socialism, and its troops are marching through the streets of America and the entire

Western world, well camouflaged by the propaganda of the intellectual mob.

Solzhenitsyn and the Religion of Revolution

The "religion of revolution" is not just a concept but a fundamental aspect at the heart of fascism, national socialism, communism, and democracy, shaping the course of history and the nature of political ideologies.

Aleksandr Solzhenitsyn, the eminent Russian novelist, essayist, and historian, deeply understood that the spirit born in France was a perpetual revolution that would give rise to radical movements and militant ideologies akin to religious fanaticism across the political spectrum worldwide. During his involuntary exile in the West between 1974 and 1994, he also discerned that among the contemporary political religions was democracy itself, a revelation that significantly enhanced our understanding of modern politics.

Even in the United States of America, a nation seemingly rooted in conservative values and born out of the Enlightenment era, Solzhenitsyn's keen eye detected the turbulent spirit of egalitarian ideals. This spirit, he cautioned, threatened to radically undermine society's traditional structure.

Alexis de Tocqueville, in his contemplation of French society during the Revolutionary era, made a striking observation in *The Old Regime and the Revolution* (1856): "the ideal the French Revolution set before it was not merely a change in the French social system but nothing short of a regeneration of the whole human race" (Tocqueville, The Old Regime and the Revolution, 2018). This quote from Tocqueville vividly portrays the all-encompassing ambition of the "religion of revolution," which aspires not just to change political systems but to fundamentally reshape society and human nature itself — humanity had to develop into "a species of religion."

None of the political religions came to power in the 19th century. However, some formed governments in the 20th century, chief among them being the communist, fascist, socialist, and National Socialist branches of the Left. The historical significance of these ideologies cannot be overstated, as they shaped the course of the 20th century.

Benito Mussolini, who began his career path as a Marxist, once stated: "Fascism is not only a party, it is a regime; it is not only a regime but a faith; it is not only a faith but a religion" (Mussolini, 1933). Although Hitler did not view National Socialism the same way, he recognized the importance of religious rituals and spectacles. By watching Leni Riefenstahl's "Triumph of the Will," the famous propaganda film of the 1934 Nazi Party Congress, one can easily recognize the ritualistic nature of that political rally, with the undertone of National Socialism being a religion.

Of course, neither fascism nor National Socialism advanced universal claims; both were national, not international. The former was Italian, and the latter emphatically German. Consequently, the political religions formed around Mussolini and Hitler also died with them.

On the other hand, communism, unfortunately, survived the deaths of Lenin and Stalin — and even the collapse of the Soviet Union — because it was universal in its claims and decidedly more religious. The Russian philosopher and theologian Nikolai Berdyaev accurately noted that "it is a property of the Russian spirit to switch over the current of religious energy to nonreligious objects" (Berdyaev N., 2015). That religious spirit was alive and well in the Russian "intelligentsia," a social class defined by its alienation from existing reality and its predilection for religiopolitical ideologies.

The religious backgrounds of Russia's 19th-century revolutionaries, many of whom were former seminarians or the sons of Orthodox priests, were not mere coincidences. Nikolai Chernyshevsky, a utopian socialist and a leading theoretician of Russian nihilism, exemplifies this. His famous novel *What Is to Be Done?* features a central character, Rakhmetov, whose revolutionary life mirrors that of the 4th-century Orthodox St. Alexius, the "Man of God" (Chernyshevsky, 1989). The irony of this historical context is further heightened when we consider that Stalin, a former seminarian, ascended to power and commissioned portrayals of his countenance akin to revered Russian icons, despite his likely lack of belief in God.

Solzhenitsyn understood all this and — although once a believer in communism — became one of the most famous critics of that political religion. On September 5, 1973, only a few months before his expulsion from the USSR, he penned an open *Letter to the Soviet Leaders* (Solzhenitsyn A. I., 1974). In it, he argued that it was not the authoritarian government but Marxist ideology and the lies, fabrications, and hypocrisy it "foisted upon us" that were unbearable.

Solzhenitsyn, in a thought-provoking contrast to the popular belief in Western circles, always denied that the evils of communism had their roots in Russian history and that

Stalin was a reincarnation of Tsar Ivan the Terrible. On the contrary, like Dostoevsky in *The Possessed*, Solzhenitsyn argued that those evils were the direct consequences of ideologies originating in Western Europe (Dostoevsky, 2015). He said more about the sins of doctrine in his *The Gulag Archipelago*:

The imagination and inner strength of Shakespeare's villains stopped short at ten or so cadavers. Because they had no ideology... It is thanks to an ideology that it fell to the lot of the twentieth century to experience villainy on a scale of millions (Solzhenitsyn A. I., *The Gulag Archipelago*, 2003).

Solzhenitsyn made a striking observation after his extensive exposure to the West, particularly the United States. He saw democracy as a political system and a surrogate faith for intellectuals deprived of religion. This insight, perhaps unbeknownst to him, resonated with the long-held American belief in their country as a "city on a hill," a phrase rooted in the Sermon on the Mount. For Americans, they were a chosen people, their nation was a redeemer, and it served as a beacon of hope for the world. Almost replacing Christianity, this civil religion had transformed into a global missionary faith, a crusading political belief system cloaked in the language of democracy, freedom, and human rights.

While he retained some respect for democracy at local levels of government, Solzhenitsyn's distaste for the democratic concept as an ideology was intense. In *The Oak and the Calf*, a memoir of his literary life, he expended no effort to praise Aleksandr Tvardovsky, the editor who published *One Day in the Life of Ivan Denisovich*, for his crucial role in preventing the thaw in the literary world that followed Stalin's death. Tvardovsky's actions effectively averted the relaxation of the revolutionary-democratic orientation in literary works, maintaining the status quo (Solzhenitsyn A. I., *The Oak and the Calf: Memoirs of a Literary Life*, 1980).

Most Western historians view Russia's February Revolution of 1917 as a tragically aborted attempt to create a democratic Russia. However, Solzhenitsyn concluded that the February Revolution was a disaster that made the Bolsheviks' October Revolution possible — in reality, inevitable. In his view, it would have been far better if a more liberal Russia, characterized by a stronger middle class and a more balanced distribution of power, could have evolved along the path of reform laid out by Prime Minister Pyotr Stolypin, a course interrupted by his assassination in 1911. Before his return to Russia, Solzhenitsyn advised his compatriots and his American audience about democracy's flaws and dangers — in vain (Solzhenitsyn A. I., *A World Split Apart: Solzhenitsyn's Commencement Address Harvard University*, 1978).

Yet revolution is the primordial political religion at the heart of fascism, National Socialism, communism, and democracy. The term "revolutionary mystique" refers to the aura of heroism, righteousness, and inevitability that often surrounds revolutionary figures and movements. This aura surrounded Oliver Cromwell, Napoleon, Lenin, Mussolini, Hitler, Stalin, and Mao — just as the idea of revolution was almost always presumed to be a desirable aspiration. One can think of the scientific revolution and other revolutions, such as new and "revolutionary" consumer products that allegedly make life easier or "revolutionary" cancer treatments designed to save or prolong life. However, none matches the allure of political revolution, for which Solzhenitsyn felt an "extreme revulsion."

In his monumental work, *The Red Wheel*, a series of novels chronicling the Russian Revolution, Solzhenitsyn masterfully captures the heady, intoxicating atmosphere of the early stages of the February Revolution, a time when hope and uncertainty mingled in the air and the fate of a nation hung in the balance:

"Revolution! The magic word! ... The marvelous flickering of red banners on tilted poles through the smoke of rifle volleys! Barricades! ... The taking of the Bastille! ... What earthly feeling could compare with that of a revolutionary? ... Revolution was greater than happiness, brighter than the daily sun; it was the explosion of a red dawn, the explosion of a star" (Solzhenitsyn A. I., *March 1917: The Red Wheel, Node III, Book 1*, 2017)!

The Russians had reached a state of religious euphoria, and Solzhenitsyn knew this from his studies. Berdyaev, who was also expelled from the Soviet Union in 1922, noted in "Spirits of the Russian Revolution," an essay published in 1918, that Russian revolutionary sanctity assumed the configuration of a cult: "This cult has its saints, its sacred tradition, its dogmas. And for a long time, every doubt of this sacred tradition, every criticism of these dogmas, and every non-reverential attitude towards these saints led to excommunication" (Berdyaev N. A., 1918).

Whatever the envisaged goal of a revolution may be — almost always equality and happiness — it is not long before it becomes an end in itself. That is why it became permanent under Lenin and Stalin: when all enemies seemed to have disappeared, the revolution started devouring its own, often by uncovering new enemies of the people. Even some early leaders fighting for the revolution turned out to be counterrevolutionaries. The most notorious example is Trotsky, who was first expelled from the Soviet Union in February 1929, then tried and sentenced to death in absentia during the first of three major show trials of the so-called Old Bolsheviks in August 1936.

In Communist China, the revolution became a dangerous permanence. Fearing a loss of control, Mao Zedong launched the Great Leap Forward (1958–62) and the Cultural Revolution (1966–76). The revolution without end led to the replacement of older comrades with power-hungry younger ones, a practice duplicated in every communist-controlled country. The dangers of permanent revolution are starkly evident in these actions.

Solzhenitsyn gave an address at Les Lucs-sur-Boulogne on September 25, 1993, commemorating the bicentennial of the counterrevolutionary Vendée Uprising (a.k.a. War in the Vendée). He told the assembled crowd he would not wish "a 'great revolution' upon any nation." Solzhenitsyn also stated France had a Thermidorian Reaction that ousted Robespierre, but no Thermidor restrained the Russian revolution "as it drove our people on the straight path to a bitter end, to an abyss, to the depths of ruin." Moreover, he observed that it was a pity no one in the audience could speak from experience of the suffering in China, Cambodia, or Vietnam and thus give testimony of "the price they had to pay for revolution" (Solzhenitsyn A. I., A Reflection on the Vendée Uprising, 1993).

As centuries have passed, people should have learned from their misadventures that revolutions pulverize the organic structures of society, disturb the natural flow of life, destroy the best constituents of the population, and give complete freedom to the worst. A revolution never brings affluence to a nation but serves only a few corrupt opportunists, while to the whole country, it brings the message of death, destruction, impoverishment, and a long-lasting degeneration of the population.

However, it is doubtful that everyone has learned the lesson, as the new wave of revolution in American streets has proven. The revolutionaries of the 1960s failed to do what the Bolsheviks could — seize power — so they had to settle for an incremental, step-by-step revolution, the "long march through the institutions." The myth, spirit, and zeal of revolution lived in the academy and governmental bureaucracies and then passed on to another generation.

Following the death of George Floyd, Black Lives Matter and Antifa were able to bring white people to their knees and beg forgiveness for the "original sin" of racism and being born white. BLM signs appeared on lawns across America, and Floyd became a martyr at the center of a religious cult. The U.S. government itself has become another cult with a barely-veiled ideology, substituting race issues for class struggle and insisting upon rituals of "self-criticism." Furthermore, there is no final goal — the

117

revolution is permanent. On Martin Luther King Jr. Day, Americans are treated to the same speech every year: "We still have a long way to go."

But Solzhenitsyn warned the West that a descent into the abyss could also be its fate.

Society, Culture, and Science

I propose a term for understanding the prevalent discord in contemporary Western culture and politics: cacophonic dissonance.

What do I mean by this? Cacophony, as I use the term, is not just sound; it combines harsh and discordant noises. For example, the mixture of different tones one hears at a busy city street corner or market, such as the sound of traffic, chattering people, working machines, barking dogs, etc., is an example of cacophony. The noise itself is a variety of usually unwanted sounds. Cacophonic noise is an unpleasant shrill that can tear thought and personality to shreds and drive one insane.

Consider the works of Beethoven, Gershwin, Orwell, Faulkner, Renoir, or Rockwell. They embody musical beauty, dramatic character, comprehensive musicianship, unique intellectual culture, natural goodness, kindness, and moral principles. They fill the concert halls, libraries, galleries, and museums with music, purpose, talent, message, and beauty, starkly contrasting the cacophonic noise of modern pretenders, hucksters, and self-promoters.

Then I think of Miley Cyrus, who has no "intellectual culture" or virtuoso performance on the violin, guitar, or banjo. The lights around her shriek, and while I can turn off the sound, I cannot escape the visual noise. Her face twists in madness and wrath; there is no smile but a petulant sneer; no blink of the eye suggests a trace of the meek, kindly, or humble. Who would allow themselves to be imprisoned in that skin?

Who are the people whose Loretta Lynn or Emmylou Harris is Miley Cyrus today? I am not referring to moral corruption or a collapse of good taste — those were common in the fall of empires and cultures before ours. But cacophonic dissonance has obliterated certain organs of intellectual, moral, and aesthetic perception. We have become so blind and deaf today that we are no longer aware of the destruction.

I cannot imagine anyone now being brought to tears while listening to a contemporary performer singing anything. There is merely the noisy dissonance, properly speaking: the decibels. The people in charge of the racket must believe that we desire relief from leisure, conversation, and silence.

The newspapers once meant to be read by farmers, fishermen, and mill workers would overtax college students' linguistic capacities today. College professors cannot write as Jefferson, Hamilton, or Madison did because they lack learning and literary skills. *The Federalist* could not be written or taught today; it cannot be taught because the dissonance would trip up the first small steps of thought. If we put Alexander Hamilton's *Federalist 6* before a couple of television personalities to discuss, they would not get far enough to debate how accurate Hamilton's account is because they do not know history. But even if they did, the shrieks would interfere.

There is a truth we are not permitted or enabled to conceive — the cacophonic dissonance always interferes. Not just the noise of the de facto mob, busying themselves as self-appointed judges and juries or rallying for or against measures neither they nor their nominal representatives have read, but the noisy dissonance of that mob in the wreckage of the soul.

Equality, equality! The journalists, politicians, and those in academia who scribble upon the walls of a dilapidated culture will fill the air with passionate vagaries. Terms like "toxic masculinity," "intersectionality," "bodily autonomy," and "social justice" might retain some semblance of meaning if subjected to careful and dispassionate analysis, but they are employed precisely to ensure that such study is never forthcoming.

Passion is cacophonic dissonance when it does not belong or is not under the strict reign of reason. The response to the viral pandemic COVID-19 provides a case in point. There has never been a rational discussion of what measures should be appropriate. Lives were at stake, and no one could know how many and whose. Since nothing can be called life that is free of danger, it was incumbent upon the state and the people to consider risks and losses in their wide variety and understand that they would suffer consequences for whatever actions they took. But there was no discussion about that because it was impossible, just as you cannot read and understand a poem while a hundred voices are shouting at you in a dark room. You cannot reason with a fanatic; if one's soul is brimming with fanatic dissonance, he cannot reason with anyone.

When people can no longer perceive the difference between saying "You are wrong" and "You are wicked," rational discussion becomes inconceivable. Narcissism, a term I use to describe excessive self-interest and self-admiration, makes much noise in fraudulent language, as its sentimentality is a deceptive feeling. The word "sexism," rather than denoting something clearly defined, such as irrational hatred of or contempt for one sex, is tossed like a match into the fire: it is meant not to initiate but to thwart discourse. One can defend oneself against an accusation by analyzing the facts or discovering an error in reasoning, but you cannot so protect yourself against a shriek — soon enough, you will be shrieking in turn. Our politics are a cacophony of shrieks.

In this respect, the schools are factories for political and counter-rational dissonance; students are taught conflicting historical narratives or presented with biased information, deliberately creating contradictory and irrational ideas. This process discourages students from forming their own opinions while teaching them how not to read. The schools aim to convey and magnify the cacophonic noise. Rather than encouraging students to pause, reflect, and consider, today's teachers drown everything in the cacophonic dissonance of politics, chattering about the natives in the New World, colonialism, and sexual power play. Why bother to read Shakespeare and have barely literate students struggle with early modern English? Will not the barely literary Margaret Atwood suffice?

Very few modern geniuses with exceptional intellectual or creative power turn to the arts — that cacophonic dissonance prevents a turning toward beauty in favor of the quick, cheap, and vain. Besides, it may not be so in absolute numbers: we may have as many people calling themselves artists as Raphael did in his Urbino — but where is our Raphael? In any case, we expect a secular age to produce more microwave ovens than Madonnas. Are we in a secular age because of clear thinking and conviction, or because of cacophonic dissonance, so that we are not what we think but what we do not think — if we think at all?

The masses create noise and cacophony, and dissonance weighs heavily upon the soul. Nevertheless, we need not withdraw from the world to be mostly free of it. Eton or the studios of Ghirlandaio or Rembrandt were conducive to learning, brilliant thought, and the making of masterpieces — such schools, studios, and universities littered the fields across Europe. Nor were such places islands unto themselves, although, in meaningful ways, intellectual wisdom, which I define as the ability to think critically and engage in rational discourse, shielded them from noise — from the cacophony of political passions, the lure of the ordinary and demotic, and the incessant and thoughtless chatter.

Let us not mistake a flurry of slogans for a true poem when it is no poem at all. Why strive to craft one small but exquisite poem like a gem when a simple costume glass sells for a thousand times more? But in this pursuit, we risk losing our discernment, our ability to appreciate the jewel. Our tastes will become debased, and we will lack the clarity and composure to recognize what is truly good and valuable.

The cacophony of dissonance demands attention; this attention, in turn, distracts the mind, leading to a metaphorical headache. This noise breeds poor quality, and its omnipresence sets the standards. If the transient content of social media shapes our viewpoints and the political fervor of a riot or the "theory" of the schools dominates our thoughts, we may never read *The Federalist,* even if we have the opportunity.

Scientific methods have governed much of popular American thinking. Empirically, scientists have advised us to examine evidence and data and then develop rational hypotheses by induction. Politics, superstition, bias, and deduction are the enemies of "science." However, Western society is regressing, reverting to a modern version of medieval alchemy and astrology, discarding a millennium of the scientific method. This anti-scientific fervor has seeped into scientific endeavors, distorting them from rewarding merit to promoting wokeness in medical school admissions and peer-reviewing scientific papers.

"Critical race theory," or CRT, preposterously tells people they must fight racism with racism. CRT ludicrously alleges that laws have no rational basis — they only reflect power inequities. "Modern monetary theory" challenges millennia of evidence, basic logic, and financial history by claiming that governments can print money without balancing expenditures with revenues or inflating the currency to devastating hyperinflation. Corporations are urged to adopt a new and woke agenda theory called Environmental, Social, and Corporate Governance (ESG) instead of adhering to market realities, due diligence, rules of investment, and economic data.

Science, the beacon of progress, is fading, and in its place, superstition is resurging — camouflaged as morality. This shift threatens to impoverish our collective knowledge, fuel our discontent, and deepen our societal divisions.

Destruction of the Western Right

In recent decades, a rhetorical style has developed — centered on warning people about a "far-right" takeover of Western countries. However, that has little to do with the present political reality or with anything that seems likely to happen.

Nevertheless, even the Western "conservative" press pulls out all the stops to ensure that culturally and politically leftist opponents win elections against "right-wing" challengers. Moreover, mainstream American and European "conservative" media also seem determined to preserve the leftist status quo in the Western world. And concerning the LGBTQ agenda, the entire Western political Left of the 1990s was still well to the right of what is today, quite ridiculously, called the "American conservative movement."

People who lived through the second half of the 20th century can grasp the magnitude of this lurch to the left. First politically and then culturally, the Left has been given a free hand for many decades in America, Western Europe, and throughout the Anglosphere. As the Left advanced, the opposition grew weaker, more intimidated, and more accommodating. Part of what fueled this development was the fear of being identified with "fascism," although that term became so loaded with ideological baggage that it eventually lost any connection to what happened in interwar Europe. In those few instances where one can locate connections between extremist movements, the anti-white, anti-Christian Left looks much more like fascists and Nazis than an increasingly weakened and retreating Right today.

There are two effective techniques for those who have no desire to reverse this continuing leftward shift.

First, one can denounce any retreat from the present degree of radicalization as a plunge into Hitlerism. The argument goes like this: "Human decency" requires us to accept everything the political and cultural Left has achieved in the last 60 to 70 years as the minimal requirement for overcoming "discrimination," "systemic white racism," and "social injustice." If we retreat from this minimal base, we will soon be living in the equivalent of the Third Reich. According to its advocates, no going back or undoing what the Left has done must ever be permitted if we wish to remain a society working to overcome its irredeemably evil past.

Second, there is a conservative movement variation on this argument, which consists of frantically and repeatedly calling attention to "right-wing extremism" while the speaker claims to represent a genuine conservative tradition. These supposed voices of moderation warn against a dangerous neo-fascist Right that is ready to corrupt both Christian humanism and "our liberal democracy." Such polemics against the right-wing "enemies of liberalism" strongly resonate in the conservative policy foundation community. Moreover, an entire industry on the genteel "moderate" Right specializes in exposing right-wing extremist dangers, and whole careers depend on this richly rewarding preoccupation.

Although there have been bumps in the Left's ascent to dizzying power, these obstacles have been at most temporary, like the hyped-up "Reagan Revolution," the proliferation of GOP think tanks in the Washington Beltway, or the supposedly transformative Trump presidency. Almost everything billed as a counterrevolution has not stopped the relentless march of LGBTQ, anti-white racism, a leftist managerial state in alliance with globalist capitalists, and, lately, a government crusade against the populist Right.

In the face of these challenges, the "authorized center-right," an exceedingly narrow political spectrum, has usually reacted by coming to terms with the cultural Left — and thereby attacking true conservatism as far-right extremism — or else by turning the conversation toward building up military defenses and fighting a mostly nonexistent Marxism.

The question is whether there will be an effective, if not cataclysmic, reaction to this leftist hegemony. Will the pendulum swing back, or will things continue as they have, with an increasingly radical Left doing what it wants without much effective pushback? Among the now-marginalized alt-right, one finds a genuine interest in interwar revolutionary nationalists and other antiliberal thinkers of the early 20th century. However, there is no indication that what little still exists of real opposition to the Left will assume the character of the interwar European Right.

When considering what a reaction to current leftist successes might entail, one should remember the political theorist Carl Schmitt's emphasis on the uniqueness of each historical moment. The political or cultural past is not reproducible because "a historical truth is true only once"

(Lievens, 2011). Nevertheless, we can take in the wisdom of past thinkers while trying to relate their observations to the present crisis. Even in uncharted waters, we still have a sketch from those who came before.

Unfortunately, there is also the possibility that the leftist, woke hegemony will continue, the social harm it has caused proves to be irreversible, and there will be no chance of redress. Nevertheless, a reaction can and should be mounted because the so-called conservative opposition to the Left will be allowed to prosper as long as it rails against a supposedly dangerous Right.

The concern about right-wing illiberalism seems exaggerated since the "extremists" are not attacking a true liberal tradition. While traditional liberalism was the worldview of the 19th-century Western bourgeoisie, today, it is a thing of the past. It is no longer "our tradition," in contrast to managerial rule, global capitalism, and government-enforced wokeness. The older liberal tradition no longer influences the current political class. Perhaps it is now even "illiberal" to mourn the passing of liberalism, Anglo-American constitutional rules, and other middle-class decencies. By now, liberalism is an idea and practice that survives in increasingly deformed manifestations while losing its hold on Western minds.

The Western world is locked in political stagnation and appears condemned to a perpetual clash between the same forces. In general terms, the "stationary ideological warfare" is between the right-wing "national conservatives," accused by the Left of wanting "to destroy democracy," and the left-leaning "liberal-democratic front" of the establishment parties associated with the Deep State that mainly align themselves to "stop fascism."

From the political impasse, as usual, the leftist front will most likely emerge victorious by introducing a "new weapon," a "new" party, or a "new" person coming in from the cold. This new leader's support will not remain confined to one group of the electorate but will extend to at least two or more other groups, embracing parties from nationalists to liberal conservatives. They will gather support from all the popular classes — from the peripheral conservative countryside through the liberal-conservative bourgeoisie to the left-liberal and radical socialist intellectuals. This makes the "new" person, in effect, able to unify the Left of the Deep State. For years, the media, "thinkers," and politicians have discussed uniting the Left, bringing together left liberals, socialists, and modern conservatives to defeat the Right, i.e., the "populist" national conservatives. However, such a synthesis has never come to fruition because no one could embody it.

Of course, when found, this "new man" will be a "media candidate" immediately; his rise will be unstoppable. His goal will be to stop the "fascism" of the Right and fight for democracy, globalism, multiculturalism, a one-world government, free trade, human rights, equality, social justice, and more. He will be a very personable intellectual, full of empathy and brilliant logic, like Obama was before. He will even pretend to fight for the foundations of traditional structures: family, nation, work, state, and school.

It will all be a façade. A new political elite will be born: on the one side, i.e., on the left, the socialists, communists, centrists, liberals, the media, artistic and financial elites, the winners of globalization, and the traitors of the Right. On the other side — there will be no "other side," only the "fascist losers."

It is a hydra that emerges in all social, political, and cultural areas. It is not a revolution like '68, which lacked substance and failed to achieve anything. It is a revolution overthrowing the regime and conquering society by turning it against the country. It is the revenge of the globalist oligarchs, the victory of cosmopolitan internationalism over the sovereign nation, the vengeance of the new managerial lords against the state, the triumph of intellectualism over populism, and feminism over masculinity.

The advertising system's glorification of homosexuality and transsexualism justifies the denigration and delegitimization of the traditional family model. Feminists celebrate the attainment of the dream: the rejection of all responsibility, sex without marriage, abortion on demand, and divorce on the spot. These transformations have led to the inevitable disintegration of the family on a scale the West has never seen before.

The Western cultural cohesion preserved despite the 19th-century immigration waves is suspect to the emerging elites. According to them, demanding the assimilation of non-Western racial and cultural elements amounts to xenophobia; attachment to history and its heroes is a testimony to Western racist arrogance.

Liberalism has a weak tradition in Latin and Central/Eastern European countries. In France, Spain, Italy, Poland, Hungary, and Russia, no strong schools of liberal thought have emerged because, for them, liberalism is the ideology of the elites indifferent to their countries' interests and full of contempt for the people.

Liberalism, using economic arguments, opened the way to mass cross-cultural immigration. The same liberalism also initiated the deindustrialization of Western countries, leaving masses of non-Western immigrants unemployed, thereby increasing the tensions between them and the society that received them. Liberal ideology is one of the major causes of the anomie into which the Western world has descended.

The European Union has magnified liberalism's catastrophic impact on the shape of Western society and economy. The Single European Act opened the way to the free movement of capital, goods, and people — but it also meant the end of sovereign, independent economic policy and national industry (European Community, 1987).

During Thatcher and Reagan's eras, their economic reforms were not just about financial changes but also accompanied a revival of patriotism and national pride. In contrast, the liberal policies implemented in France and Germany, usually characterized by bland slogans devoid of patriotism and a perceived surrender of sovereignty, led to a different narrative, one that lacked a sense of national identity and belonging.

The liberals, in their pursuit of global economic integration, sacrificed European and American industries. The once proud "national champions" were no longer national, and the onslaught of outsourcing and competition with China profoundly reshaped the Western industrial sector, leaving many feeling deeply lost and betrayed.

When implemented wisely, protectionism can be a beacon of hope for a nation's economy. It is not just about economic or financial principles and concepts; it is about empowering citizens to be more than just consumers but proud members of a national community. The historical examples of Jules Méline and Friedrich List, who ended the reign of free trade in France and Germany and introduced protectionism and tariffs that led to a revival of the economy and industry, should inspire confidence in the potential benefits of protectionism (Smith, 1992) (List, 2013).

I am an open enemy of the political European Union based on leftist ideology. Not only do I believe that the European community is a cover for a globalized, multicultural, and supranational one-world government, but what is more, it is the ultimate expression of the oligarchic tendencies of a managerial elite. Globalist dignitaries govern the Union without ever being democratically elected; they are carefully selected officials who do not feel accountable to the people. In 2010, when "save the euro" was on the lips of all EU officials, even the last scruples disappeared — the European Commission stopped pretending to respect and heed national parliaments and started openly dictating its terms and conditions. When the Greek prime minister urged a referendum on leaving the eurozone, Germany and France forced him to abandon the idea and resign — the notorious "Couple Franco-Allemand" was at work.

Contrary to the myth of a harmonious French-German partnership, the reality is starkly different. "Couple Franco-Allemand" is a French construct, not a term used in German public debate. The French may have hoped for a united

Europe that mirrors an extended France, but the reality is that Europe has become more German than French. German hegemony in Europe is now unquestionable, with no critical decision made without Berlin's approval. This dominance has significant implications for the EU's governance and decision-making processes.

The surrender of national sovereignty to the EU and its subordination to Berlin are not just political decisions but also acts of betrayal by the elites. Jean-Claude Trichet's first official statement when becoming president of the European Central Bank (ECB) encapsulates this shift. His words were in English: "I'm not French" (Le Monde, 2003).

I condemn the renegade elites' revolt, their admiration for Germany, and their joy at the West's defeats. They reveal the genealogy of liberals and progressives who incessantly seek a foreign master while renouncing their own homelands. Elitist intellectuals, cosmopolitan captains of industry, actors, singers, writers, journalists, and politicians speak with one voice, defending globalism, multiculturalism, and wars against nation-states in the name of peace, love, and tolerance.

It is not conservatism but populism today that is the cry of those nations that do not want to die. A populist will side with and feel for the people; the horizontal divide between the Left and Right has lost any meaning. But there is a different divide, a vertical one today: the oligarchy, leftist intellectuals, and the winners of globalization on one (usually the left) side versus the ordinary people, the losers of globalization and multiculturalism.

Preserving the identity of Western civilization by opposing mass immigration and the growing influence of non-Western culture, mentality, and values must be a priority. One must choose which side to fight in the clash of civilizations on Western soil.

If any European nation wants to regain sovereignty over immigration, tariffs, and industrial policy, it cannot do so without leaving the European Union or changing the treaties. European politicians are reluctant to tackle that problem because they risk losing support among the part of the electorate they so desperately need — the well-to-do city bourgeoisie, the finance and high-tech oligarchs, and the progressive intellectuals — all in the service of the Deep State elites. After World War II, the communists successfully used "salami tactics" to take power in Eastern Europe. It is called salami tactics because of the attempt to cause division within an opposing political party by finding and emphasizing splitting issues on which its members disagree, effectively slicing the adversary into sections or segments that oppose each other instead of working together.

Using this method, the communists gradually discredited all opposition on the right as already tainted with fascist associations after World War II. They repeatedly characterized non-communists as "fascists" and, in some way, linked them to Hitler's Third Reich. They kept slicing away at the margins of their opposition, turning all mainstream political establishments against their right flank. Using a fictitious guilt-by-association strategy enabled the communists to discredit any resistance trying to prevent them from assuming total control. The German slang term *anbräunen* ("browning") depicts how the already dominant Left uses everything that opposes it with the hue of the Nazi Brownshirts of the Third Reich.

Whether communist or woke, the totalitarian Left has never abandoned the privilege of deciding what is fascist or pro-Nazi for the Right. Those availing themselves of this privilege always conceal their ultimate goal, total domination, achieved by smearing their opposition with the Nazi brush. In the end, the retreating opponent surrenders everything out of fear of being identified with fascism, antisemitism, or its updated version of "systemic white racism."

Here, I return to the modern conservative establishment, which continues to retreat until it has become the "Latecomer Left." Comparing or equating anything the Left does not like with the swastika or antisemitism represents the woke progressives' attempt to "Nazify" something they wish to render unacceptable, and such moves usually meet with no significant pushback from the Right — from the "modern conservatives."

The phony Right finds it almost always inappropriate or dangerous to make a needed distinction regarding anything the Left attacks. This fake conservative Right has become cravenly gutless and always gives ground to the Left. And with such pseudo-conservatives, the salami tactics will continue until an already weakened opposition no longer looks remotely credible.

The Role of Professional and Managerial Elites in Destroying Capitalism

It is crucial to note that the social and electoral base of the new revolution, which began with the student revolts in 1968, shifted from the working class to the elites — the professional and middle classes. Although some transformation had started earlier, this shift marked a significant turning point in the political landscape.

The strength of the Left lay within the world of intellectuals even before World War II and began to grow with managers, business leaders, and white-collar workers soon after the end of that war. Within its democracies, the European Left developed a public ownership and responsibility model based on businesses being accountable to governments. This model freed specific industries, public utilities, and public services from the marketplace's strictures, discipline, and competition. Instead of market pressures, the model instituted intervention by politicians and trade unionists in the operations of these companies and introduced comparatively lower levels of compensation for their managers than were available for managers in the private sector.

Simultaneously, as amalgamation continued in the private sector, managers began to seek new markets, new ways to free themselves from shareholders' influence, and methods of reducing competitive market pressure. They did not yearn for interference by politicians or unions but envied how their colleagues in the public sector could receive state subsidies while getting others (taxpayers) to bankroll any losses.

In their quest to circumvent accountability to shareholders and the marketplace, private-sector managers devised various strategies. They utilized dispersed share ownership to evade shareholder scrutiny and employed creative accounting to bypass market pressures. Their resourcefulness was further demonstrated when they managed to secure state subsidies during the financial sector's crisis in 2008, a feat their public sector counterparts had never achieved before.

However, public sector managers also found some exit doors out of their problems. Occasionally, quasi-privatization enabled them to manage natural monopolies without accountability to the state or the marketplace. In other cases, this was accomplished by shrewdly distancing themselves from the policy-making process and developing complicated structures such as "quangos," i.e., state-funded, semi-public administrative bodies outside the standard civil service.

Politicians found the emerging arrangement agreeable for avoiding responsibility and accountability. This was accomplished primarily by privatizing or dispersing policymaking to quasi-independent institutions. For example, the most significant development has been the growth of the European Union's complicated and bureaucratic structure, which enabled politicians at the national level to hide behind decisions made at the European level and blame others for them.

In the liberal-democratic Western world, a circle of irresponsibility and unaccountability has emerged in which politicians and public and private corporate managers operate. Unsurprisingly, this arrangement has led to the severe disillusionment of the broader public. The non-executive workforce and small- and medium-sized businesses have had to work in a market environment where a pyramid of public and private corporate debt has severely impacted their living standards and quality of life, leading to unemployment, cuts in public services, price increases, and higher taxes. Of course, top managers and politicians have protected themselves, including their pensions, salaries, and bonuses, against these consequences.

The managerial class now views the globalization of the economy, the internationalization of government, and the creation of a multicultural world as the primary means of exercising and retaining power. Differences between the political parties of the Left and Right have, by and large, become entirely irrelevant to them. Anyone attending the gatherings of transnational organizations, such as the World Economic Forum or the Bilderberg Group, could not tell who, theoretically speaking, was from the Right or the Left of the political spectrum. Their goal is to empower international institutions to operate, thereby taking away or at least obscuring national-level responsibility. The managerial class is also preoccupied with the functioning of global institutions such as the World Bank, the IMF, and the EU.

Through this globalization process, the managerial class's ultimate objective is to create a condition in which the mountains of accumulated debt will be absorbed in a coordinated and organized manner by joint guarantees of international institutions or, in less favorable circumstances, through coordinated devaluation — although it would be challenging to align the factional interests involved. If this process fails, the contingency would be military action, which would create demand during and after the conflict, eliminate surplus labor, and allow for extraordinary measures to deal with debts and dissenters. Nevertheless, this would likely be the weapon of last resort (pun intended).

What I have outlined here is not a mere conspiracy but a fascinating and intricate interplay of the interests of managers from the public and private corporate sectors and politicians. These individuals did not consciously orchestrate this situation. However, now that such a circumstance has taken hold, it is in their interests to preserve it and prevent any potential uprising by those who oppose them and whose interests are adversely affected by this emerging paradigm.

Such leading managers and politicians have several instruments of persuasion and coercion. For instance, persuasion occurs with the help of the media and through electoral bribes, such as promises of favorable policies or financial support for campaigns. Coercion, in turn, transpires through surveillance, the judicial system, and law enforcement, which can be used to intimidate or punish dissenters. If the harmony of persuasion and coercion is disrupted, the system stops functioning. Another threat to this equilibrium is potential "strife at the top," whereby the benefactors of the new managerial model begin to fight among themselves for the spoils — if there are not enough spoils to go around.

Traditional capitalism seems to be on the brink of extinction — not due to the workers but the managerial class. The revival of genuinely free and functioning capitalism could only occur if the current paradigm crumbled. However, such a collapse would likely be more detrimental to those opposing the prevailing model than to those who support it.

Ultimately, the burden of the crisis would fall on the poor and small businesspeople.

The collapse of command or planned economies and one-party, socialist, Bolshevik, and pro-communist states was a setback for the Left — a term I use to refer to political ideologies that advocate for social equality and government intervention in the economy — but only for a short time. In the long run, getting rid of an obsolete model based on autarky, heavy industry, and an outdated Rust Belt even benefited the Left. It could concentrate on trying to achieve "real" communism — this time without the working class and its hang-ups about the nation, family, and gender issues. In attacking the church, family values, and the nation-state, the "Left of the West" now has the most potent ally: international and multinational corporations, for whom families, religion, heavy industry, national boundaries, and limitations are obstacles to development. They desire a globalized world in which the movement of labor is free so that they can keep costs down.

In the meantime, politicians from traditional political parties also began to see advantages in supranational solutions, i.e., passing responsibility to others for unpopular decisions and building niche electorates. These strategies involve focusing on specific issues or demographics centered around, for example, gender politics, multiculturalism, and ecology (to accelerate the dismantling of heavy industry). The supranational solutions allow traditional political parties to maintain their power and influence, even in changing political and economic landscapes.

The Left would encounter significant resistance only by attacking the military with pacifism. Interestingly enough, pacifism is the one strand of communist thinking that has been "forgotten" ever since the collapse of the USSR. Western communists no longer favor the one-party model of "socialism with Chinese characteristics" that prevails in China today, nor do they have much time for Islamism. But they will not confront them because the primary objective of the Left is to concentrate on seizing and retaining power in the West rather than waging war on the West's enemies.

The methods of the "21st-century communists" have been not just practical but also remarkably versatile and effective. They rightly saw that the old forms of their political organization would not work in the new post-industrial order — the mass parties and trade unions of the Left are a non-issue. Instead, ingeniously, they sought ideological hegemony through what Gramsci called the "march through the institutions" (Kiska, 2019). The Left achieved that by working in smaller circles or cells of influence — in the humanities, media, education, the professions, and emerging civil non-governmental organizations (NGOs).

The 21st-century communists have proved far more flexible, pragmatic, and intelligent than the old communist parties of the 20th century. They are more prepared to infiltrate existing political structures and collaborate with the most unlikely allies. They exert massive influence on the political scene in Europe, with their ideas accepted by governmental forces that comprise the socialist, liberal, green, and even right-of-center European parties such as the Christian democrats. The British Conservative Party has endorsed parts of that agenda; in the United States, the ideas of this program are now widely approved by the Democratic Party. There are few strongholds of politics, commerce, the professions, the media, or show business where leftist, socialist, or communist views are not dominant. They have defined political correctness and control the language and agenda of political discourse today.

The philosophy, ideology, and culture of the largest supranational structure, the European Union, are no longer aligned with Robert Schuman but rather with Karl Marx. Of course, Eurocrats talk of universal liberal values such as human rights — but communist conceptions of the human person increasingly define these values.

Conservatives in the United States and Europe have been retreating throughout the 21st century. The times of Reagan and Thatcher are long gone, although Brexit, Trump, Orbán, and Kaczyński are evidence of some remaining resistance. The dilemma for American Republicans, British Conservatives, and national conservatives in Hungary and Poland, among others, is that they must face and fight not just external foes who oppose the nation-state, religion, and family, such as the European Union and its minions, but, first and foremost, communist ideas attacking them from within — and on a scale that Reagan or Thatcher never had to confront.

Although Orbán, Kaczyński, Trump, and the Brexiteers in the UK have provided some breathing room for those defending sovereignty, Christianity, and nationhood, if other conservatives elsewhere in Europe do not get their act together, they will not be able to hold out forever.

Today's communist revolution is far more challenging to overcome than the one advanced by the "socialist" states in the 20th century. The first step to bolster the fight is to admit that the entire Western world faces a revolution aimed at moving the world toward communism. And since this revolution has communist objectives, let us call them and their advocates by that name. Today's communists must not be allowed to triumph or escape the legacy of the 20th century, with its many failed and brutal attempts to create a communist paradise in the USSR, Eastern Europe, China, North Korea, or Cuba.

The transition from a traditional capitalist society, with its socially impaired leverage and altered weights of governmental and private enterprises, to a managerial society represents a significant shift. This new order, led by managers and their political associates, has taken over as command slipped from the grasp of capitalists.

Following the politically and socially induced breakdown of capitalism, the state assumes a more prominent role, merging with the economy and expanding its functions to control it. This shift is the only viable solution to restore the economic structure, effectively placing managers in the position of the ruling class.

It is essential to reiterate that truth is not a matter of belief but of evidence. This fundamental principle forms the basis of this book's analytical approach, which aims to stimulate critical thinking about political and economic changes and their implications.

Chapter 3

The Crisis of Democracy in the American Republic

Anyone can see that the American government is not only broken but dying. Whether or not one understands the U.S. Constitution, we all intuitively know that something is wrong. And it is not merely that "the government spends too much money" or "the government should be doing X" — it is hard to explain why the political system is not working.

Of course, several trends explain a great deal, such as the origins of the Second American Party System in the late 1820s, the growth of the patronage or "spoils" system, the increasing irrelevance of the House of Representatives in recent decades, and the recent cowardice (or ignorance) of state legislators. These developments are only samples of U.S. history, but it is imperative to understand how America got here and why simple adjustments in the electoral and legislative systems will not lead to any real difference — short of revolutionary changes.

In 1820, New York State Senator Martin Van Buren and Thomas Jefferson perceived that the Missouri Compromise would inexorably lead to civil war. The Missouri Compromise eventually allowed a half-dozen new free-soil states that prohibited slavery in their territories to gain admission to the Union. However, these free-soil states and their allies would quickly gain majorities in the U.S. House and Senate to pass antislavery laws, and when that occurred, the South would have no alternative but to secede (Forbes, 2007).

Van Buren's solution was a paradoxical compromise, both brilliant and disastrous, which would typify America's future political landscape. He argued that the Democratic-Republican Party was no longer viable, and a new, more effective political party would require a commitment to prevent any national discussion of slavery in any official capacity. His approach, which could be seen as both hypocritical and an oxymoron, involved rewarding individuals for not discussing slavery with political jobs within the party or the government. As a result of this strategy, the government's size swelled with each election. Candidates had to promise new jobs to secure votes. This spoils system, initiated by Van Buren, became known as the Albany Regency, a term that reflects the significant impact of his political maneuvering (Mowry, 1966).

The newly formed Democratic Party under Andrew Jackson adopted a system known as patronage, where political appointments and favors were distributed based on loyalty and support. Once the Whigs, a competing party, also emerged, they had no choice but to adopt the patronage model, leading to its widespread use in American politics.

The tales of corruption that marred the patronage system were not just whispers but well-known facts even in Lincoln's time. In an effort to curb this, Congress enacted the Pendleton Civil Service Reform Act in 1883, which mandated standardized tests for various government positions. This marked a significant shift — to join the Civil Service, one had to pass an examination rather than rely on political favoritism (U.S. Congress, 1883). Following the landmark Pendleton Act, a significant shift in the distribution of political power occurred. This Act replaced the spoils system with a merit-based civil service. However, instead of promising a handful of jobs to their supporters, politicians had to direct their disbursements to large "interest groups." This change led to a transformation in the lobbying landscape, with farmers, teachers, autoworkers, and retirees advocating for government benefits such as subsidies, price controls, and minimum-wage laws. The outcome remained the same, with subsidies being distributed, but the beneficiaries were now entire groups rather than individuals.

So, America's legislative structure rests on a winner-take-all, i.e., single-member district system with no proportional "seats" or representations in Congress. The majority vote gets the seat, whether it is a few votes or millions that win it. One either wins or loses everything, but you must promise more "goodies" than your opponent to win. These goodies can include promises of job creation, tax cuts, or increased government spending in the district.

This power escalation presents a formidable challenge for third parties to make headway in this system. To distribute jobs as a member of the House, one must be part of the majority; therefore, one will either be a Democrat or a Republican — no Libertarians or members of the Reform or Green parties need to apply. A party struggling in the 5-percent electoral range would need to double its turnout in four consecutive elections to reach majority status — a feat that is not feasible for most.

The implications of the current U.S. legislative politics are stark. The system inherently discourages concentrated efforts to "reduce the debt," "control the budget," or "cut expenditures." Instead, it fosters a culture of "giving away jobs" or "giving away anything," a tactic that predominantly aligns with leftist behavior based on entitlements. Unless radically changed, this political landscape is not conducive to the country's long-term stability.

Another development that would have made the Founders' heads spin is that the House of Representatives has virtually become irrelevant. That deterioration began in the Reagan era when the Democrat-controlled House refused to balance the budgets. President Reagan, desperate to impose fiscal restraint, asked for the line-item veto, which Congress rejected. Everyone knew nothing would happen unless a two-thirds majority of budgetary conservatives were in each House.

During President Obama's term, first with a two-thirds majority Democrat-controlled House and then with the Republicans controlling both Houses, Congress did virtually nothing. Even with supermajorities, President Obama could hardly get more passed than a stimulus package and Obamacare. Republicans assumed control in 2011 when it was abundantly clear that the House had only two choices: a government shutdown or impeachment — with the GOP unwilling to choose either.

Thus, for over 25 years, the Representatives' power had atrophied. Then, with Donald Trump in the White House and a Republican-controlled House, Senate, and presidency, the House of Representatives could manage only a single tax-cut bill, a failed repeal of Obamacare, and an unbalanced budget that President Trump, trying to woo the Never-Trump House Republicans, reluctantly signed. Then, Nancy Pelosi's House made itself even more irrelevant and impotent than ever. It wasted two years on impeachment and other questionable investigations, pausing only for a COVID-19 stimulus bill, frittering away the House's most important power: control over the budget.

The above has led to a significant shift in the legislative power of the House, a departure from the original intentions of the Founders. The U.S. Senate has emerged as the pivotal chamber, a reversal of the English system, where the "upper house" of the Parliament (House of Lords) became irrelevant while de facto primary power shifted to the lower house (House of Commons). Ms. Pelosi solidified the final transfer of power from the House of Representatives to the Senate, which now controls the job of confirming appointees and judges. Starting with Obama and continuing with Trump and Biden, actual "legislation" — rather "non-legislation" — now originates from the president's executive orders, followed by passive approval from the Senate, with the House observing this transformation.

The death warrant to federalism and the separation of powers has involved another, more recent shift: state legislatures willingly ceding their control to governors. For instance, in the Commonwealth of Pennsylvania, the legislature backed off as the governor unconstitutionally changed the law in the summer of 2020. This trend was not isolated, as governors across the country turned into autocrats, changing laws and trampling on civil rights during the COVID-19 lockdowns. Only months later did some state legislatures dare to bring up gubernatorial impeachment as the lockdowns wore on, destroying state economies across the United States. Until the end of 2021, no state governor who imposed draconian but illegal measures had been reproached, impeached, or even seen their power abridged, save for a couple of state supreme court rulings.

Moreover, in the ambiguously contested and fraudulent-smelling 2020 presidential election, when it was the right and duty of state legislatures to challenge some governors' last-minute electoral laws, demand the full auditing of the votes, withhold certification of the election, and otherwise stand up to the fraud, not one did so.

These acts are not merely cases of cowardice but profound betrayals of the very principles the Founders laid out for the American Republic. The deliberate dismantling of legislative bodies at all levels has paved the way for executive despotism. The long-term consequences of this failure undermine the checks and balances that are the cornerstone of the Republic, leaving the country vulnerable to the whims of those in power.

The American system of government, which should be a beacon of constitutional governance, has instead devolved into a corrupt system that rewards people with government handouts and makes "spoils" the focal point of politics. This shift in focus has led to a situation Winston Churchill famously defined as "a riddle, wrapped in a mystery, inside an enigma," referring to Russia at the time (Darrah, 1939). But I will call the United States of America, and with it, the entire Western world, the actual mysterious lands — deception, hidden in hypocrisy, inside a pretense — made deliberately unknowable by their own rules, usually to the detriment of those who choose more genuine regulations. The rulers have thoroughly corrupted the Founders' concept from within.

Although there have been some minor signs of life in the corpse of "American democracy," e.g., possible new election integrity laws and a bill blocking big tech from blacklisting residents over political views, none of the new initiatives have anything to do with budgets or radical reform of the patronage system. At the same time, the Right is already too late, finally becoming aware of the danger facing the republic.

The Washington Beltway is the land of the Swamp and the monsters in it who have given us the Full Spectrum Dominance doctrine and the notion that we are exceptional by birth (Engdahl, 2011). Accordingly, Beltway denizens are supposed to be the appointed leaders of the international community, sympathetic to LGBTQ+ "rights," a light to the world, good, virtuous, and free to destroy those who beg to differ.

The U.S. government is a peripheral theater in the hubristic neoconservative-neoliberal-globalist scheme to control the world. It is the black hole where trillions disappear to no good effect. It is one of America's primary sources of evil, the hydra of self-serving malevolence, and the enemy of the American people. Telling lies is the usual manner of operating for the U.S. government and its media servants.

It is a thought-provoking question: when did the U.S. government assume the role of a global moral authority, dictating the political systems of other nations? Who granted the American missionaries this authority to write the moral code for regimes that govern lands far from its shores?

Yet no rulers bristle more than America's when they discover that foreign regimes meddle in their politics or presidential elections.

Looking back at history, the U.S. has not only formed alliances with democracies but also with autocrats, dictators, monarchs, and tyrants. From Joseph Stalin and Chiang Kai-shek to the Shah of Iran and the Greek colonels, from Latin American generals to African kleptocrats, the U.S. has aligned itself with anyone supporting at least some of its causes — and they did not have to be democrats. In times of crisis, the U.S., like any other country in trouble, has often found allies in autocrats and dictators while democracies remained neutral. This historical perspective reminds us that nations often judge friends not by ideology but by behavior when a crisis comes.

Lately, the U.S. has been preaching the superiority of its democracy as a political system for all peoples, as it manifests "universal values." But if tomorrow the kings, princes, and emirs fell to popular rebellions for "freedom and democracy," how beneficial would this be to the U.S.? When did the political systems of foreign countries that do not threaten or attack the U.S. become an American concern? When did they become part of America's business?

Stalin imposed communism on the eastern half of Europe during the Cold War, and Nikita Khrushchev said, "We will bury you!" (TIME Foreign News, 1956). But Russian President Vladimir Putin does not promise that our grandchildren will live under communism, autocracy, or

Russian rule. China is communist with its very own characteristics, but it does not impose its ideology outside the territories it claims as its own.

Under President George W. Bush's leadership, the United States championed a global mission for democracy. This commitment is evident in the support the United States provides to color-coded revolutions aimed at toppling regimes in the Balkans, Caucasus, Near East, Eastern Europe, North Africa, and other regions. America, a global powerhouse, persistently intervenes in the internal affairs of other nations, driven by its globalist, left-liberal, and "democratist" ideology. This active role in shaping global politics underscores America's influence and reach.

Interestingly, most "autocrats" are not transnational crusaders but nationalists. Presidents Putin, Erdoğan, and Xi are not the primary drivers of global division based on ideology, adding a layer of complexity to the international political landscape.

Only America wages relentless ideological wars in the power struggle between the United States, Russia, and China. Ideological battles often end in shooting wars.

Tocqueville and Totalitarian Democracy in America

American democracy has proved successful in representing interests but fails to promote citizenship. It has safeguarded some civil liberties while allowing others to erode. However, we must remember that institutions alone are not enough for a republic to succeed — civic virtue is also necessary.

In recent times, the political establishment, the mainstream media, Big Business, the Tech Giants, and the intellectual elites have conspired to achieve the American presidential election result they wanted, while the judiciary disqualified itself from protecting the electoral process. Many Americans wonder whether liberal democracy can guarantee individual liberty and constitutionalism. In 1840, Alexis de Tocqueville warned about what America would become due to the very nature of democratic peoples, a warning that seems eerily relevant today:

"I think, then, that the species of oppression by which democratic nations are menaced is unlike anything that ever before existed in the world; our contemporaries will find no prototype of it in their memories. I seek in vain for an expression that will accurately convey the whole of the idea I have formed of it; the old words despotism and tyranny are inappropriate: the thing itself is new, and since I cannot name it, I must attempt to define it" (Tocqueville, Democracy in America, 1969).

No previous tyranny, autocracy, or dictatorship has been willing or able to exploit so absolutely, penetratingly, and expansively its power: the power that destroys everything in society that is spontaneous, autonomous, and pluralistic and takes over anything private or politically social. No autocrat, despot, or monarch, dead or alive, ever attempted to "subject all his subjects indiscriminately to the details of a uniform rule" (Tocqueville, Democracy in America, 1969). Reflecting on history, we find that even under the autocratic rule of the Roman Emperor, his subjects could maintain their diverse traditional customs and way of life. Although all provinces under Roman control owed allegiance to the Emperor, most ruled themselves autonomously. The Emperor and other autocrats were content with exploiting a few, sometimes mercilessly, while leaving the rest to their own devices.

Today, in America and the Western world, I see the development of a totalitarian democracy, a concept that Tocqueville warned about. It is not a traditional dictatorship but a system where the government, allegedly and ostensibly elected by the people, exercises extensive control over their lives and suppresses dissent. This observation is not made lightly but is rooted in my personal experience of living in socialist Central Europe for twenty-five years under the ideological dictatorship of the Communist Party. That experience and fifty years of witnessing a quixotic political, cultural, and social predicament in America and Western Europe have led me to a disconcerting realization.

"Democracy" becomes autocratic when decision-making emanates from the apex of the official hierarchy, with the executive process remaining unaccountable to anyone else while the other authorities that are supposed to share power in the government exist in name only. Consider the regimes of China and the European Union — the difference is merely procedural and deeply concerning, as the actual ruler or group of rulers wields absolute power in determining what is in the public interest and enforces that decision with full authority, leaving the public with no choice but to obey.

Tyranny or dictatorship can be the rule of only one or a few, the privileged elite or the many, and the license to select leaders or rulers through voting in a democratic system is not tantamount to the people ruling themselves. Americans and Europeans are bound by a gigantic and intricate web of regulations, such as tax laws, environmental regulations, and labor laws, formulated without any consideration for the public will. Whether violent, crude, or subtle, governmental terror is absolute when it succeeds in coercing people into compliance and obedience.

Accordingly, people will be left alone wherever their actions pose no threat to the rulers and their system. The officials of that system will not bother to mold anyone's behavior through, say, anti-harassment training or shape one's thinking through critical race theory. Western totalitarians are more "humane" and refined, yet equally tyrannical and frightening. Even if well-intentioned, a call for "anti-racism" can be intellectually misguided and, what is worse, morally tyrannical. When the official doctrine of "diversity, inclusivity, and equity" dictates that white society constantly checks its "privilege" (however that term is defined) and participates in self-criticism and re-education, the aspiration to nourish genuine civic affection — the foundation of civil society — is destroyed.

20th-century totalitarianism was steeped in terror and mass killings committed by a handful of murderous dictators. But that does not mean that tyranny must be acute, brutal, or bloody — it can be mild, seductive, and insidious. The democratic dictatorship does not aim to kill, torture, or exploit people as Hitler, Stalin, Mao, or Pol Pot did; instead, it seeks to equalize and infantilize its citizens.

This totalitarianism does not decimate the population or torment the people but truly "degrades" men (Tocqueville's apt word). It softens the will. The intellectuals and the "educated mob" have developed a vulgar, conformist, and acquisitive culture. It is horrifying that middle-class children are now crying out for safe spaces on college campuses. Meanwhile, the new totalitarianism mysteriously nurtures a cheap passion for petty causes in today's American youth. Following "nonevents" flooding their consciousness, pseudo-concepts such as "white fragility" or "body positivity" now reign supreme over the moral sense of education, pop culture, and social movements. That is tutelary totalitarianism seeking to protect its tutees from harming themselves or each other. It aims to satisfy their needs and provide them pleasures, relieve hardships and shield them from danger, train them in the correct manners and thoughts formulated by the righteous "schoolmaster" (in Tocqueville's words) who, of course, knows better, and secure for them an existence on equal footing, provided they accept the master's unquestionable authority and obey all his decisions.

Ultimately, all people are "socialized": equally well-fed and well-sheltered but tamed, timid, and never daring to leave their "schoolmaster." "Meanwhile, they are hypersensitive, easily outraged, extremely fragile, unreasonably entitled, profoundly ignorant, and stupid. I do not suggest anything about these people's intelligence but simply an unwillingness, inability, and fear of failure to think for themselves. What is the purpose of free will when one constantly hears how to live his life from officials, experts, and influencers? What is the benefit of free will when the "schoolmaster" eliminates the burdensome responsibility of thinking and the hardship of life for you?

Although "totalitarian democracy" might seem an oxymoron at first, democracy, by its very proposition, is vulnerable to tyrannical solutions in politics. Democracy

155

presumes and preaches that every person is equal; therefore, it requires power to constantly distribute and redistribute resources in society, shaping and reshaping reality for the presupposition to hold. In a way, democracy is a gentle but interminable revolutionary movement that continually overturns the status quo — a status quo that naturally ensues from spontaneous, instinctive, and autonomous actions in human society. The more progressive a democratic society becomes, the quicker it overthrows the status quo.

For example, although same-sex marriage took a few decades to become a constitutional right, it took just a few years for transgenderism to prevail. Thus, modern liberal democracy gradually but effectively drives politics to take charge of society. Nevertheless, this is not a goal that any particular form of governance can achieve unless there is an incessant movement toward an idealistically set target destination where all people are supposed to be equal and alike. Totalitarianism, seen from this perspective, is a never-ending revolutionary movement — just like democracy.

Besides the democratic assumption, an equally significant second force fostered totalitarian democracy in America: liberalism, the American republic's founding ideology. Compared to the two totalitarian ideologies, fascism and communism, liberalism is less obvious and more nuanced. It consists of three elements fundamental to its dogma: the ideal, the practical, and the doctrinal.

Liberalism, just like its rivals, delivers a myth about human nature and society that its devotees take as a self-evident truth and intends to transform all facets of human existence according to a utopian scheme. Liberalism assumes man is independent of pre-existing associations, a pre-political creature, free, and bearing natural rights. Though false narratives of reality, all three ideologies are seductive because they offer some irresistible idealization that appeals to humans' righteous minds or covetous hearts. The fascist state flatters its subjects with membership, the communist state with egalitarianism, and the liberal state obtains loyalty with a cheap version of liberty and rights — instead of civic duties.

At first glance, liberalism seems to be a powerful check on totalitarian impulses. Whereas totalitarianism is an autocratic rule that is absolute, penetrating, and expansive, liberalism speaks the opposite language: limited government, freedom of thought, and individual sovereignty.

So, how do I arrive at totalitarianism from liberalism? There are three connections linking the two.

First, liberalism conceptually liberated humans from pre-existing constraints. It demolished irrational and artificial ways of living such as religion, ritual, and custom, and unshackled rejected associations and binding relationships. Thus, liberalism has transformed the individual from a historical being into an existentially naked person by reducing him to his natural essence: a rational being — stripped of accidental attributes. According to Rousseau, this naked individual is happiest and sound in the state of nature, and according to Rawls, capable of justice behind the veil of ignorance (Provencher-Gravel, 2008) (Rawls, 1999). Furthermore, the naked individual is said to be the building block of society, and his well-being (however defined), i.e., individualism, is the foremost concern of the state.

Individualism is a milestone, a stage of advancement toward statism, first vividly delineated by Hobbes in his thought experiment *Leviathan* and later empirically proven with Barack Obama's notorious, progressive, and deviously misleading political campaign "The Life of Julia" (Hobbes, 2017) (Jasso, 2019).

Second, the relationship between individualism and statism is stark: In the absence of intermediate institutions like the family, affiliation, and church, the state emerges as the sole community where the individual can thrive. As a result, the state's power becomes the individual's lifeline to advance his well-being. In the liberal state, the people are independent of one another but forever bound to the state.

On the other hand, liberalism presents a stark contrast with its idealistic view of liberty, often seen as the absence of restraints from arbitrary forces. Figures like John Locke paint a picture of "a perfect freedom" in the state of nature — a concept that contrasts with the intricate realities of governance — arguing that government is created afterward, by consent, for the sole purpose of protecting and expanding individual liberties, a notion that may require a more nuanced examination (Locke, 1980).

However, reality does not reflect Locke's theory. Assuming that self-limitation is impossible and that cultivating virtue is unrealistic — as splendidly argued by Machiavelli and Hobbes — the state develops into the sole arbiter of conflicts that arise when individuals freely exploit their liberty. These conflicts could include property disputes, public safety concerns, or even societal unrest. Without self-regulated behavior or self-control, authority and the instruments of power must be combined in the sole judge, i.e., the state, to produce peace and order. That is the rationale for the modern state, which effectively fulfills its role as the arbiter of conflicts by enacting laws. These laws, however, come with a necessary caveat: they put strict limits on individual liberty. As Hobbes states, freedom exists only "where there is silence of the law" (Hobbes, 2017).

Thus, liberty has become a political conception — a state-issued license. Therefore, indeed, it is the state that creates liberty. This "liberal version of freedom," which is primarily concerned with individual rights and limited government intervention, fails to expand individual liberty — it certainly injures it.

In the third and final instance, liberalism claims the existence of natural rights — false again. There are no natural rights, only political ones. However, the moral degradation that liberalism induces is more significant when it hypocritically advocates for protecting rights in the political sphere while maximizing self-interest in the economic domain as the state's primary goals. This paradox, where liberalism champions individual rights while promoting self-interest, starkly contrasts with ancient political philosophy's advocacy of cultivating virtue in the citizenry.

This premise of natural rights has found its way into the two propositions of the American experiment with democracy: utilitarian liberalism, which prioritizes the greatest good for the greatest number, and Kantian liberalism, which emphasizes individual autonomy and respect for human dignity.

The utilitarian school, a moral philosophy that seeks to maximize general welfare, postulates that maximizing this welfare is the highest moral principle. However, this school is far worse than merely a precarious moral philosophy that fails to respect the individual as an end in himself because, insofar as one is in the minority, his welfare can cede to the collective or common good.

The Kantian school strives to rescue liberalism from the utilitarian notion that views individuals merely as a means to the happiness of others — whether they are a majority or a minority. Kantianism presents a value-free framework in which the right precedes the good, allowing individuals, as free moral agents, to choose their own goods. However, this value-free ethics leaves liberalism with little room to maneuver, as it does not provide a theoretical basis for public policy debate. Ultimately, as independent and sovereign beings, we are citizens of a polity and cannot adequately justify any public policy without explicitly referencing the common good and its ends. The one who wields the power to coerce has the final say. Society becomes a mere battleground where individual, group, and class preferences, ambitions, and wills vie for supremacy, underlining the pressing need to address the potential for power abuse in a rights-based political system.

Rights-based politics falls short of fully representing the citizenship and community in which we exist. As the history of totalitarianism has revealed, when shared meanings and significance lose their unifying power in a mass society, isolated and fragmented individuals are left exposed and vulnerable to the totalitarian political solution. Rights-based politics dismisses the common good and moral virtue, blurring the lines between beauty and ugliness, temperance and indulgence, and nobility and debasement. It also fosters an unwarranted sense of entitlement, transforming citizens into government consumers — an insidious yet potent way to debase the citizenry and demoralize private individuals.

Tocqueville observes that such a totalitarian democracy had never happened in the past due to "the want of enlightenment, the imperfection of administrative procedures," and "the natural obstacles created by the inequality of conditions..." (Tocqueville, Democracy in America, 1969).

Indeed, he is correct; this principle emerges only in a democratic society where individuals are equal and indistinguishable. Tocqueville cautions, "The more equal men are, the more insatiable will be their longing for equality." And because "democratic institutions awaken and flatter the passion for equality without ever being able to satisfy it entirely," democratic people quickly become frustrated, anxious, and angry when confronting real or perceived inequality. Consequently, they are more inclined to demand aggressive and radical interference from the "schoolmaster" to level the playing field or attain social justice. By design, the word "equity" has now been smuggled into campuses, academia, and industry, supplanting "equality" — and the equality of condition delineates this natural trajectory.

Whether by design or not, the pursuit of equity is expected to eventually merge and amalgamate the nation into a homogenous entity where every citizen shares "the same opinions, the same passions, and the same interests" — a concept that James Madison identified as the second means to the end of eliminating factions in *Federalist Paper 10* (Hamilton, Jay, & Madison, 2014).

Not surprisingly, Madison considered this method "impracticable" as long as a man "is at liberty to exercise (his reason)." But little did he know: unfortunately, the concept is indeed practicable when a totalitarian mind, a dictatorial system, overcoming the "insufficiency of enlightenment," regards the first objective of government as no longer to safeguard and preserve "the diversity in the faculties of men" but to establish a uniformity of interests. Moreover, it is practicable when the mass media apparatus, once a tool for information and education, now aims to indoctrinate the public; it is achievable when the public mind is constantly monitored and controlled by the latest information and communication technology and molded by elitist cultural institutions. This should raise a red flag for us all, as it signifies a dangerous shift in power and control.

The vulnerability to totalitarianism is not a mere possibility but a stark reality, particularly in a society that is increasingly secular, materialistic, alienated, and bored. When the pursuit of complex and profound questions is abandoned, the mind is left to grapple with immediate, trivial, and mediocre concerns. In such a society, individual gains and losses take precedence, and the meaning of life is reduced to material acquisition. Pleasure is fleeting, and displeasure is enduring, further exacerbating societal vulnerability to totalitarianism. The potential consequences are dire, as healthy individual freedoms are suppressed, and a uniformity of interests is enforced.

In *The Origins of Totalitarianism*, Hannah Arendt harshly criticizes "bourgeois individualism," attributing the rise of modern totalitarianism mainly to the "acquisitive society of the bourgeoisie," who were habitually apathetic and even hostile toward public life, prioritizing private calculations over civic duties. They first recklessly ceded their power to the autocracy and later demanded an aggressive foreign policy, preparing Europe for the rise of dictatorship, whereby a "strongman" assumed the burden of conducting public affairs. However, these "bourgeois attitudes" eventually led to the downfall of their class, and the masses emerged from the ashes of the class society (Arendt, The Origins of Totalitarianism, 1973).

Arendt characterized the masses as apolitical people who "cannot be integrated into any organization based on common interest" and lack "specific class articulateness which is expressed in determined, limited, and obtainable goals." Also, the masses are indifferent to political endeavors that require meaningful and considerable participation. According to Arendt, totalitarianism is a mass movement — either on the right or left — driven by ideology and seeking to dominate society by perpetuating the crusade.

Arendt also mentions that the triumphant advance of modern totalitarian movements in Europe shattered the long-held and deliberately propagated misconception that the majority rules in democratic nations by actively participating in government. American "democracy" seems to have proceeded under the same illusion. Paradoxically, as voting privileges and other social measures concerning equality kept expanding, majority rule became less factual and more ceremonial. The history of American governance points to a direction where more and more public affairs are governed by laws and regulations created by an administration in which a few representatives of the rulers hold sway without accountability to "we the people." In Tocqueville's words, the polity has evolved into a system that is "republican at the head, and ultra-monarchical in all the other parts..." (Tocqueville, Democracy in America, 1969).

Sometimes, I cannot help imagining that I am the modern Tocqueville visiting 21st-century America and its Western subsidiaries. In that state, I am also crestfallen to see many of his insights becoming a reality and the ever-diminishing difference between the Western world and the old Soviet Bloc.

American "democracy" has proven successful in representing interests and a failure in nurturing and refining citizenship; it has maintained some civil liberties while permitting others to erode, particularly in recent decades. One lesson from its almost 250-year history of triumphs and failures is that for a true republic, i.e., having a shared public life, to succeed, institutions are not enough and may not even be necessary. What is needed is civic virtue.

Accordingly, the nature of democracy, in conjunction with liberalism's 500-year predominance in the West, has prepared the ground in America for the coming rule of the totalitarians. The old words of despotism, autocracy, or tyranny no longer work. I have been trying to think up a new description to reflect the insanity that prevails in Western society today and can only describe it as *bizarrely demonic*. It is demonic for a people who used to live under the freedom and prosperity that Americans have, like no other people anywhere in recorded history, to willingly become slaves to an ever-expanding, totalitarian leftist government that is incrementally leading their country toward one of the worst forms of life ever invented by man. A "new and improved" way of life, which technology will control, that only the devil could conceive to re-engineer humanity into some hybrid machine: human at first, then gradually more diabolical than our present mind can even fathom.

Francis Fukuyama's tranquilizing "End of History" thesis, heralding a post-historical Eden where liberal values like free-market capitalism and parliamentary democracy would reign supreme and unchallenged, is on the retreat, if not defunct, today. The reasons for that change range from the revival of Russia and China through their effective use of "authoritarian capitalism" and "illiberal democracy" to the corruption of the liberal and democratic ideals within the very same states that initially gave life to them — proving the inadequacy of the liberal worldview itself.

It is important to note that Mr. Fukuyama did not claim that the "end" of history would bring about a utopia free from conflict or the tragedies of the human condition. His thesis posited that at the "end" of history, society would have discovered its "formula" in liberal democracy and resolved its "big questions" once and for all (Fukuyama, 1992).

But would a static vision of life devoid of conflict and the potential for "serious moments" ultimately satisfy the human spirit? As Mr. Fukuyama suggests, the end of history may be where "there will be neither art nor philosophy, just the perpetual caretaking of the museum of human history." While seemingly peaceful, this notion leads to a sense of emptiness, as it removes the opportunities for growth and self-discovery that conflict often brings.

As many conservative thinkers have recognized, the "result" of the end of history is that comfort and freedom, while pleasant, are not lasting sources of fulfillment — our yearning for a higher meaning and purpose is what truly resonates with us. We aspire to be part of a narrative that transcends our individual lives, one that is larger than ourselves and does not revolve solely around us.

Citizenship Dies, Intersectional Constitution Lives

In its 245th year, America is dangerously divided and chaotic. I can only conclude that the United States does not function as it once did and, at the same time, works all too well in frightening ways. It is a multifaceted system collapse.

Despite the nightly shootings, gang violence, and stories of economic recession from the pandemic's dislocations, Amazon's founder Jeff Bezos has doubled his fortune during the quarantine to become the wealthiest man in the history of the world, with a reported $180 billion in net worth (Au-Yeung, 2020).

Millions of Americans are moving to a "red," i.e., Republican-controlled, state that better fits their ideology or dropping out of political and civic life altogether. Idaho, Wyoming, and Montana lure city dwellers from Los Angeles, Seattle, and Manhattan by being perceived as antidotes to the New York of Andrew Cuomo and Bill de Blasio.

Others suffer psychological damage due to anger or retreat into a monastery of the mind. Millions of unhappy people tune out the incessant proselytizing of professional sports, the evening news, network sitcoms, dramas, commercials, and Hollywood releases.

Globalism enriched the informational, investment, and professional classes with new markets and billions of consumers. Yet, institutionalized outsourcing and offshoring have insidiously enervated the American and Western interior's industrial and manufacturing base. Politics has become topsy-turvy. The once middle-of-the-road political parties, such as the Democratic Party in the U.S., have moved far more to the left than conservative parties, such as the Republican Party in the U.S. or the Christian Democratic Union in Germany, which, if they moved at all, also moved to the left. In the new century, the Democratic Party embraced open borders and new tribalism, becoming the party of the wealthiest intellectuals and the poorest illegal immigrants — both of the Left. The old Republican establishment of the Bushes, John McCain, and Mitt Romney was vaporized by furious Make America Great Again populism. The Trump phenomenon accelerated the conservative and patriotic transformation of the middle classes from working-class-issue Democrats into populist Republicans.

Yet both parties — in addition to Bernie Sanders and Donald Trump personally — acknowledged that the U.S. was becoming more volatile, unhappy, and unfair. The Left now, in conspiratorial fashion, points to a supposedly iconic January 6, 2021, "insurrection" as the moment when the republic changed into something else.

The Right argues that the legal exemptions far better epitomize lawlessness and insurrection, given the four months of rioting, looting, arson, and protests during the summer of 2020. COVID-19, the lockdowns, the self-induced recession, the rioting of 2020, the controversial elections, and the January 6, 2021, assault on the Capitol were the matches that ignited the combustibles of the last 20 years.

America's malaise, divisions, and obsessions with national decline led to a loss of citizenship and the feeling of (not) being part of a (non) nation — the original glue that once, long ago, held together the American experiment. Perhaps we assume that a "citizen" of a country is a natural concept that arose organically with the ascent of civilization itself. It did not.

For generations, unique laws, customs, and traditions, such as the Bill of Rights, the right to bear arms, and the tradition of peaceful transition of power, united the citizenry, distinguished them from their neighbors, and ensured civic solidarity and security. Ancient tribal loyalties slowly eroded, were relegated to chauvinistic myths, and were superseded by shared fealty to constitutional states.

The Hellenic states thrived and preserved their freedom against the overwhelming forces of the transcontinental Persian Empire for a while. Yet, the richer but more internally divided Greeks of the 4th century BC lost their freedom to the Macedonians. An erosion of Greek citizenship perhaps best explains the fractious Greek states' failure to unite, sufficiently arm, and confidently meet the invaders.

The classical Western traditions of Greek consensual government and Roman republicanism were not just distant echoes, but living legacies that deeply influenced the American founding classes. They sought to emulate checks on the use of government power. The Founders divided the government into legislative, executive, and judicial branches and institutionalized personal freedom — all in reaction to their contemporary history and the classical warnings from the past.

They designed the newly formed American Constitution to ensure that the small property-owning, common-sense classes formed the backbone of the new nation. Like the classical world, Americans incorporated inherent mechanisms for challenging and questioning the status quo into their new governance system, in the tradition of unique Western self-criticism and reexamination, a practice where societies reflect on their actions and beliefs to improve and adapt.

Despite the numerous upheavals and transformations brought about by the vast frontier expansion, waves of immigration, the Industrial Revolution, the Civil War and Reconstruction, World War I and World War II, the Great Depression, the suffrage, labor, and civil rights movements, and the countercultural revolutions of the 1960s, America not only survived but emerged as the freest, wealthiest, and most powerful nation in the history of civilization. The key to this remarkable achievement was the resilience and the rights and responsibilities of American citizens.

However, the middle classes have suffered from stagnant incomes, even as the country has become more prosperous. Middle-class and poor students owe $1.7 trillion in aggregate college debt, the average net worth of Americans at retirement is plunging, and about 40 percent of American adults can only make minimum payments on their mounting credit card debt (Horch, 2020).

The age at which Americans marry, have their first child, or buy a home has risen to new highs as American fertility rates reach modern lows. The 19th-century Americanophile Alexis de Tocqueville's fear of government-induced dependency, resulting in prolonged adolescence replacing self-reliant citizens, is becoming a reality.

Some twenty million foreigners remain in the U.S. illegally. The idea of a southern border has been reduced to a mere postmodern construct — as if countries need no formalized demarcations, or it is racist or xenophobic to think they do.

America's once-thriving melting pot of integrating, assimilating, and intermarrying legal immigrants has turned into sheer chaos. Although millions of immigrants vote with their feet for better lives in the United States, tribalism — the incendiary stuff of all empires and the former Yugoslavia, Iraq, Rwanda, Ukraine, or Yemen — is returning with a vengeance that supersedes mere hyphenated names and identity politics. Race and "identity," not class, are considered the more immutable and desirable divide.

According to the new and woke creed, one must embrace *good* bias, i.e., reversed discrimination, to fight *bad* discrimination. Or, putting it another way, one must first become obsessed with racial differences to curb racial obsessions.

Few will reflect on the fact that a large, developed, multiracial democracy is history's unique artifact and that until recently, America was about the only society in history that had even tried such an ambitious project. However, this ad hoc attempt has resulted in the continuous erosion of the chief principles of citizenship. The weakening of the middle class, the porous borders, and the idea that race is merely incidental, not essential to who and what people are, occur almost organically. It seems that America is reverting to a premodern, pre-civilizational region, or territory of peasants and dwellers rather than a modern industrial country of empowered citizens on whom the free world can rely.

Simultaneously, the ruling elites are making a more deliberate effort to curb citizenship: federal government employees often infringe upon citizens' rights not to be subjected to government surveillance and hounding, government warping of their private tax information, radical challenges to their elections, and infringement on their constitutional protections.

Economic globalization often conflates with envisioned global political harmonization. Global and Westernized elites talk of a future "Great Reset" in which nations adopt top-down reforms of their economies, base their energy use on transnational norms, and implement global guidelines on everything from corporate governance to reparatory diversity policies.

No nation has a longer history of uniquely stable constitutional government than the United States, yet American customs, civic education, and commonly shared traditions are rejected today as toxic because they are not perfect. But few acknowledge that the glue holding together an otherwise unruly and once-tribal America was the shared national and religious holidays, the collective respect and pride for American values, icons, emblems, and traditions, and the knowledge of and appreciation for the reasons why most immigrants come to the United States and why so few Americans leave for homes elsewhere.

In short, without popular allegiance to viable middle-class values, a defined and shared space with secure borders, and a joint investment in an America that transcends particular tribes, there can be no citizenship. Nor can American citizenship survive if the ruling elites entrust its governance and protection to the unelected and unaudited millions, or if they seek to alter the Constitution or change time-tested customs and traditions for ephemeral political advantage or modify the American idea of governance and its ancient traditions to align with global but self-serving trends.

Without viable citizenship, America can no longer exist. A society adrift from its origins and foundational principles of citizenship has real foreign policy consequences. For that reason, it was only a matter of time before the U.S. faced tragedy abroad, given the unhinged assumptions it was operating under at home.

Is the truth too bitter to swallow? Namely, the "elites" are hardly elite and have not been so for generations. Retired Pentagon generals rotate in and out of defense contractor boards on their way to multimillionaire status. They gain exemption from the once anti-corporate Left by sounding "woke" in promoting race, class, gender, diversity, equity, and inclusion agendas, in which military efficacy is not defined by victory on the battlefield or at least U.S. strategic advantage, but rather by approbation from the Left and the administrative state.

In 2020, one hundred twenty days of rioting, looting, arson, and billions of dollars in losses convinced even the medieval Taliban that America is a hopelessly adrift society and would prefer to be a victim than unapologetically retaliatory. Did the Dark Ages win an existential war between the premodern and postmodern? Or, put another way, do those who believe fiercely in something pre-civilizational defeat those who hesitatingly, tentatively, might believe in something post-civilizational? We have gone from a movie audience idolizing Gary Cooper, Clark Gable, and Jimmy Stewart to one more comfortable with Tom Hanks, Hugh Grant, and George Clooney.

Two million people are expected to cross the southern border of the U.S. over 12 months — *en masse* and illegally. The new arrivals' first act is to break American law by entering the country illegally; then, they violate the law again by residing in the U.S. illegally. On top of that, they will find and even get help to find false identification, fake documents, and other illegal means to continue breaking the law. A guest does not arrive in a foreign country only to immediately violate the laws of their host — unless one holds those laws in contempt.

The cynical logic and immoral rationale of illegal immigration do not care about the would-be legal immigrants or U.S. citizens. The new arrivals will depend on the state and thus become loyal constituents of progressives who engineered their presence in the first place. However, the issue is not illegal immigration per se. If protests continued in communist Cuba and one million Cubans fled to Miami, the progressive Left would immediately stop the influx, horrified that so many anti-Communists might tip Florida to the right forever.

Crime is another everyday absurdity, with internet videos depicting young people, disproportionately African-American males, stealing, looting, or robbing luxury goods, clearing shelves with impunity, or assaulting Asian Americans. Though these archetypal moments may be unrepresentative of reality, given the frightening statistics of significant increases in violent crime in certain cities, a particular popular conception was born and entrenched worldwide. According to that perception, walking in major American metropolitan areas is dangerous, day or night. Chicago has already reverted to a state reminiscent of Tombstone, Dodge City, and the OK Corral, with a solid racial overtone in the popular imagination this time.

Moreover, scarier still is the realization that if one is mugged, assaulted, or finds their property vandalized, almost certainly, the miscreant will never be held to account. Either the police have been intimidated, pulled back, and found arrests of criminals to be a no-win situation, or radical district attorneys view the law as a critical legal or racial theory construct and, therefore, will not enforce it. Alternatively, the criminal may still be arrested but also released within hours.

Thus, a subculture has developed among Americans, passing information about where it is safe to go and where it is not, where one can go and where one cannot. This state of affairs is not what America used to be but something bizarre out of São Paulo, Durban, or Malmö.

The death of the sainted George Floyd has provided the ideal pretext for the Left to dismantle the signs of American historical identity.

With generous corporate and philanthropic support, radical activists are "resetting" America. That means mandating the instruction of critical race theory (CRT) in public schools, replacing Old Glory with the rainbow "pride" flag, restricting social media and newsroom language, overwhelming the southern border of the U.S. with unvetted illegal immigrants from Mexico, Central America, and elsewhere; removing allegedly racist statues from public spaces; and rendering former President Donald Trump *persona non grata*. All this deconstruction is building toward the ultimate path to power: a new Constitution.

Rewriting the basis of law and country is a formidable task. Nevertheless, radical egalitarians, whose ranks seem to be swelling by the month, have become convinced over the last few years that this mission is both doable and overdue. In their minds, the U.S. Constitution is the obstacle to their ideal of complete racial and gender equality of outcomes. Since the Framers of the Constitution overlooked including such provisions in America's founding document, it has no legitimacy.

Advocates of such interpretation are blunt about their desire for an inclusive replacement or, failing that, a wide-ranging amendment that would permanently alter the character of American daily life. Either way, the rule of law, due process, and property rights would not figure into this.

Instead, the repugnant moral paladins of the campaign to reset the U.S. Constitution demand to include the following totalitarian instincts in that newly fashioned document:

· To mend the original sin of racism, Americans should pass an amendment to the U.S. Constitution that enshrines two guiding anti-racist principles: racial inequity is evidence of racist policy, and different racial groups are equals.

· The amendment would make unconstitutional racial inequity over a certain threshold and racist ideas by public officials.

· It would establish and permanently fund the Department of Anti-Racism (DOA), which would comprise no political appointees but formally trained experts on racism.

According to Black Lives Matter activists, the U.S. Constitution is the root of virtually all their problems in America. As they wrote in a 2015 article, "A New Constitution or the Bullet," "Our Black Lives Matter protests have stormed the country, yet cops continue to kill us daily, and the judicial system continues to justify our deaths with acquittals, non-indictments, and light sentences — all in the name of upholding the Constitution" (Simons, 2015).

A blogger named Victoria Abraham posted the following barely readable list of clichés for *Teen Vogue* in June 2021: "Black Americans experience persecution based on race and reasonably fear such persecution by the American government, and if they lived in another country, it stands to reason America would grant them asylum. The extent of America's oppression of Black people means that to dismantle systemic racism, America must begin by replacing the U.S. Constitution with one based on equality and human rights, like South Africa did after the end of apartheid — a system of racial discrimination and segregation that has been compared to America's Jim Crow laws" (Abraham, 2021).

Consequently, white governors, mayors, and judges practically kneel before Black Lives Matter. Agitated as these passages are, they reflect the view that government authorities should restructure the legal system to eliminate differences in income, wealth, and power. Since the Constitution, by design, restrains this impulse, the radicals would reject it outright. Few things provoke the race and gender police more than the thought of one of their ploys being ruled unconstitutional. To them, the Constitution is a musty and outdated impediment to fulfilling the American national promise.

Those progressives who call for the repeal of the Constitution are fully aware of the barrier that is the current U.S. Supreme Court. Any jurist could recognize the ulterior motive behind wanting to expand the Supreme Court from 9 to 15 members, ban the filibuster, federalize state election laws, end the Electoral College, and admit the District of Columbia and Puerto Rico to the union. Although the Democrats are willing to paddle through these radical waters, the court's originalist majority, however tenuously, is likely to block their program.

While a constitutional reset has a long way to go before execution, it is now within the realm of possibility — and Broadway also plays a role in it. On March 31, 2019, a play titled "What the Constitution Means to Me," written by and starring actress and playwright Heidi Schreck, was introduced at the Helen Hayes Theater following a successful off-Broadway run the previous year (Stasio, 2019). Playing nightly to packed houses filled with enthusiastic audiences created an impetus for challenging the Constitution. This is a clear example of how progressive arts can shape public opinion and influence political discourse, a fact that should not be overlooked.

As the title implies, "What the Constitution Means to Me" is less about the Constitution itself than about its creator's emotional connection to that document. The mostly one-person show is constitutional law recast as psychodrama. Critics, like audiences, raved. It is undoubtedly a landmark work, but in an unintended way: Schreck's character arc mirrors millions of radicalized Americans steeped in histrionics and moral self-righteousness. She has exposed the deepest desires of the Left's post-communist "intersectional" coalition, mainly through the backstory featuring a recreation of her youthful promotion of the very thing she rejects today. No matter the issue, her verdict is always the same: The Constitution, despite its possibly good intentions and elegant prose, has not protected vulnerable and defenseless Americans — those who are not white, male, or heterosexual.

The entire drama negates the Framers' intent in designing the U.S. Constitution to discourage direct majoritarianism, i.e., the belief that those with a simple majority should make and abuse the rules for all members of a group or nation. The Constitution is meant to protect against the majority and their potential for mob rule, endless bandwagon appeals, and the setting of boundaries for political discourse. Admittedly, the delicate balancing of interests collapsed during the secession crisis and the Civil War of 1861–65. But looking at the broader picture, all those seemingly pesky checks and balances have warded off tyranny. Without the Constitution's current separation of powers and delegation of authority to the states, some sinister inquisitors would surely enjoy a far straighter path to absolute power.

Heidi Schreck's play misrepresents the Constitution for agitprop purposes aimed at a hipster crowd. Using the Constitution as a pivotal reference for a personal odyssey sounds disingenuous, insincere, and contrived.

The U.S. Constitution — the result of months of heated debate and reluctant compromises, not to mention 27 subsequent amendments — defines the contours of workable political order and nothing more. And that is the way it should be; it is not a master plan for solving social issues or protecting each of us from fortune's slings and arrows. If leftist radicals want to solve social or personal problems, they should rely on markets, legislation, courts, philanthropy, and emotional maturity.

The U.S. Constitution is more than a foundation for law and politics — it is an expression of American identity, as much as the English language, baseball, and Old Glory. Therefore, the people must stop America's multicultural radical Left from using a new, "living," whimsical, and intersectional Constitution to become a mega-factional Leviathan that lords over their political rivals. Replacing the Constitution in the manner envisioned by the radicals, far from "completing" our country, might finish it off — which is, of course, their ultimate goal.

The American Descent into Madness

I prophesy what a socialist government of any color and name will do by the force of its logic. Instead of dwelling on the alleged victory over Bolshevism, Marxism, communism, socialism, the Soviet Union, the Warsaw Pact, et al., and touting America's and the West's unique achievement that commanded the support and participation of all peoples of freedom, I predict the deadly danger of Leftism, its violent aspirations, and denounce the current popular path of appeasement — similar to that in the 1970s and 1980s. Socialism, in any form, inevitably leads to a politicized police force that may be benevolent at first but will inevitably turn into a Gestapo.

Some people may think that I paint myself as mentally disturbed. They will claim that Britain's Labor governments and prime ministers, Germany's social-democratic party and chancellors, France's socialist presidents, Italy's socialist and leftist presidents and prime ministers, and the democratic socialists of the Netherlands and the Scandinavian countries all worked together seamlessly, effectively, and selflessly to win that ostensible victory by sharing the hard work of bringing down the communist dictatorships.

But I say that underneath it all, the above heroes, or their present-day successors, would turn the world, including the United States, into the same type of socialist police state they had "sacrificed so much" to defeat.

I declare that no socialist system can ever exist without political police, despite what those intellectuals advocating socialism, democratic socialism, social democracy, or voting "socialist" may still claim today. This is because these fanatic idealists or short-sighted and naïve left-liberals cannot see where their theories lead them.

No socialist government of any form conducting and governing the life and industry of any country could afford to allow expressions of public discontent or effective opposition. Any such government will stop criticism as it raises its head and will gather all the power of the Supreme Idea and party leaders.

Governments have to be competent to serve the people, but socialism accepts no limitations on the power of the government it would run. Nothing will be allowed to stand in the way of achieving socialism's ideology and social visions. Any other source of power, e.g., emanating from individual liberties, religions, alternate political parties, or even families, will have to be co-opted, intimidated, or eliminated. Once the socialist ball gets rolling, it will never stop itself.

Consider present-day America and its contemporary cancel culture. It was first prevalent in academia, which had stood for freedom of inquiry and civil discourse in recent memory. But all that matters now is the attainment of the approved social outcome. Because of that, even the merest toleration is afforded only to those politically correct followers who are in continuous and unquestioning ideological compliance.

Consider the Justice Department directive threatening FBI intervention in local school board politics, whereby the attorney general raised the specter of parents' much-belated opposition to school board policy as "domestic terrorism" (Benner, 2021).

Consider the unleashing of the FBI on an opposition journalist in a raid at the crack of dawn (Wulfsohn, 2021). He had once held in his possession a text delivered to him by a source claiming it was the notebook of the president's daughter. Since the journalist could not authenticate the papers, he never published them but turned them over to the police. The FBI attack is a blatant attempt to terrify anyone bold enough to challenge or present a possible danger to the regime's political power.

But anyone following the sordid affair of the Steele Dossier, also known as the Trump–Russia dossier — although it would be more appropriate to call it the Trump-Russia-Clinton dossier — knows that the conversion of the FBI into the forefront of a police state did not start with this latest attack on the journalist (Cohen, 2021).

The U.S. may not yet have a Gestapo, and all this may seem quaint and outmoded to the already corrupted elite believing their propaganda and acting as if they were accountable only to their social program. But it is enough to persuade anyone that America went from the happiest, wealthiest, and freest country in the world in the 1950s to a repressive, frightening, and semi-third-world place by 2021. How did that happen?

Civilizations have often gone mad in months — at least temporarily. The French abandoned their idealistic revolutionary project and turned it into an atrocious slaughterhouse for a year between July 1793 and 1794. After the election of November 1860, Americans went from thinking secession was unthinkable and something not allowed to killing the highest possible number of their fellow citizens in a matter of weeks — before reemerging again during the Reconstruction Era. The China of Mao Zedong went from a failed communist state to a horrible hell, consumed by the Cultural Revolution in 1966 — before slowly starting to reemerge in the 1970s. Some other countries, such as Nazi Germany or the Soviet Union, could never manage to overcome the madness — and disappeared forever.

The United States has been on an ever-declining slope for many decades. However, in the last six to eight months, we have seen absurdities approaching madness that have never quite been witnessed in modern America. All these disorders have three characteristics: the events are unsustainable and will either cease or destroy the country as it is; the law has been chiefly rendered meaningless, and leftist political agendas justify any means necessary to achieve their goals.

Americans have seen the CIA wrecked, the FBI ruined, and the military tarnished during this entire descent into madness. There is a massive reeducation and indoctrination campaign draining scarce resources, targeting, and defaming the same white working class that disproportionately died in the civil and foreign wars. Today, policing the thoughts of U.S. soldiers is more important than fathoming the minds of America's enemies on the battlefield.

The Left has finally revealed what I have always known since coming over the Iron Curtain in 1972: a purely ideological view of legal and illegal immigration. After opening the U.S. southern border to pseudo-political refugees, the U.S. Administration is terrified that thousands of real ones might come to Miami in the same fashion it invited millions to storm into Texas. Its immigration policy hinges only on whether immigration alters the demographics of the electorate in the "proper" way.

Finally, almost all Americans agree that the U.S. Constitution is unique and guarantees personal freedom in a way the United Nations charter cannot. But the U.S. The Secretary of State has invited the UN to assess whether the United States meets global standards of justice or is racist and in need of international censure: "I urge all UN member states to join the United States in this effort and confront the scourge of racism, racial discrimination, and xenophobia" (Reuters Staff, 2021). What a confession of failure and evidence of incapacity. That is akin to asking Osama bin Laden's Al-Qaeda in 2001 to assess whether U.S. anti-terrorism training met proper standards or having the Soviet Union adjudicate the conditions in U.S. prisons.

The reality is not just that the West is eroding the value of money — the skyrocketing prices of gas, food, appliances, lumber, power, housing, and stocks are threatening to overwhelm the entitlement machine, even with near-zero interest rates — but also that the "Wise Men" of the West are constructing a facade of economics, bolstered by pseudo-finance, to justify their nihilistic approach.

The witness of this age can observe a multitrillion-dollar borrowing spree beyond the American multitrillion-dollar debt to build "infrastructure," a notion that includes just about anything other than roads and bridges. This infrastructure is financed by "good debt" since it is supposed to pay for itself in the future — an often-heard socialist vow from the past when the state took the people's money for "industrialization," "nationalization," and other "socially just redistributions"; all wasted without ever turning a profit. The state then squandered the worthless money on useless projects — and when the system collapsed, the perpetrators claimed it had not been "real socialism."

America has moved much further left and become stark-raving mad.

The universities have been intolerant, radically leftist, and increasingly anti-constitutional over the past 40 years. Moreover, they have fostered a cash-cow scheme that the administrators dare not damage, given the golden gifts of federally guaranteed student loans ensuring zero academic accountability while sending tuition costs to stratospheric heights. There was an acknowledged belief that any college degree, of any major, was the ticket to American success. At the same time, people skeptically shrugged, as they still do today; most prestigious institutions were little more than mere stigmatizers that stamped graduates with seals that conferred unearned privilege for life.

By now, universities are determined to strangle their golden goose. The public, including parents, is becoming repulsed at the woke culture on campus and will be even more turned off when, at Ivy League or major state university campuses, admissions will no longer be based on proportional representation in the context of affirmative action but will increasingly be defined by an even more discriminatory, reparative character.

The grades, test scores, and "activities" of white and Asian male college applicants are becoming less relevant.

Only those "privileged" white males who fortuitously possess sports skills and connections or whose families have donated significant amounts of money are exempt from the biased racial reparation quotas. Ironically, the new woke admission policy targets the suburban, liberal-intellectual professional family, the Left's constituency, whose lives obsessively focus on whether children graduate from Ivy League or similar campuses. Given the radical change in new student profiles — thousands of fresh enrollees do not meet the entrance requirement standards of just two or three years ago — the faculty will increasingly have to choose between allegations of racism or grading regardless of actual performance. Since wokeism has always been a top-down business of the elites, minority progressives will still battle white leftists in disputes over titles, salaries, and managerial posts. Good for them.

Perhaps the public will eventually ask why they are subsidizing student loans, why multibillion-dollar endowments are not taxed, and why anyone thinks a B.A. in sociology, psychology, or gender studies is an "investment" that would prepare anyone for anything.

No healthy society is sustainable with a Maoist creed such as critical race theory, which destroys citizens for thought crimes. Obscurantist commissars do not produce anything or serve anybody; they only monitor thoughts and speech to ascertain the purity of ideology, equity, diversity, and inclusion. They are a drain on the healthy functioning of society and will insidiously destroy it, as their acceptance ensures a timid obsequiousness and banal orthodoxy.

From the ignominious French Revolution to the failed Soviet system, society's most mediocre people became its most eager auditors of correct behavior. The arbiters of proper thought — the self-righteous sycophant, the perpetual victim employed in service to government payback, the freelancing snitch — have always been the scoundrels of freedom, efficiency, and humanity, whether it was about the killing off of Alexander the Great's inner circle, the forced suicides of the Neronian ring, the Jacobin murder spree, or the nightmarish world described by Aleksandr Solzhenitsyn (Solzhenitsyn A. I., The Gulag Archipelago, 2003).

In modern America, in Cuban fashion, millions of judge-jury-executioner online snitchers, encouraged by a progressive government, will help root out incorrect thoughts at light speed.

American State Security and Media Service

Is there still any freedom of speech in America?

Today, *The Washington Post, The New York Times,* ABC, NBC, CNN, CBS, and others present a matrix of constructed reality. Together with the collaborating American intelligence community, they form a gigantic apparatus capable of infringing upon our freedoms by controlling and surveilling every spoken and written word everywhere.

This apparatus targets white Americans who support Donald Trump and are therefore considered would-be "homegrown" extremists and terrorists. If you are a white, heterosexual male, perhaps even a practicing Christian belonging to an evangelical denomination, you are viewed as suspicious and potentially liable to surveillance. In a tweet and on its website, the FBI asked Americans to spy and report on their neighbors, acquaintances, co-workers, and even family members for so-called "suspicious behaviors" potentially conducive to homegrown violent extremism (Murica, 2021). The FBI also embraced the material concocted by a particular former agent of an intelligence service and duly packaged it into a dossier at the behest of Hillary Clinton's election campaign. That once highly regarded organization treats the mere questioning of the legitimacy of Joseph Biden's victory in November 2020 as a red flag, emblematic of the claimant's path to radicalization. All this is genuinely worthy of George Orwell, the Gestapo, the current German police state, and the Stalinist Soviet Union.

Although "Deep State" is the established term, I prefer to call it a "sensed but not seen state." It is a profoundly ideologically committed part of a complex mechanism that sees in Donald Trump a temporary aberration that must not be permitted but removed instead. Their actions make it evident that the security services and law enforcement agencies are prepared to use any means to discredit and politically destroy those who do not think as they do. At the same time, they faithfully serve their ideological allies and order-givers — and even protect them from well-deserved criminal prosecution.

The question arises as to what the actual role of these agencies is and how powerful they are.

With the support of the media, we have reached the point where any mention of any fact that is at odds with today's approved narrative is portrayed as fake news, outright lies, incitement, or hate speech — without any prior analysis of their veracity. This excludes any possibility of debate.

The BBC, Voice of America, Agence France-Presse, and Deutsche Welle are government-funded entities that present their countries and governments in the best possible light to the world. In that respect, they are just like Sputnik News, which the Western mainstream media routinely calls a "Russian propaganda outfit." Like Sputnik, the Western government-funded, sponsored, or indirectly influenced and privately owned media employ seasoned professionals and produce quality programs. Just like Sputnik, RT News, or Global Times, their more astute audiences rightly perceive these outlets as information and propaganda conduits of their respective governments.

However, the Western mainstream media outlets pretend to be something other than "propaganda outfits." The affectation is pathetic; the core claim is clear: we are good, they are bad. We educate; they corrupt. We stand for "all things bright and beautiful" — whether democracy, left-liberal values, LGBTQ+, open borders, globalism, or multicultural harmony. On the other hand, they are the totalitarian, drunk, reactionary Russian, Chinese, North Korean, or Eastern European barbarians, irrationally, hatefully, and obstinately opposed to our values. Only we tell the truth; they always lie.

In reality, everyone "lies," deceives, misleads, and distorts by not allowing mere facts to obstruct their fabricated or desired "reality" — the Brits are pretty good at the game, based on their long experience. By "quasi-reality," I refer to a narrative that, while not factual, is constructed in a way that appears plausible and convincing. Their quasi-reality

189

constructs sometimes even ring true to the naïve, and their polished accents and urbane fabrications also help.

The Russians are far less ideologically zealous these days and, for that reason, do not need to lie much — because they have observed an exciting role reversal over the past few decades. When the Bolshevik state emerged as a revolutionary project more than a century ago, it was determined to shatter the old order. However, following the USSR's disintegration, Russia has struggled to protect its core and traditionally understood national interests — no quasi-reality needed. Sputnik and RT have given their contributors a global platform to express their thoughts when asked — and that can no longer happen in the Kremlin-on-the-Potomac, New York, or Berlin.

"The West" has transformed into the greenhouse of bizarre posthuman projects and overtly aggressive geopolitical designs — the rise of transhumanism and the expansion of NATO are just a few examples of these projects and designs. Whether Joe Biden would be able to move on, unite the country, and heal America's wounds when so many people deny his legitimacy, I can say the following:

The mainstream media machine has acted as an integral, symbiotic part of the "Deep State" and has wholeheartedly supported Biden's team. That machine treated all claims of irregularity in the presidential election as baseless, insignificant, and inconsequential fibs, acting as an inseparable arm of the Biden campaign. That same media machine denied President Trump's legitimacy throughout the entire process while covering up the scandals concerning Hillary Clinton's servers and emails and the dubious business dealings of Hunter Biden, the president's son, in Ukraine, China, and elsewhere. Had it been the other way around, had there been any accusations of wrongdoing by Republicans or even the slightest hint that the GOP was manipulating the election process, *The New York Times*, *The Washington Post*, CNN, MSNBC, and the other suspects undoubtedly would have been highly diligent in not leaving a single stone unturned.

But Donald Trump — unlike Biden — did not have the "Deep State" on his side. The American Deep State, which includes the military-industrial-congressional-media complex but is not limited to it, sees the return of the left-liberal interventionists to power as an almost-lost opportunity to continue where the dreaded Trump had stopped. They want to reaffirm the strategy of global hegemony, liberal democracy, multiculturalism, and nation-building with missionary zeal, which will produce wars, conflicts, and upheavals like the ones Bill Clinton engineered in Bosnia and Kosovo, George W. Bush in Iraq and Afghanistan, and Barack Obama in Syria, Libya, Yemen, and Somalia. Donald Trump did not like any of that, and his audacity was unacceptable to the establishment.

The third, but by no means least important aspect, is that President Trump assailed one of the unassailable holy cows of the left-liberal establishment: the cult of open borders of an "open society" and immigration reform that would legalize illegal immigrants — probably forever. Biden will persevere with that agenda, especially since the Democratic Party sees a way to cement its advantage in this course. It knows that naturalized nonwhite immigrants have voted overwhelmingly for Democrats in recent decades. They are the immigrants who rely on the federal government to help them along, unlike the old-school immigrants from Europe who relied on their fingers, muscles, and brains to establish a new home and better life for themselves and their families without needing or expecting any mechanisms of public assistance and government social programs.

Given these circumstances, it is inevitable that millions of Trump followers will remain convinced of the deliberate, systematic, and premeditated manipulation of the electoral process. These mishandlings, which also have a constitutional component, were observed in various executive, legislative, and even judicial institutions in Wisconsin, Michigan, Pennsylvania, and Georgia, where the rules of the game were changed at the last moment. Despite these blatant violations of the law, Trump supporters feel that the mainstream media machine of the Deep State is ignoring their concerns. The real frustration, however, lies in the inability to articulate this righteous anger in a systematic, coherent manner that could disrupt the Biden administration's ability to execute its various designs. With the loss of Georgia in the Senate races, it seems the Republicans have little to prevent the Democrats from having a free hand to implement the Biden team's agenda unhindered on all fronts.

The "Disunited States of America" Is the Soviet Union's Successor

Just like the Soviet Union, the U.S. is suffering from "depressive hopelessness." The Cold War ended with a failed and bizarre coup in Moscow thirty years ago, confirming Marx's dictum that history repeats itself as a farce. That proved true for the Soviet Union, the state defined by Marxist ideology.

In August 1991, while the reforming General Secretary Mikhail Gorbachev of the USSR holidayed in his Ukrainian dacha, hard-liners tried to seize power. Under house arrest, Gorbachev learned that Boris Yeltsin, President of the Russian Federation, courageously stood in front of Moscow's White House in defiance of the plotters, surrounded by supporters flaunting the old Russian flag.

Perhaps it was not clear to everyone that Yeltsin was drunk for much of it. The plotting conspirators, it turned out, were also generally drunk. Having begun a botched and unusually amateurish coup, the ringleaders appeared on television looking ashen-faced and almost pathetic, some shaking nervously. Most of all, though, they seemed to be old, much beyond their years, the faces of a fading empire built on faith no one could believe in anymore.

One of Gorbachev's most impactful decisions was to raise the tax on vodka, a move intended to address the country's catastrophic drinking problem. However, the Soviet Union was already in the grip of alcohol, and any attempt to curb it proved futile. This societal issue, along with others, played a pivotal role in the demographic collapse that preceded the political fall of the USSR; the decline in life expectancy affected not only the elderly but also the middle-aged. The stark reality was that people were drinking themselves to death out of hopelessness. A country where life is becoming shorter, more hopeless, and miserable for its citizens has a bleak future.

Russia's birth rate had also long collapsed due to several causes that once drove higher fertility in wealthy countries, such as security, family, religion, optimism about the future, and affordability.

A similar trend can also be observed in the United States. If both partners of a couple must work to make ends meet, fertility rates will likely be significantly lower. While the U.S. may have more extensive daycare provisions, they often fall short of compensating for the lack of adequate wages, ease of divorce, and freely available abortion. Raising just one child can be a significant challenge, even for a married couple in the United States. These societal challenges, among others, are indicators of a future that mirrors the decline of the Soviet Union.

Liberalism faced challenges in America in the late 20th century. Ideology defined the United States, just like the Soviet Union, its main adversary in the Cold War; liberalism was enshrined in America's foundation. But starting in the early 1960s, a new way of thinking began to predominate in the U.S. that was not liberal at all, although its opponents confusingly still referred to it as such. The same applied to free-market capitalism, which has been neither, but that did not stop its leftist opponents from blaming everything on it.

The new way of thinking was most hostile to freedom of speech, and its supporters began chasing "deviant thinkers" out of academia. This started in the late 1960s and would heavily reduce political diversity by the 21st century. The new attitude promoted personal sexual freedom, as did liberalism, along with radical ideas, including outright hostility to the family. As for freedom of association, liberalism was also incompatible with a new worldview that prioritized equality over liberty.

This new orientation — progressivism is probably the best term to describe it — is far less tolerant than liberalism. It is closer to the totalitarian tradition in its hostility to freedom of speech, its suspicion that its opponents are all "fascists," and its belief that politics should be inserted everywhere, from science to children's books. American progressivism is not communism any more than its opponents are Nazis; the U.S. has become ideologically, politically, and culturally more left-wing while right-wing economic policies have still dominated the Western world — globalization being the common theme linking them together.

However, globalization came with a price, with millions of jobs lost after the trade deal with China in 2000. In the former industrial heartlands, people first noticed an epidemic of drug-related deaths that has become one of the most significant social disasters in history. This epidemic took so long to make an impression because of the drug problem's solitary and sometimes legal nature — unlike AIDS, it did not affect too many celebrities. Four decades after its superpower rival, the United States had become a country where people were dying younger, driven by overdoses and suicides. The victims were predominantly white Americans living in rural areas, neither powerful themselves nor championed by influential supporters.

Like the Soviet Union, the U.S. has also developed a system in which some social classes and races are officially acknowledged as favorites while others are disfavored —

reflected in post-war legal innovations such as affirmative action.

The U.S. government introduced affirmative action as an antidote to official or unofficial segregation, but its purpose evolved as bureaucracies grew. Today, government interference in society and private institutions mainly aims to achieve equality.

However, it is not the liberal concept of equal opportunity but the more ambitious equality of outcomes, or "equity."

Equality is achieved through inequality. Under this theory, each racial group must have equal representation in elite institutions. Depending on their race, Americans may score differently in gaining acceptance to and attending specific colleges. This concept is illiberal and un-American, not unlike the "nationalities policies" created by communist ideologues under which the USSR officially discriminated against the Russian majority for certain positions.

The policies of Soviet nationalities, viewed in their historical context, allowed minority groups recognition and a certain degree of self-rule while ensuring that their elites remained safely under the control of the Communist Party. This approach, while seemingly inclusive, also had its limitations. Specific groups, such as Ukrainians, Tatars, and Jews, were at times disfavored due to their perceived anti-communist or disloyal stance. However, it was Russian identity that was actively discouraged, as Stalin denounced the "Great Russian chauvinist spirit," viewing the nationalism of the majority as the greatest evil.

Nonetheless, that did not lead to the brotherhood of men either. The ethnic spoils system significantly benefited the party and minority members but not the majority. The benefits of diversity, just like the benefits of liberalism, capitalism, or democracy, tend to be a non-zero-sum game: migrants always benefit from moving to a more prosperous or safer country, but it is hard to determine whether the host population also gains from their skills or cultural niches at all — it depends on the migrants.

Equity is similarly a non-zero-sum game: someone must lose, and if one group is favored, sometimes even sacralized, others have to suffer, whether with tangible matters like jobs, college places, or simply status and prestige.

Today, the focus of America's intellectual discourse and public opinion is often on white nationalism. White supremacy is regularly denounced as a grave societal threat. The U.S. has become a country where certain institutions are accused of discriminating against the majority, and group members are sometimes viewed as so tainted and wicked that the media frequently denounce whiteness. This situation has led to numerous individuals attempting to distance themselves from this perceived taint, even resorting to faking their ethnic origins.

There are striking parallels between the Soviet empire and contemporary America. For example, Soviet thinking was based on the "blank slate" theory: life outcomes are determined almost entirely by social forces rather than genes.

Likewise, American progressivism today also rests on a blank slate, as in the USSR. There, belief in Mendelian genetics led to internal exile, while today, American social scientists offering any genetic explanation for outcomes face ostracism. Privately, many people will agree, but they are afraid of losing their jobs and career prospects if they speak out. Moreover, their publishers will drop them, or it will only embolden the "enemies of the cause" and endanger the noble goals of progressivism.

Communists saw their ideology as so all-encompassing that they even politicized science: if science contradicted the goals of communism, it was not science. Similarly, the slow death of liberalism has resulted in the blatant politicization of science in the U.S., to the extent that, as in the USSR once, scientists teach untrue things because it supports the prevailing ideology. Then there are the mainstream media parroting the Left's party line with almost embarrassing but extremely annoying "Comrade Stalin has driven pig iron to record production" levels of conformity. Therefore, if you want to hear the truth, your work is cut out for you in a "free and liberal democracy."

Once the most trusting society, today's America is heading in the same direction as the USSR, which was one of the least trusting societies. Once the most demographically vibrant Western country, the United States has suffered a spectacular collapse in white fertility. This dramatic decline is primarily attributed to stagnant wages among middle-class people, who can no longer sustain a family with a single breadwinner. People have lost optimism in the future and the ideals of their country; perhaps they have even lost faith in themselves.

The Soviet Union, ruled by geriatrics, broke into 15 pieces, and the transition was largely peaceful.

Today, people talk of secession in the United States, escaping a crumbling superpower ruled by geriatrics. Maybe this seems very unlikely, but a little more than a generation ago, few "experts" would have foreseen the Soviet Union crumbling due to the incompetence of some old fools, well-meaning idealists, and dying jerks in a haze of alcoholic despair.

Has the "United States of America" ever been more divided — or uncivil? Public discourse in the United States has taken a distressing turn. Whether walking down the street or turning on the television for the news, a movie, or a talk show, one is bombarded with profanity and hears the "F-word" almost as often as the definite article. This statement is not a mere exaggeration but a reflection of the increasing use of such language in public conversations. Our "America the Beautiful" has become a rude, broken place marred by division.

The problem is that people differ violently over what, when, and how broken they are, never mind how to fix it. The political, legal, and education systems, schools, and other fundamental institutions are all defective, and their flaws directly contribute to real unresolved societal problems, including racial, political, and economic issues. No other countries in the Western world currently face such controversies; no other place is so unhappy with itself that it resorts to intellectual incest as a palliative.

There is a troubling "schooling by ideology" trend in the United States today. Depending on their socioeconomic status, American children receive vastly different content and quality in their education, a far cry from the principles of a fair and just civil society. This disparity is evident in the housing choices families make, opting for either available private schools that cater to their specific needs or public schools dictated by location. Those schools used to teach "citizenship," the role an individual played in a constitutional republic and not a liberal democracy where elections no longer have much to do with democracy.

Increasingly, more people have given up to the point where it is newsworthy if just a little more than half of the eligible voters participate in a presidential election. Furthermore, the election process is only "fair" when the outcome is to "our liking," further eroding the public's faith in the system.

The process is complex; few people understand it, resulting in the "legal" and illegal manipulation of the rules, which are then doctored again if the judiciary finds them "unjust." Voting is based simply on mainstream and social media propaganda, which describes a dying democratic system.

Many want to "fix democracy" by using direct election, packing the Supreme Court, or ending the filibuster; it is nothing more than trying to sell something as "progress" that will aid only their candidates. It does not even matter because people no longer expect the truth. They do not know how to discuss things or disagree because they hate people with different ideas. Disagreements end with one-word pronouncements, such as "racist!" or "fascist!" instead of better ideas. Therefore, people do not speak to one another, or if they do, the range of conversation topics narrows down more and more for fear of offending someone, facing a summons to human resources, or receiving a lawsuit.

Entertainment is primarily social justice memes childishly presented and force-fed to the audience. There is no way to disengage — people can no longer ask to be left alone. But they can video everything, hoping to settle matters by embarrassing someone virally. Strangers accuse others of wanting to kill their children with a virus they do not have.

In the context of the American Civil War, the North and South were bitterly divided, even to the point of armed conflict. Yet, arguably, the average Northerners and average Southerners shared much more in common than the average conservatives and leftists today, at least in terms of underlying values.

Both the North and South were Christian. They revered America's founding and its Founding Fathers, and both believed theirs was the correct interpretation of the spirit on which the country was founded. In many ways, they were not so much divided by different values and belief systems as by dissimilar interpretations of the same values and belief systems.

Turning to the present, our political landscape is not just marked but deeply scarred by a fundamental divide between the Left and Right that surpasses the historical divisions of the North and South. They have increasingly opposite beliefs on everything from God to the differences between the sexes. The South thought secession was in keeping with what our Founders did when they split from England; the modern Left says, "To hell with the Founders," and advocates burning down the whole system.

As Americans, we have not descended into armed conflict yet, but that does not mean we are less divided. While we might not actively profess a rigid ideology, we are generally more polarized than we admit.

A person who has never voted for a Republican and embraces every leftist proposition, from support for LGBTQ+ rights through defunding the police and redistributive taxation to socialized medicine, would see himself as "center-left" when he is a polarized liberal who cannot admit it to himself.

He would maintain that the "hard right-wing" in America plays the lead role in rudeness, and that it is not the Left that loses elections and then "without evidence" claims fraud. And no one could convince this individual on the "center left" that it is the Left that has spent a century declaring an all-out war on religion, morality, patriotism, the traditional family, private enterprise, and everything else on which America, or perhaps any functioning society, is built.

The Left burns buildings and rampages through department stores while calling for the police it wants to defund to defend it. How else can the looters be characterized as leftists? They neither support nor share the values of the Right, vote Republican, or consider themselves conservative.

The Left refuses to enforce the borders and immigration laws but seeks to give the right to vote to non-citizens.

The Left wants to declare the entire American project more or less irredeemable and impose an ideology of generational racial guilt, which it considers a good thing.

It is the Left that wants generations of white American children to grow up hating themselves, their ancestors, and the society they live in, spending their lives finding it harder to get jobs, obtain admission to universities, and otherwise move up in the world — because of their skin color.

The current escalating contention in the U.S. is not a result of both sides becoming equally extreme, nor is it solely the consequence of the Right's actions. It is, in fact, a product of the Left's systematic abandonment of the principles that once united the country and held it together.

Wokers' Paradise, Where Barbarism Is Alive and Well

When Soviet Bolshevism fell, liberal democracy and capitalism stood ready to replace it. But thirty years later, they are not far from following those comrades into their workers' paradise.

Liberalism and liberals do not come off well in my books. Liberalism, with its reforms, has always hastened any system's fall, including its own. The political aspect of this dynamic is clear: when dissent is finally allowed in a once-illiberal country, discontent grows until it takes on its own momentum and finally becomes unstoppable. Political and economic liberalization are destabilizing; they are merely transitional steps leading to the next phase of development that liberalism cannot control. Furthermore, most liberals are ineffective, abusive, and insulting toward anyone who disagrees with them.

The much-desired private enrichment is often achieved more easily and quickly through corruption than through honest capitalist efforts. After the collapse of the Soviet Union, this was evident in Central and Eastern Europe in the 1990s, when quasi-privatization led to the rise of oligarchs, not entrepreneurs. Merely applying the liberal rules of the free market is insufficient without the underlying classical liberal culture to sustain capitalism. Ironically, the practices of liberal democracy will undermine and destroy capitalism itself, leading to a shaky and unstable cycle until it becomes anarchy or develops into an illiberal democracy with managed capitalism. Russia has already traversed this path assigned to it by the West, and the U.S. is currently teetering on the edge of such disorder.

No one had predicted the fall of the crumbling Soviet empire until it happened, and no one who lived through that time can analyze the collapse of socialism without thinking of the decaying American empire of today. The American political system is outdated, dysfunctional, corrupt, and run by a gerontocracy — President Biden was older when inaugurated than Leonid Brezhnev, Yuri Andropov, and Konstantin Chernenko were when they died in office several decades ago.

The American constitutional system, once a symbol of stability, is now a mere relic, if not already dead, and the legislature has become a theater for racial equity and political correctness. The judicial system, once a bastion of justice, is now tainted with prejudice; the mainstream media, once a source of unbiased information, is now shamelessly biased and propagandistic; big business, once a driver of innovation, now slavishly follows state orders predicated on social justice; the educational system, once a place of learning, has become a compilation of training institutions for leftist ideology; store shelves, once stocked with abundance, are now intermittently empty, and there are even show trials on television.

One other point of resemblance to the USSR is the rebelliousness of a resentful majority. The Soviet Union, like the U.S., was racially and ethnically diverse, with Russians as the predominant nationality, albeit suffering a demographic decline — similar to whites in the United States. Russian nationalists began to demand why Czechoslovakia, Poland, or Hungary enjoyed higher living standards than the Russians to whom they belonged. Americans, primarily liberal intellectuals, have begun to ask why Europeans, mainly Scandinavians, live better than the citizens of the leading country in the Western world.

The assumed still-majority in America is not in a position to secede the way Russia was able to free itself from the USSR and thus bring down the empire. The distinctions between the First, Second, and Third Worlds blur in contemporary United States, where the competencies of fifty individual states stretch in various odd and tyrannical directions while leaving the essential functions of government untouched. The resulting misalignment of priorities could not only delegitimize the government in the eyes of the citizenry but also lead to unforeseen and potentially disastrous consequences.

The post-WWII political landscape, a time of relative transparency, starkly contrasts with the present. The "First World" nations of the West — the U.S., United Kingdom, France, and so on, including Japan — portrayed relative political and economic independence, capitalist material prosperity, and legal probity. Then, there were the communist dictatorships of the "Second World," where the government exercised near-total control over its citizens, the state dominated the media, and a single political party enforced its own ideology-driven laws. Filling out the picture was the "Third World," notable for autocracy, corruption, poverty, disease, and crime.

Ideologically and intellectually impaired Western experts assumed an inevitable transition of Third World countries (even those under communist control) eventually becoming First World nations. Although there was some progress as capitalism became more widespread, this Third World-to-First World transition did not occur as those theorists had anticipated.

Now, the America of today seems to be combining critical elements of communist-style dictatorships with Third World human misery and a Western intellectual morass to create a startling hybrid.

Most evident is the gradual slide toward enhanced state power once associated with communist governments, i.e., a totalitarian creep toward socialism. This encroachment includes politicizing the security and intelligence agencies and government permissiveness as social media companies censor and defund organizations disputing government claims. The transgression also involves exaggerating crises to expand bureaucratic control, political show trials, transforming education into indoctrination, rewriting history, the state co-opting the mass media, encouraging mobs to threaten ordinary people, manipulating elections via controversial regulations, and an Orwellian obsession with criminalizing language.

America and the Western world have become not the Workers' Paradise of yore but the Wokers' Paradise of today, in which parts of the U.S. merge the worst of the Second and Third Worlds.

In supposedly First World cities, dozens of ill-kempt, homeless drug addicts might invade your front yard, mug you, and set up camps — and trying to evict them is a risky business. Yes, the state-run stores in old East Berlin had empty shelves, but the odds of your Trabant being carjacked with you in it were zero, and the Stasi happily ignored your choice of pronoun.

The contradictions concerning the present government's power are staggering, but the most disturbing is the disconnect between the energy devoted to stamping out constitutionally protected political dissent and curtailing criminality. There are cockeyed priorities, and their pursuit may ultimately delegitimize government authority. Physical protection and public safety are the first obligations of any government, and chasing imaginary, politically created enemies inflicting imperceptible harm undermines its core mission and credibility. Imagine the chagrin of those watching the U.S. Secretary of Defense announce that combating white supremacy is the Pentagon's number one job while thousands of illegal immigrants stream unhindered across the southern border of the U.S., smuggling drugs and child prostitutes. It is comical and sad, bizarre and outrageous, and, after a point, no one can still respect the military or its blundering commander-in-chief.

Picture this: I am sitting in a coffee shop, trying to enjoy my drink, but my peace is shattered by the blaring of rap "music." The same "F-word" — the one that rhymes with muck and yuck — that I hear in this supposedly peaceful setting, I also overhear in children's play and municipal workers' conversations in town. It is used as an adjective, a noun, and a verb, infiltrating our everyday language.

This crudity of language is merely one symptom of America's descent into barbarism, while a disheveled fashion sense is another. However, the most alarming and pressing sign of our societal drift toward brutality is the so-called Women's Health Protection Act, a bill passed by Democrats in the House of Representatives in September 2021 (Chu, 2021). This act, if passed, would immediately override state laws on abortion, including mandatory waiting periods, requirements involving ultrasound tests, and informed consent — and allow abortions through nine months.

What kind of hell is this in America? What kind of people will chop up an eight-month-old baby in the womb? The fact that this bill passed the House of Representatives not only condemns the United States of America but also labels it a country of barbaric pagans. This stamp places it in the company of the ancient city-state of Carthage, known for its brutal child sacrifices, pre-Columbian cultures practicing similar atrocities, and even Nazi Germany, which valued human life discriminatively.

"Americans" are fond of condemning the past today, tearing down monuments, revising history books, and attacking the forefathers who founded the United States and made the country attractive to millions of immigrants. But what will their children's children, those fortunate enough to be born and see the light of day, think of a people who condoned and approved such atrocities?

Real Americans must embrace a moral way of life and not act as if they believe in the left-liberal values and mores of modern Western civilization. A return to our ethical values is paramount to prevent further societal decay.

Supposedly, *The Times* of London once sent the following brief inquiry to several intellectuals and acclaimed authors: "What is wrong with the world today?" G. K. Chesterton, writer and philosopher, responded with a two-word answer, "I am." This simple yet profound response serves as a reminder of our individual and collective responsibility in shaping the world we live in, especially in the context of the societal issues we are currently facing. Ideally, those in government, corporations, schools, universities, and the rest of American society would exercise the same sense of humility. In that case, they might turn away from their current trajectory, which is leading us down a dark path of moral decay and societal disintegration.

However, I am a realist, not an idealist.

In my almost fifty years in the West, Uncle Sam has repeatedly endured challenging and unpleasant experiences. The first such episode included an enfeebled America that had just lost a war in Vietnam, suffered from cultural collapse and double-digit inflation, forced a great president to resign, and allowed its diplomats to be confined in a foreign land, with U.S. authorities unable or unwilling to do anything about it. Oil prices quintupled practically overnight, and the good uncle became a laughingstock.

Then came Margaret Thatcher and Ronald Reagan. The Iron Lady turned the screws on left-wing unions sabotaging the British economy without even enjoying approval from most of their members. Endless strikes became illegal, and the Brits have not looked back, becoming one of the five largest world economic powers based on nominal GDP shortly after Thatcher's tenure. Reagan installed Pershing II medium-range ballistic missiles and ground-launched cruise missiles (GLCMs) in Europe and raised the stakes in the poker game with the Soviet Union. Bolshevism folded its hand ten years later.

After those two political giants passed, it was natural for the governmental nincompoops to follow. The post-Cold War period saw the rise of the neoconservatives with their catastrophic foreign policy, causing the good uncle to stray from his innate opposition to unchecked power. Suddenly, there was no national purpose, just blind recklessness, imperialist fanaticism, and idealist shortsightedness that have led to the present. The three decades since the "victory" in the Cold War, a period marked by the collapse of the Soviet Union and the end of the bipolar world order, have been one long American defeat.

Looking back at Afghanistan, had the U.S. confined its mission to kicking out the Taliban and denying the 9/11 perpetrators a haven, the present would look vastly different. A proposed deal with the Taliban, limiting American presence to only three months as brokered by Hamid Karzai, was outright rejected by the neoconservative fanatics. Instead, the Afghan War was disastrously expanded into nation-building, just as in Iraq. This imperial arrogance, as history has shown, often leads to the downfall and collapse of empires.

And the downfall was severe and tragic. As the Afghan National Army did not fight for the kleptocracy in Kabul, so America's NATO "allies" will be unwilling to defend the uncle's nation-building efforts around the world in the future.

So, what is the U.S. to do?

· The United States should consider the potential benefits of aligning with the Russian Federation. This alliance could serve as a powerful strategic counterbalance to China in the East and the EU in the West, potentially preventing the European Union from linking up with China economically and shifting further to the left politically. This Russo-American alliance could open new avenues for diplomatic and economic cooperation, fostering a more balanced global order.

· The U.S. should stop trying to change, directly or indirectly, the governments of other countries, e.g., Syria, Iraq, Afghanistan, Iran, or Ukraine. Instead, the U.S. should make peace with Iran and issue a robust and unequivocal warning to those regimes financing terror and corrupting Washington even more than the Israeli lobby.

· The U.S. must take decisive action to halt the woke-inspired nihilistic destruction that poses the greatest, if not the only, existential threat to America. Today, American elites and liberal intellectuals subscribe to theories that demonize races and consider the loathing of Uncle Sam a badge of honor. This trend must be reversed to safeguard the fabric of American society.

If America survives in its current form, which I seriously doubt, people will wonder years from now how society was enslaved by a minority of privileged individuals who would surrender at the first sign of resistance or an attack on them. They will also wonder how a leftist, cunning, and amoral hustler like George Soros could be allowed to use his wealth to undermine American institutions, beliefs, and values. They will also be amazed why Americans allowed the predominant and racist viewpoint on college campuses that everything is the fault of white men. The ancient Greeks had Socrates drink poison for decidedly less.

Is Uncle Sam beyond cure, and is the entire Western world falling apart with it? Yes — unless something "substantial," radically new, and brutally effective happens soon. "Because of the blood and sweat and tears, the labor and the anguish, through which, in the days that have gone, our forefathers moved on to triumph." – Theodore Roosevelt (Davidson, 2003)

America's Principles Versus Prudence in Statecraft

The paradox of liberalism is encapsulated in its brave mantra, "question authority," a call that seems to be in contrast with its own demand for passive obedience to its authority. This paradox is further underscored by its display of the most abject intellectual conformism.

In many respects, present-day modern liberalism of the Left is more radical than communism. For instance, communists never entertained such delusions as the current pretense that there are no fundamental differences between the sexes or that same-sex marriage is a desirable policy goal.

Rabid left-liberals, who want to change the world, seem to think of democracy as a substitute for socialism, as though all wealth would naturally belong to a shared pool, and a true democracy would distribute it equitably. Many people in America find themselves saddled with this unremitting, burning sense of grievance, but one has to be both well-off and well-educated to reach that mental state.

Many American politicians, regardless of their affiliations, argue that America's belief in the universality of its founding principles compels the U.S., as an ethical imperative, to intervene in different parts of the world. Progress toward freedom is the calling of the United States. Americans are supposed to believe that liberty is the design of nature, the direction of history, and that freedom is not for them alone — it is the right and the capacity of all humanity.

The United States of America was born with the belief that Americans' conception of a just political regime derives its legitimacy from "an abstract truth," in Abraham Lincoln's famous turn of phrase, "applicable to all men and all times" (Lincoln, https://www.abrahamlincolnonline.org/lincoln/speeches/, 1859). This belief in the universality of American principles justifies any American intervention worldwide, including military actions. Yet, America's ideals require substantial moral commitments to the liberal world order and democracy. Is it possible to reconcile our commitment to the abstract truth, i.e., "that all men are created equal, that they are endowed by their Creator with certain unalienable Rights," at the heart of our politics with prudence and restraint in statecraft on the international stage (Adams, Franklin, Jefferson, Sherman, & Livingston, 1776)?

The tension between these two notions is difficult to overcome. Liberal universalism inevitably leads to cosmopolitanism, a belief in the importance of the individual and the idea that all human beings belong to a single community, and supranationalism, the idea that there should be a higher authority above the nation-state, which inclines toward an international political order incompatible with a foreign policy that upholds national sovereignty. Internationalism is a necessary outgrowth of liberalism that traces back to its foundations in the political philosophy of theorists like John Locke.

According to Locke, the individual has obligations to any human community only because of his consent and approval. However, in the real world, shared loyalties bind human beings into families, communities, and nations, and each person receives a particular religious, cultural, and civilizational inheritance as a consequence of being born into such collectives. Therefore, Locke's conception of human communities undermines the most fundamental bonds that hold society together. His emphasis on the abstract-choosing individual as the predominant metric does not allow for considerations of national sovereignty or the political and cultural diversity between nation-states. Instead, Locke's liberal theory leads to a cosmopolitan international order that seeks to centralize authority in a supranational body intolerant of regional distinctions.

Proponents of the liberal construction endorse a single imperialist vision, wishing to see a world in which liberal principles are systematized as universal law and imposed on nations, if necessary, by force. This "one world," they agree, is what will bring universal peace and prosperity. Unfortunately, the universalist implications of liberal political thought necessarily erode national distinctions; the declarations of unalienable rights and equality inherent and essential to all of humanity lead to intolerance for any regime but the singularly liberal one, thereby undermining the unique cultural, political, and social characteristics that define different regions and nations.

The likes of Woodrow Wilson — famous for being one of the pioneers of liberal internationalist foreign policy — often made a case for such a uniform world order while carefully presenting their reasoning in the language of universal rights derived from John Locke and the American Founding Fathers. Wilson drew a straight line between the universality of liberal principles and his foreign policy aspirations, justifying the projection of American military power in the global arena and establishing transnational institutions like the League of Nations in the context of the American political tradition. Wilson argued that the principles that animate the American system — the abstract truths of equality, liberty, and the pursuit of happiness, first laid out in the Declaration of Independence — require the interventionist foreign policy he advocated (Lynch, 2002).

But are Wilsonian internationalism or Bush-era neoconservatism inevitable outgrowths of the liberal regime? Or are they a misinterpretation of how to apply America's universalist principles in the material world?

The "just war theory" tradition aims to answer this question by combining abstract principles with political prudence. Allegedly and pretentiously, a "just war" is directed and informed by "universal ideals" but mediated by practical considerations.

In reality, particularly for a nation dedicated to an abstract truth such as the United States, not all "theoretically just causes" necessarily entail military interventions. Thus, the task of American statecraft should be to reconcile the U.S. commitment to universalism with the worldly conditions in which America finds itself. In accordance with the "just war" theory, this requires a set of moral obligations that govern our behavior, but not the utopian cosmopolitanism of liberal universalists or amoral realpolitik. Positioning the "just war" approach in the space between the two extremes, the "just war theorist" must incorporate a conception of the function and value of the nation-state.

However, when we rely solely on abstract liberal principles such as life, liberty, property, and equality among all people, we tend to view the world as a collection of abstract individuals rather than a community of nations. To develop a foreign policy that truly reflects these liberal principles, we need to go beyond the confines of liberal political theory and delve into the complexities of statecraft and diplomacy. This shift toward a more realistic and restrained approach to foreign policy is a pressing need in the current global scenario.

Prudent liberal foreign policy requires, among other things, the development and sustainability of a coherent idea of actual national interest. Many of the United States' modern problems stem from losing a shared conception of this interest, which traditionally helped counterbalance the universalist temptations in American politics. The loss of a coherent national interest — resulting from the triumph in the Cold War, namely defeating communism, and from internal political, social, racial, ethnic, and cultural divisions — has left the U.S. in a state of significant disarray, drifting between conceptual images of a globalized utopia and political realities disclosing little more than that one endless war is the precursor to the next.

This lack of shared awareness of the national interest manifests a more significant loss of direction in American foreign policy. "Just war theory" cannot provide us with the tools to renew our sense of purpose. For example, American lawmakers have often overlooked the generally accepted "just war" principle of legitimate authority in the last few decades, with the executive branch repeatedly bypassing Congress to use military force in war zones abroad. In the United States, sovereign power is supposed to lie with the people, whose elected representatives in Congress express their will. America's "forever wars" are far more unpopular with the average voter than with the political elites who continue to engage in them. However, multiple presidential administrations have waged those wars for decades without the consent of Congress and, consequently, the people.

The insights presented above are at odds with the abstract truths enshrined in the Declaration of Independence. While "just war theory" theoretically acknowledges the universality of justice, the virtues of pluralism, subsidiarity, and the contextual nature of certain questions, it often serves as a cover for liberal hypocrisy when put into practice.

To recognize the injustices perpetrated against humanity's universal rights by illiberal regimes while refraining from intervening to correct them requires a restrained worldview and an acceptance of human nature's imperfections and tragedies. Moreover, it also requires a commitment to justice tempered by an understanding that injustice is a constant feature of our human condition. Liberals claim that they adopt this humility and are capable of restraint and prudence in foreign policy, while their more radical counterparts are not.

I do not see it this way. As "just war theory" suggests, combining abstract principles and political prudence will inevitably lead to confusion and complications. An allegedly "just war" is directed and informed by universal, i.e., missionary, ideals, which one can hardly perceive as mediated by practical considerations. Particularly for a country such as the United States of America, which is dedicated to abstract truth, it should not mean that "theoretically just causes" necessarily involve military intervention. The United States exists neither as a mere abstraction alone nor has it been a nation for a long time, if ever. Yes, the U.S. is a real country with borders and interests and conflicts with others in a fallen world. But how could American statecraft reconcile the mistaken commitment to missionary universalism with the worldly conditions in which the land and its people find themselves? By intellectualizing "just war theory" or politicizing moral obligations in line with liberal globalists versus illiberal nationalists? Indeed, the Locke-Wilson-Bush line directly led to the "forever foreign wars," with all their "just causes," color revolutions, nation-building, et al. — without the consent of the American people or much, if anything, to show for the costs, lost opportunities, and sacrifices.

A prudent liberal foreign policy subject to objective national interest instead of lacking a shared conception sounds good. Unfortunately, modern liberals are not known for their deep humility and moderation; they have repeatedly exhibited a complete lack of restraint, prudence, and maturity in foreign policy, among many other fields. They have put the U.S. train on the same tracks, heading in the same direction, driven by the same dogmatic fanaticism and missionary zeal mixed with the despair of hopelessness, where the Soviet train pulled by the communist locomotive passed a few decades ago. The million-dollar question is whether we can still find a switch to avoid hitting a hard, non-theoretical stop at the end. One vital lesson from the numerous missteps of the last thirty years is that U.S. foreign policymakers are never more unrealistic than when they think of themselves as realists.

Chapter 4

American Identity Dilemma

I defend the past because it reveals the world and man's place in it as it was and will always be. Moreover, I have no explicit expectation of better things in the future.

I am not a Christian but a philosophical dissenter who knows that idealism lies and Marx's dialectical materialism is a disguised form of idealism. Idealists are ultimately fantasists, with some being earnest fanatics willing to kill anyone instead of clearing the ground to recover. They are fools and idolaters whose object of worship is their own ideas and projects, which, however mutable, mistaken, or contradictory, are presupposed as the ultimate and highest law.

Driven by their pioneering experience and domestic success, Americans have paradoxically become materialistic idealists. They aspire to reshape the world in the image of the United States, a belief that contradicts the very essence of American exceptionalism. They mistakenly assume that their unique experience and success can be replicated elsewhere or even perpetuated once their country is fully populated, built, and prospered. This paradox, a fascinating conundrum, has profound implications for American identity and its global influence.

Americans assume that the past need not concern them because they are too busy or have advanced so far beyond it that it is now only of antiquarian interest. So, another American characteristic has come into play, which has always been present as an inheritance from England and purposely planted on American shores: a divinely appointed national mission.

However, national messianism is a form of collective idolatry — a tool of idealism in a different guise. For a nation to believe it has a divine destiny, it must be dominant and warlike — otherwise, the claim is preposterous. Universal ideals always necessitate a military force to enforce them, as they are never globally accepted. This destructive nature of national messianism challenges the notion of a divine national destiny.

Only warlike nations and cultures with a sense of destiny build empires. By their very nature, these nations are expansive and hostile toward all dissenting forms of existence, including any people or country obstructing their power — and counting the one whose blood and treasure created it, i.e., their own. The new conquests and alliances of the country will leave the people who built it and helped obtain the power for its rulers neglected and absorbed into a large empire where their national identity is destroyed, their traditions are despised, and their freedoms are lost.

Every government, particularly in its imperial form, tends to solidify into a material entity with its own origin, life, and inclinations. However, the only force capable of effecting change from within is the emergence of an entirely new government from the midst of the people. Such a drastic action eventually becomes a painful necessity and the only means to restore something precious, invaluable, and delicate that has been lost, such as order, tranquility, security, and liberty. This agonizing step is never a joyful leap into the future, as the idealist imagines with his dreams of unlimited power over creation.

Therefore, it is unsurprising that a hundred years after World War I, the United States of America, no longer united by anything but a name, could be ruled by a government that is not only casually oppressive but ideally perverse.

The proverbial "melting pot," rather than bailing out and removing the poisons, would collect and concentrate them, becoming like a cauldron of boiling toxins. Nations are natural formations, not metaphysical constructions; they are creations of time and cannot absorb an infinite infusion of heterogeneous elements and remain themselves. They cannot be built and razed, deconstructed and reconstructed, stripped naked and refashioned at will to suit the fancies of project managers or to gratify the envy of those who hate the excellent original design.

The loss of national unity, which indiscriminate and continuous mass immigration has helped bring about, has rendered a republican government unworkable. Without a foundational agreement, there can be no consensus on anything — rather than settling anything, elections merely initiate a new struggle whereby one side appeals to the right of resistance while the other enforces repression. The resulting tension and continuous conflict are not sustainable, leading to either the dissolution of the state or the imposition of one side's will.

Another American characteristic that causes concern is innocence. Innocence, in its two forms, is a hallmark of American society. The first form, typical of fanatical reformers, is a self-justifying will that refuses to accept any responsibility for the consequences of their actions. The second form is a kind of national naïveté that views the American flag as a sign of a rainbow in the sky, promising that the storms are over and better times are to come. This form of innocence leads to complacency, thoughtlessness, and optimism, which can be detrimental in the face of real-world challenges.

This mentality is the product of national good fortune and spacious, protective geography. But what happens when the two oceans can no longer protect the land of the brave, when the once unspoiled and empty places are crowded and polluted, and when good luck turns bad? Liberalism has merely cleared a field where every soul and corporate interest may fight with every other for domination. The winner of the struggle will put an end to liberalism.

Chaos, turmoil, and anxiety are humanity's natural states, and tyranny is the usual remedy. That is why perfect order is so rare and precarious and why the human race must closely guard the few islands of permanence and beauty lest they, too, become engulfed. And sure enough, American patriotism has become debased and confused by being mixed with the pride of the empire.

There comes a time in a people's life when the accumulated illusion suddenly collapses, and then, for the first time, they rub their eyes and notice what they see and think. This moment signifies the breaking of a spell, revealing the governing class as incompetent fools who have grown rich by betraying their country. Their time is passing, and we must act.

Thirty years ago, the "victorious West" proclaimed a unipolar world with the United States on top. Yet, the world has never quite figured out what that means.

The British have long been accused of suffering through identity crises. Since WWII, India, Suez, European Communities, Thatcherism, or Brexit, the United Kingdom has never determined its place in the world compared to the vast empire it once commanded. The Union Jack soars, "Rule Britannia!" plays, and the British are still proud — but it all seems like sentimental nostalgia in contrast to a time when Britain's role was much more clear-cut and well-defined.

Americans are currently grappling with what can be termed an "American identity crisis." Though not openly acknowledged, this crisis is a significant societal issue that has been brewing for some time. The "America First" movement, a political rallying cry that prioritizes American interests over global concerns, is just the latest manifestation of that hesitant metamorphosis. So, what does America look like in 2021 amidst this identity crisis?

The answer was seemingly clear during the Cold War thirty-some years ago: The U.S. was at the forefront of the free world, a champion of democracy and liberalism fighting against the dark hordes of Bolshevik totalitarianism. However, the reality was far more intricate. America endured the revolutions, discontent, and anxiety of the 1960s and the consequent upheavals, hangovers, and uneasiness of the 1970s. These events, along with crime, social unrest, racial troubles, deindustrialization, Vietnam, Watergate, stagflation, and gas lines, tarnished America's image and bred self-doubt, significantly impacting its self-perception.

Nevertheless, due to the fortuitous existence of an easily definable Soviet enemy, an antithesis of the USSR, capitalism, prosperity, and free-market materialism helped patch together another *virtual identity*. Then, in the 1980s, America the Free finally found her moment: The Berlin Wall collapsed, the socialist East with it, the champagne corks came flying, and liberal democracy seemed to lead to a new "unipolar world," a term used to describe a world with a single dominant power, in which nothing could hope to challenge American power.

But then, what has become of the United States? A swaggering, free-trading, and rapidly secularizing Moloch with an amoral society deifying materialism propped up by capitalism, simultaneously starry-eyed about the future and blind to the present. "The end of history" had arrived; there were no more enemies, and liberal democracy was the world's future, so what was the hurry? The Gulf War, the Soviet collapse followed by the Russian financial collapse, and the Yugoslav Wars all showed that the U.S.-led Western world was on a roll — no country, ideology, or military could survive by resisting this superior power.

Then came September 11 — and suddenly, a revision was in order, no matter how haphazard, accidental, and amateurish. Like the one-eyed Cyclops blinded by Odysseus, a raging America would blindly respond to the attacks ("Who and where was the enemy, why did it strike, against whom?"). It would unsheathe a crusader's sword, go to war, and bring democracy to the most squalid ratholes on earth. "Our responsibility to history is already clear," announced

President George W. Bush pompously, "to answer these attacks and rid the world of evil."

Unfortunately, by 2008, America's own naïve, idealistic, and missionary zeal had led to entanglements abroad, particularly in the Middle East, economic wreckage at home, institutional distrust, and snowballing debt — quagmires everywhere. Then a new enchanter stepped into the circus ring: Barack Obama's appeal manifested in simple emotional slogans like "Yes, we can!" "Hope" and "Change" were rooted in his promise of a better, greener, and more egalitarian future. The difference this time was the promotion of federal power: while Bill Clinton once announced that the era of Big Government was over, Obama would use the state to reanimate the economy and save the planet.

However, the U.S. experienced the slowest economic recovery since the Great Depression, which hurt the white lower middle class more than anyone else. And when a particular TV and real-estate mogul decided it was time to run for president, he promised not just a repudiation of Obama's legacy but of Bush and Clinton's as well, including, to a certain extent, all the globalist trade policies and trappings of an empire that had arisen during the Cold War and gone into self-destruction since then. Donald Trump's answer was this: America would use its power to benefit its own people — a heresy for globalists. I do not think, as many others do, that Trump believed in the unipolar world — he frequently talked about American might and spent money on the military, but only as a deterrent and reminder that the world should take the U.S. and its president seriously.

Moreover, he rejected the imperial idea that the United States should exercise leadership over the entire planet.

In 30 years, the U.S. has undergone significant ideological and political transitions, from neoliberalism to missionary democratism to neoconservatism to progressive renewal to national conservatism. These transitions were not isolated events but reactions and counter-reactions that fed off each other. George Bush's failure led to Bill Clinton's missteps, and then George W. Bush's blunder led to Obama's disarray. The seemingly schizophrenic nature of these transitions has caused Americans to lose their sense of patriotic continuity and become indecisive about their country's modern identity.

What is America's self-told story now? Who are the American people beyond trite, self-satisfying titles such as "the leaders of the free world" and "defenders of freedom, democracy, and human rights"? They are in the midst of an identity crisis, grappling with who they are today and waging a culture war in pursuit of an answer. The British cousins, America's racial and cultural forebears along the path of history, struggled to find an identity after their empire collapsed — and they are still wrestling with the answer. Their successors, the Americans, still have to contend with an imperial standing, yet they do not seem to know what that should resemble.

Two Americas in a Split Western World

The United States has already split into factions congregating in two major camps, and the entire Western world is breaking into two civilizations with fundamentally different characters. The United States of America is no longer a nation (if it ever was) — it is now two Americas, merely a country at war with itself. The Western world is no longer one civilization — it is two, simply a geographic entity with two cultures engaging in a deadly struggle with each other. Politically, this war plays out over electoral irregularities, ideological divides, progressive rules, COVID-19 vaccines, and lockdowns. Yet this divorce is more than a political break-up; it represents a fundamental shift in the character of the American people, splitting into two separate camps within the U.S. and creating two civilizations with fundamentally different views.

It is vital to grasp the complexity of the issues arising from America's "blue-red" division and Europe's "progressive left-liberal vs. national conservative" split. The underlying causes of both chasms are essentially the same: "Leftist" vs. "Rightist" ideologies. The "leftist" terminology signifies globalism, socialism, multiculturalism, diversity, equity, inclusion, etc., while the "rightist" wording represents national identity, conservatism, sovereignty, tradition, family, faith, etc.

Progressives feel justified in punishing supposedly disloyal Americans, Poles, or Hungarians who defend their identity, electoral integrity, national culture, personal responsibility, and institutions such as the family. They believe these old traditions are not suited to the new order they have built over several decades and generations.

This progressive order, initiated with public policies promising safety, prosperity, and social justice in exchange for the people's submission to "experts" telling them how to live their lives, has had a profound and far-reaching impact.

The bureaucratic, elitist mentality has permeated Western political, cultural, and educational institutions, gaining momentum with the New Deal and President Lyndon Johnson's Great Society programs. Public and elite private schools have indoctrinated generations of children with an ideology that condemns American society as inherently racist, sexist, and homophobic. Its petty commissars have replaced independence, patriotism, and public service with fear, hate, and loathing as necessary virtues in Western and American society, rendering roughly half of the Western world's population unfit for and even hostile to their inherited constitutional order.

Depending on where we live and how we were raised, we are either controlled by a tradition based on family, faith, and freedom or governed by the abstract ideals of the administrative state. The first is a constitutional system of limited, decentralized, separated powers that protect the more fundamental institutions of local life. The second focuses on "diversity, inclusion, and equity," implemented by a centralized state that protects people against disease with lockdowns, safeguards them against crime (including "domestic terrorism") with a surveillance network, insulates them against poverty with the welfare state, and shields them against dangers to life, limb, and self-esteem with a web of administrative institutions and rules.

Resilient and steadfast, those who uphold the first idea of constitutional order demonstrate an unwavering commitment to living harmoniously within their families, churches, and local associations. In contrast, the progressive order relies on a societal structure that places undue trust in a centralized government, its officials, and technocrats to dictate individual lives, thoughts, and actions, all in the name of safety, equality, and happiness.

Beyond the metropolitan and coastal "blue" zones, most Americans attend church, enter into marriage, work diligently, and devote themselves to supporting and spending time with their families. They prioritize integrity over advancement and actively engage in their communities, fostering a sense of connection and shared responsibility.

The other half of America — mainly in the "blue zones" — and most Western Europeans no longer live or value such a life. Instead, they prioritize comfort and status and consider manual labor an insulting burden. They may marry and have children, but their lives focus on self-improvement, health, exercise, and supporting politically correct opinions on race, gender, climate change, and public safety. They may even attend church occasionally, but only to commune with a God who would tell them to remain true to themselves and bring more social justice to the world. These "blue zones" play a significant role in shaping the societal divide, with their distinct values and lifestyles.

"Blue America" and the "blue West" also include many people who have no real attachment to the constitutional order, even refuting the justification for its existence. Instead, they want a "living constitution" — laws they can reshape at any time to suit their goals of the moment. But no system of law could long survive the absolute power of a government and political, business, and cultural elite that can lock the people down (or up), make a mockery of their elections, take away their rights, and otherwise control their lives while "canceling" those who speak against the wrongdoers. No people can remain free and self-governing once the progressive globalists have transformed them through massive immigration and population exchange, while unskilled laborers are dependent on government support — and no-work welfare. Extreme public health policies displacing millions from independent livelihoods and forced propaganda sessions against racial "privilege" in schools and social media facilitate the transformation of society. This transformation will remake the character of Americans and others in the Western world who have not already submitted to the technocratic elites. Those who oppose these programs are likely to be publicly shamed and shunned. That goes beyond "cancel culture" — and one must take these people at their word with the caveat that a house this divided cannot stand long.

At this critical juncture, America, and ultimately the entire Western world, faces three diverging paths:

- Restore traditional values and, with them, America's constitutional order.

- Accept continued political dominance by a new culture associated with progressive or leftist ideologies and an unconstitutional order, which refers to a system of governance that does not adhere to the principles of the constitution and rules a new, unfree people.

- Split the United States and the rest of the West into separate political entities, with some remaining political ties, so that each culture and people can peacefully pursue their own path.

The first option sounds excellent but is reactionary, so it is no longer feasible unless new or modified values are also accepted, together with a reworked and altered U.S. Constitution, i.e., the "rightist" camp is willing to compromise.

Potentially catastrophic, the second option could be averted if the "new culture" of political domination, i.e., the "leftist" side, is willing to engage in meaningful compromise. The last option is unfortunate and, one hopes, unnecessary — it should only be implemented if the first two options do not work.

However, the Western world will not and should not survive if it cannot fully grasp and embrace the idea that "ordered liberty," a term used to describe a society that maintains order while preserving individual freedom, is more important than remaining under one government if that means surrendering who we are.

The leaders of the "Blue World," a term used to describe the progressive or leftist side, must realize that at a certain point, radical assaults on the rights of Americans and Europeans, particularly Eastern Europeans, as well as their churches, communities, and states, may delegitimize the regimes in Washington, Brussels, Paris, and Berlin, and spawn genuine (initially nonviolent) resistance. The individual states of the U.S. and the European nation-states must fight against unconstitutional orders and laws to save their constitutional freedom. It is time for states and citizens to make clear that even the most patriotic Americans and Europeans will choose their way of life over cultural death within the confines of a regime that has made a mockery of their constitutional system.

Americans are polarized: red vs. blue, conservative vs. progressive, rural vs. urban, Fox News vs. MSNBC. The United States has all the prerequisites for a civil war today except for one: the willingness to fight for the sake of disunity.

There was a riot at the U.S. Capitol on January 6, 2021. Yet the mob violence lacked guns and gunfire — at least on the intruders' side. Whatever one thinks of the overall gravity of January 6, the charge on the Capitol was not the revolutionary raid on the Bastille or the seizing of the Winter Palace.

Still, the federal government is increasingly recognized as a Blue System. In the view of Red America, it is an occupying force controlled by the woke. The Deep State — a term used to describe a network of government officials and institutions thwarting the will of the people, undercutting the constitutional authority of the elected president, and operating outside the law to influence government policy — has now risen in all its horror. In response, Republicans in red states have built their independent institutions, including new red universities and social media platforms. Florida will even set up a new military unit because one never knows what will happen.

But there is still no real prospect of a "blitzkrieg." If anything, it would probably be more like a "sitzkrieg," i.e., a phony war or stalemate, with nobody wanting to fight.

However, what will happen if the U.S. becomes two states, Red America and Blue America? The answer could hopefully be that the two sides develop a *modus vivendi*, a Latin term meaning "way of living together" or "compromise." In this context, it would imply a peaceful coexistence and a system of mutual agreements, even if the two states remain politically and ideologically distinct. After all, it would take a long time, perhaps forever, to sort out the property and custody concerns.

Could the disunited fate of the United States be a lesson waiting to be learned from history? The Austro-Hungarian Empire, a significant European power from 1867 to 1918, could provide valuable insights. It was a unique entity that managed to maintain unity despite being composed of two distinct states, much like the potential division of the United States into Red America and Blue America. By studying its history, we can gain a deeper understanding of the challenges and potential outcomes of such a division.

The House of Habsburg had ruled an empire for six centuries but was defeated in a brief and decisive war against Prussia in 1866, losing leadership over the German Confederation. This defeat marked a significant turning point, leading to what is often called the "crisis of the old regime." After this crisis, the Hungarians, the most important minority within the remaining parts of the Habsburg realm, demanded shared political power.

Despite their tumultuous history, the Austrians and Hungarians found a new path in 1867, one of conciliation rather than conflict. This rapprochement led to an *Ausgleich*, a compromise settlement, which transformed the Austrian Empire into the Austro-Hungarian Empire. The *Doppelmonarchie,* or Dual Monarchy, symbolized this new arrangement under the Austrian Emperor, who also held the title of King of Hungary. The Hungarians were now theoretically equal partners, even though the Habsburg dynasty retained both crowns within the family.

For the next half-century, Austria-Hungary flourished under the benevolent rule of the Habsburgs. Their 52 million subjects (in 1914) enjoyed significant economic freedom, underpinned by the rule of law and varying degrees of regional and local autonomy. To maintain the empire's unity, the Habsburgs had to practice relative tolerance and pluralism. This meant respecting the diverse cultures, languages, and religions of their multiethnic and multicultural lands, a stark contrast to the rising intolerance, racism, nationalism, and even genocide in much of the world.

Fin de siècle Vienna, the empire's capital, was a cosmopolis of culture, housing a prosperous middle class that could afford operas, theaters, museums, and even psychoanalysis. Budapest, the Hungarian capital, was also a growing and cultured city of one million, boasting the continent's first subway system.

Nevertheless, Austria-Hungary was torn by ethnic tensions, racial issues, and the rising nationalism of its constituent parts, a peaceful land without a peaceful future.

In 1914, the Habsburg Empire finally plunged into a catastrophic war that was a suicide of choice. For the Dual Monarchy, defeat in World War I spelled the end, the final collapse. The Habsburgs were deposed, and the treaties of Saint-Germain and Trianon ultimately dismantled their empire. Its fragments became four new countries, with portions of the Habsburg lands added to four other countries.

Therefore, while the story of the Austro-Hungarian Empire may not be a perfect guidebook for America, it serves as a reminder that even in the face of significant challenges, a peaceful and prosperous future may still be possible for the United States.

However, the general condition of the former Habsburg provinces has improved only in recent decades. Ironically, that improvement is partly due to the European Union — a hodgepodge of a political-economic entity resembling the old Habsburg regime's structure and diversity. Few countries in the European Union are flag-waving loyalists today, but few want to exit. The EU is rich enough that even Hungary's conservative leader, Viktor Orbán, a vociferous critic, expresses no desire to take his country out of the Union. In this, Orbán evokes the memory of Ferenc Deák, the Hungarian statesman who brought about the compromise with Austria in 1867, which kept Hungary within the greater Austrian ambit.

As I contemplate all this muddled history, one should remember that the issue is not what people want in an ideal world but what they have in this real world. And here, America has been dealt a set of cards that make it resemble the old Habsburg model — a rather dreary prospect. The U.S. is a mongrel society comprising multiracial, multiethnic, multinational, and multicultural elements, which is not about to change. America has more internal schisms than external threats, which is not bad since the country has never had the right stuff for imperialism.

Statecraft must know one's time, and strategy's first task is correlating goals and means. However, America's statespersons and strategists should recognize that today, the country is not in an 1860s crisis, and the solution this time is neither Habsburgian nor Lincolnian. In the meantime, there is no ideology, dogma, religion, cultural unity, political force, moral crusade, or any other inspiration — other than the temptation and fleeting enjoyment of momentarily "free" money — to unify the country by word or sword. Without any common cause, no textual *Ausgleich* can hold together a mongreloid, non-cohesive mixture.

The United States is at a crossroads, and although change is imperative, the country should refrain from trying to follow the Austro-Hungarian way directly. Lawlessness, chaos, terror, anarchy, disorderly conduct, destruction, looting, and more are rampant in the cities of America — all the signs of a degenerate, decaying, life-weary, left-liberal, and globalist society hiding behind "democracy," "equality," and righteous ideology — it is an ideological-cultural conflict. And how could American statecraft reconcile the mistaken commitment to missionary universalism with the worldly conditions in which the country finds itself? It is time for a new direction.

One of the primary goals of the Entente Powers, including the United States, was the final defeat, overthrow, and dissolution of the Austro-Hungarian Empire in World War I. And they were right: the lessons not learned from all empires in history, including the Austro-Hungarian, Soviet, European "Union," and, finally, the American ones, is that many disparate races, nations, and cultures cannot stay under one political umbrella for long.

As someone who was born in Soviet-occupied Central Europe a couple of years after WWII and later fled to the U.S. at age twenty-five, I never thought I would encounter the same mentality, ideology, and propaganda here by the time I retired. It is disappointing that during my lifetime, the U.S. has made several significant choices, mostly bad ones, eaten its cake, and is now looking for it. But it is gone — just like the un-American Austro-Hungarian Empire. From my perspective, if the American elites are the new Habsburgs, they face both peril and promise. So here are three lessons that the past might offer:

First, the internal divisions of the Habsburg dominions inherently undermined their military power. That is one reason they never pursued overseas colonies, saving them all the grief, guilt, and stigma suffered by more aggressive states. That is what America must finally learn from all the once-great and once-militaristic states: It is time to end the force projection. Learn the lessons the Swiss, Swedes, Germans, and Austrians have discovered before — defense, yes; offense, no.

Second, in the absence of hard power, stick to what you do well. The world's peoples, from Vietnam to Somalia, Lebanon to Afghanistan, and Libya to Iraq, have shown that they do not want the U.S. to invade their countries. But even after beating back American hard power, they are enticed by American soft power: computers, smartphones, aircraft, innovation, medical devices, science, and even pop culture.

Third, fight against over-centralization — of any kind. Pursue decentralization and subsidiarity — at any cost. Practice healthy distributism and allow for planned compartmentalization — free America from an unhealthy subservience to a central authority. Respect and facilitate local ways and prevent the over-concentration of power at the top. The overstaffed, ever-expanding managerial elite has already mutated into a parasitic caste destroying its host, the wage-earning national majority. Fight back against the bureaucratic and technocratic soul-suckers. The woke Left has seized control of every major institution in the Western world and turned classrooms, boardrooms, and newsrooms into ideological re-education camps. However, conservatives should plan, organize, and manage an overdue decentralization campaign in the West's centralized economy and culture.

The U.S. is not likely to stop the further fracturing of the country, red against blue, in the years to come. Therefore, American nation-building must occur at the local level at home, not abroad. Americans in Florida and Texas should build their states, and Americans in California and New York should do the same. Red and blue states should bravely grow apart, following their ideas, goals, and values, and loosely and cautiously come together in a confederation like the Swiss cantons.

That is not a formula for heroic feats but a proven formula for dualistic flourishing (in Canada or Belgium) or multiple thriving (Switzerland). As the past has demonstrated, surviving is winning, and this approach offers a solid foundation for future success.

Woke, Do-Gooder, Loyal, or Authoritarian

The current American regime, its entire system, and the underlying philosophy, ideology, and policy are no longer sustainable. Despite its apologists rationalizing that as long as the U.S. remains the world's top economy, as long as the people's basic needs are met, and as long as liberal-democratic decadence remains, there is no reason for the U.S. and the Western world to fall any time soon, the clock is ticking. History is full of unpredictable challenges, unexpected calamities, and preordained disasters.

Donald Trump was not supposed to become president of the U.S., Brexit was not supposed to happen, COVID-19 was not supposed to occur, and it will not be long before the next major crisis accelerates the "process of elimination" even further. The operative question is, who and when will provide the much-needed wake-up call to the masses and mobilize the Right to take the fight straight to the Left?

It is crucial to note that when I write these lines in the middle of 2021, the ubiquitous and ever-so-robust Left, referring to the globalist, progressive, or liberal political spectrum, is spreading the news that the anxious and decaying Right, referring to the national conservative political spectrum, is embracing authoritarianism, and the danger of dictatorship is imminent and very real. According to the Left, white nationalism is taking root in some areas on the right, and white nationalism, or any racial nationalism, is inherently authoritarian.

Many conservatives and a broad spectrum of non-leftists are as exasperated with democracy and liberalism as the leftists — except the Left is further along the timeline. I believe that liberalism, even classical liberalism, is an excellent enabler of what has emerged from the Left. It is no wonder many have lost faith in the Western political system, leadership, and future, searching for better and preferable societies. The current Western system is the Left's answer to their defeat, more precisely a temporary setback, in the Cold War — and, due to the Right's incompetence, short-sightedness, and ignorance, they have successfully turned defeat into victory. But if the non-leftists reject this leftist answer, the Left immediately blames them for supporting authoritarianism, totalitarianism, or illiberal extremists. It is a sad state of affairs that non-leftist individuals have essentially given up on America, Europe, and the Western world and would like to see them fundamentally transformed into something else.

Significantly, I observe the emergence of four distinct ideological and cultural camps in the coming rift:

- The Woke (Radical) Left: This group, which requires no introduction, is a formidable force in the political arena; given its combative nature and potential influence, it belongs to the *fighting category*.

- Left-Liberal-Socialist "Do-Gooders": Mildly utopian mainstream intellectuals, armchair theorists, and well-meaning, innocuous, but manipulable middle class — these "useful idiots" belong to the *non-fighting category*.

- "Loyalists": These are the remnants of the classical liberals who, despite their diverse views, still believe in the American experiment and the U.S. Constitution, embrace American history, and want to see the United States stay together. Many naïve, primarily white Americans are proudly part of this group — which also belongs to the *non-fighting category* of "useful idiots."

Their influence could be significant in shaping the future of the United States.

- Authoritarian Right: Much like the Left's acceptance of dictators, the desperate and hopelessly outgunned Right also accepts authoritarian leaders and finds something feasible in them. Many within this group would also approve of breaking up the United States — however difficult and messy this would be, even if done peacefully — and belong to the *fighting category*.

While most Americans may not align with these groups yet, their perspectives will likely fall within these four factions. The question remains: which of these factions will they ultimately gravitate towards, or will the Deep State's influence guide them in a different direction?

For now, it would take a race war, general civil disobedience, a total breakdown of law and order, catastrophic economic collapse, or another domestic calamity for the Right to be motivated, organized, and finally carry the fight to the Left. At this time, the Left is too powerful, and the Right is far too fractured, foolishly arrogant, and still too invested in an America it thinks it understands.

The Left's surge began when it had to reorganize in the post-Cold War period, make a clean break with its pure communist-Marxist-Bolshevik ideals, and redefine its strategy. The Right's rise will also begin when they must make a clean break in the same way. But the reality is — and will remain — that both sides, the opposite poles, want an altogether different country and world.

In the philosophical, ideological, cultural, and historical sense, America is an "exceptional" country — like every country is. For example, Hungary is not the "far-right dictatorship" run by a corrupt "fascist leader," as it is unfairly and deliberately portrayed by the leftist Western media, just as Sweden is not a socialist state. Like any other, these two countries are the product of their particular circumstances, unique cultures, and past experiences, with little to no precedent in America. Therefore, I caution against wanting the United States to become like Hungary, Sweden, or any other state or country. We must be careful about societal transformations and the potential loss of our unique American identity.

I can say only this — one day, America, as we know it, will be no more. Whether the U.S. ends up as a country broken into pieces, perhaps one or more of which becomes a Third World or authoritarian state, it will not be the country it was when the Cold War ended. Having been disappointed in socialism, democracy, liberalism, and the Deep State, I understand why those on the Right want their own "leader." Having been disappointed in modern conservatism, capitalism, and the "one percent," I understand why those on the Left want their own political, social, and economic system. It will be a heavy price to pay; it will not be possible to hold something together that has already fallen apart.

However, I will not take part in condemning the United States of the Founding Fathers and the American people. It is worth fighting to protect my family, myself, and my way of life, but not for another "idea" of a "better society" or yet another experiment that is supposed to "improve" the one that is best for the rulers. And I know that my objective is already a purportedly "national conservative," therefore "rightist," concept.

A multiracial, multiethnic, and multicultural society is possible but neither necessary nor desirable — one can no longer speak of a "nation" when nothing holds the people together. What kind of public culture can those people assume with whom they disagree? How can we live together amid racial, religious, and cultural differences when our traditions, history, and languages are all at variance? The fact that the once-glorious Western world has an existential problem today is rooted in its willingness to relinquish its identity — but for what purpose, reason, or basis? It is sheer idealism to think and hope that respect and affection for those very different from me, with whom I share nothing, will somehow create the best possible arrangement we can expect in this fallen world.

The fundamental philosophical, moral, and cultural consensus binding native, essentially similar people with the same culture, history, language, or ethnicity has largely dissolved. I am not a defender of liberal democracy because I hold it partly responsible for our current plight and do not see how it could work going forward. Furthermore, I do not see it as the epitome of possibilities, nor do I believe that all the natural alternatives are necessarily worse.

Envisioning a redefined American political landscape, I advocate for a shift toward a set of specific policy positions that will steer us to a more balanced and sustainable future:

- Anti-globalist — no trade pacts and political arrangements that hurt the national interest defined by something broader than the GDP.

- Pro-national and pro-sovereignty — allowing other countries and states whose customs, laws, and beliefs do not agree with ours to have their way.

- Pro-family — defending the traditional family in law and policy, including economic policies, instead of supporting gender ideology.

- Skeptical of Big Business — ending the privileging of economic actors.

- Pro-business — acknowledging the legitimacy of business activities that correspond to the interests of society.

- Defending the nation and its culture — opposing open-border migration, trade deals that hurt the domestic economy and customs, woke attacks on national and civilizational (including religious) identity, and attempts to destroy museums under the banner of "decolonization."

- Pro-education — recognizing that universities are currently originators of toxic, society-destroying ideology; therefore, using power is necessary to rein them in.

- Pro-heritage — the Left is dismantling our civilizational heritage, and the Right is allowing it to happen.

- Pro-fighting — taking politics and lawmaking seriously and having convictions and principles to win intelligently.

Alas, the items outlined above cannot be executed within the framework of liberal democracy because they require courage and vision among leaders and followers, which are not attainable or even expected under current American and Western conditions. Although Donald Trump finally broke the GOP Establishment, for which the country should be grateful, he was a political amateur without the background, skills, experience, and discipline to be an effective leader of the Right-of-Center against the leftist Deep State.

Some government policies that would not be feasible or reasonable in one country make sense in another — and this is something the U.S. and the Western world should realize and respect. The policies followed by the American, Hungarian, or New Zealand governments might make sense within the local political and cultural context. The messianic attitude, both Left and Right, holding that the rest of the world should adopt American ideals, principles, laws, and way of life, is offensive and wrong. It led the U.S. from the Right into the foolish cause of turning Iraq and Afghanistan into liberal democracies and from the Left to make enemies where America should have none.

Decline and Rage — A Patriotic Partisan's Viewpoint

There is a destructive impulse on both sides of the aisle, a rage symptomatic of politics' failure to contain the

American and Western cultural division in the hearts of people for whom politics has become inadequate. Rage and frenzy can destroy in half an hour what prudence, deliberation, and foresight built up in a hundred years.

Over the last 50 years, a fault line between opposing forces, a divergent boundary in the country's cultural tectonics, has widened into a rift between irreconcilable concepts of America. Demands and demographics change, but the friction is permanent, leaving few places undisturbed in our personal and public lives. Amid the political violence, we talk less but more past each other. The cultural divergence discourages inquiry into how we might come together, leaving many questions about when the entire system will come apart.

And during the early 1970s, it almost did. Then, the outlooks of hippies and "hard hats" were nearly inconceivable to each other. The hard hats, i.e., construction workers, were angered by the revolt of the overprivileged — not unlike the catastrophizing "snowflakes" marching for social justice today. The hard hats represented the flagging fortunes of the white working class, its overrepresentation in fighting the war in Vietnam, and its "old-fashioned" values. Hard work, duty, and service to one's country were the values under attack by the anti-war Left.

Many hard hats were veterans of WWII, Korea, and Vietnam — they were not pro-war but opposed the blatant anti-Americanism and nihilism of the anti-war movement. Moreover, they saw through the grating hypocrisy of the New Left's tendency to become imperious and overbearing about American imperialism while remaining silent on the terrors of communism and waving its red flags. Students waving the communist Vietcong's flag while desecrating their own was too much for the hard hats to endure — violence exploded the next day, known ever after as "Bloody Friday." Hundreds of construction workers confronted the student protestors; chaos ensued as students chanted, provoked the hard hats, and threw bottles. The construction workers then chased them down and beat them to a pulp. The police largely stood by while thousands of spectators filled the streets, some merely to watch, others supporting the hard hats. Local businesspeople, investment bankers, and even a thousand clerical workers joined the "hard hats parade" through Lower Manhattan.

Over the next few weeks, hard hats and their supporters held marches and rallies in New York and nationwide.

Long before it was canceling the "unwoke," *The New York Times* already condemned the hard hats, of course, but with surprising consistency. The workers, the paper wrote, joined "revolutionaries and bomb-throwers on the left in demonstrating that anarchy is fast becoming a mode of political expression" (Bigart, 1970).

It was precisely anarchy that the Left was after — the goal was to shut down Washington, D.C. Their mantra, "If the government won't stop the war, we'll stop the government," fueled the flames of discontent.

The 1970–71 protests were highly coordinated, resulting from months of planning at the national and regional levels. But America's oppressed did not bother showing up — one could only view a sea of white faces everywhere. And despite the Left's lip service about equal rights for women, they left planning and decision-making to the men.

Tens of thousands of people were ultimately detained, and President Nixon was proud of how he handled the attempt to shut down the government — the authorities released most of those arrested the following evening.

The leftist BLM/Antifa riots and the U.S. Capitol riots by the Right are the latest flare-ups at the divergent boundaries of American culture, with rage being the magma that fills the rift now — and political solutions are no longer adequate. The entire political system is flawed and incapable of mediation — no wonder Americans have lost hope. Their country is not the America to which I immigrated. I was once willing to give my life for what I believed this society stood for. Today, I would give my life to protect my family from what this country has become.

If the American Right feels pinned down and crushed by a barrage from the institutions it has traditionally associated with and defended, it is because that is happening. The academia, media, popular culture, most intellectuals, and government institutions have abandoned the ship of the Right and gone over to the other side. The Right has perceived the military and law enforcement agencies as civilizational backstops that provide order and authority in case of chaos. But even this illusion is quickly evaporating, exposing these force-wielding branches as the gaping maw of the managerial regime. It is a feeling of abandonment and injustice that the Right is grappling with.

Even law-abiding Americans are subjected to the anarchy of the mob and the tyranny of law enforcement, which primarily turns against decent citizens. There is an absurd combination of oppressive government power directed at the innocent, law-abiding, and intimidated inhabitants and, simultaneously, a bizarre paralysis of the will to use that power to carry out the primary duty of government — the protection of public safety. It is a situation that defies belief and reason.

Law enforcement across the U.S. has retreated from policing violent crime for fear of triggering media outrage and Black Lives Matter riots. As riots swept the country, FBI agents, police officers, and National Guardsmen kneeled with Black Lives Matter agitators. The federal government sees no real enemy on the left. That is because so much of the Left's agenda dovetails with the regime's interests, from the empire business under the guise of humanitarianism to expanding the surveillance apparatus. Indeed, a surveillance effort by the U.S. Postal Service has revealed that analysts comb social media sites searching for "inflammatory" postings, which they then share across government agencies (Melchiondo, 2021).

Law enforcement and intelligence agencies, together with the military, operate as enforcement arms of the managerial regime, or what is commonly referred to as the "Deep State" — a term used to describe a group of influential individuals within governmental organizations who are believed to be involved in the manipulation of government policy. They serve to intimidate, surveil, and punish those who defend themselves from violent criminals — particularly violent black criminals — and even those who dare to defy the illegal, arbitrary, and permanent COVID-19 mandates that have little to do with public health but more with the power of modern, progressive absolutism. The above institutions are not immune from the same rot afflicting virtually every other organization.

The political order in the United States seeks no peace agreement with America's partisans on the right. Therefore, the Right must take up new, nonviolent campaigns, such as a new effort to cut the Pentagon's budget and defund surveillance agencies. It must also target universities' endowments, where many ideas antagonistic to the Right originate, and embrace punitive measures against corporations cooperating with or promoting surveillance or censorship.

Partisan war has always been an inevitable form of struggle, which must be, and can only be, fought by disabusing oneself of preconceived principles and illusions. Do those seeking a transformation of American society believe in American exceptionalism? American exceptionalism is the belief that the United States inherently differs from other nations, often due to its unique history, political system, and values. Is there American exceptionalism at all? If the answer is in the affirmative, what is it?

Yes, American exceptionalism exists since every country is unique in its makeup and system of fundamental principles governing it. The document embodying these principles is called the "Constitution." Accordingly, that is why the U.S. Constitution is an exceptional document. Every country is exceptional in some way; the United States of America is no exception. Citizens of every nation can rightly think there is something "exceptional" about their land, so what is fundamentally different, that is to say, exceptional about the United States? It is not the banal "American dream" that is at the heart of American exceptionalism, but what made it possible, what made it such a cliché for so many worldwide. In brief, American exceptionalism has been the American experiment's conception, implementation, and management, a project in which we all have a stake and a role to play.

That means an American experiment in limited and federal self-government over a free and virtuous citizenry. To be sure, not everyone was free at the beginning of this experiment — and that is one of those characteristics that made the trial so painfully unique. However, the process has gradually evolved into a system filled with opportunities.

There is no virtuous citizenry without freedom, but not all free citizens are virtuous. As John Adams put it: "Our Constitution was made only for a moral and religious people; it is wholly inadequate to the government of any other" (Adams, https://founders.archives.gov/documents/, 1798).

Each country develops its own traditions, culture, and civilization that will affect its politics, but no country is exempt from history and economics. Modern progressives and some pseudo-conservatives seem to believe in their naïve, even Pollyannaish, version of American exceptionalism that it exempts the U.S. from history's account. They are in for a rude awakening — sooner rather than later.

The American Deep State and Its Environment

It is 2021, and the CIA is operating against the American people. The intelligence community employs the media to manipulate the American public and pressure elected politicians. The media, pretending to see only one side of the CIA, play a dual role — they profit from the CIA's passive concealment of information while actively participating in operations designed to influence events in America.

The one-time director of the CIA, Leon Panetta, explained openly that the Agency influenced foreign media outlets ahead of elections to "change attitudes within the country." The method was to acquire such media within a country that could deliver a specific message to influence those who may own other media elements to "confirm" and disseminate that original message (Goldsmith, 2020). Since the aftermath of WWII, the CIA has engaged in a continuous series of operations aimed at influencing foreign elections.

The goal is to command information as a tool of influence. Sometimes, the command and control are direct, but the media outlet operated by the intelligence agency can be easily exposed, destroying credibility. Therefore, a more effective strategy is to become a source for legitimate media so that the Agency's (dis)information inherits the media's credibility. Allegedly, but not surprisingly, the most effective way is when one CIA operative is the initial source while a second CIA guise acts seemingly independently as a confirming source. The Agency can push information to the mainstream media, which can then "independently" confirm it, sometimes unknowingly, through the Agency's secondary agents. Thus, the CIA can write tomorrow's headlines.

Other techniques include:

- Exclusive and accurate information is blended with disinformation to demonstrate credibility.

- Legitimate sources, such as embassy spokesmen, are used to "inadvertently" confirm sub-details.

- Covert funding is provided for research and side appearances to promote academics.

- "Experts" are quoted to discredit counter-narratives.

From the end of WWII to the Church Committee in 1976, all the above was dismissed as a conspiracy theory: the U.S. would never use the CIA to influence elections, especially in fellow democracies, would it? Of course not — except when it did. Real-time reporting on intelligence is naturally based on limited information, albeit marked with the unmistakable fingerprints of established tradecraft. So, always give yourself a chance to explain later.

Under the covert operation known as "Operation Mockingbird," the CIA utilized the services of over 400 American journalists as "direct assets" — a fact that was seldom publicly acknowledged. With the approval of America's leading news organizations, these journalists carried out their tasks for the CIA (Hadley, 2019). *The New York Times* alone provided cover for ten CIA officers and kept quiet about it for decades — typically for the paper, "for patriotic reasons," you understand.

Long-term relationships are a powerful tool, so feeding a colossal story to a young reporter to get him promoted and buying him off is part of the game. One should not forget that the "anonymous source" who drove the Watergate story was an FBI official who, through his actions, shaped the careers of neophyte reporters Woodward and Bernstein. Bernstein proceeded to champion Russiagate, and Woodward became a Washington hagiographer.

The problem for America is that the tools of war abroad had come home, just as when the National Security Agency (NSA) turned its antennae inward post-9/11. The intelligence community, joining the Deep State, is operating against the American people using the established mainstream media.

The CIA has always planted stories abroad for American outlets to pick up and influence public opinion. They lied to journalists in the lead-up to the 2003 Iraq war and spread false information about "Russiagate" when they knew it was all fake. Although based on nothing but disinformation, the American press swallowed every bit of it to maliciously convince the people that a Russian asset ran their country. Robert Mueller, whose investigation was supposed to drive all the empty nonsense into impeachment, turned out to have the last bits of political courage Americans will ever see by stopping short of a coup and refusing to go any further. The Deep State's mainstream media knowingly, willingly, and deceitfully disseminate complete lies. How do you confirm a lie? Ask another liar.

The New York Times stated in June 2020 that, according to the CIA, the Russians "secretly offered bounties to Taliban-linked militants for killing coalition forces in Afghanistan — including targeting American troops" (Fredericks, 2020). The story ran next to another article claiming President Trump had spoken disrespectfully and rudely concerning fallen soldiers. While neither allegation was true, they broke around Trump's announcement about withdrawing troops from Afghanistan and were aimed at discouraging pro-military voters.

One can only wonder how all these media outlets keep making the same dishonest "mistakes" with their sources, always in disfavor of the "Right," conservatives, Trump, et al. — and never the other way around. They have become more like automatons and less trustworthy than the spies on whom they rely.

The American system once envisioned an adversarial role for the media — not today. Journalism is devoted to eliminating those practitioners who criticize the media for accepting Deep State lies as truth and running smear stories. The most significant Trump-era alliance was between corporate outlets and state security and intelligence agencies, whose evidence-free claims they unquestioningly disseminated. Even the most honest and careful journalists sometimes get things wrong; trustworthy journalists issue prompt corrections when they err. That behavior should be trust-building instead of being used for chicanery.

Those media outlets continuing to use the same reckless and deceitful tactics — such as claiming to have "independently confirmed" each other's false stories when they "confirm" nothing — strongly suggest a complete disregard for the truth and show their willingness to serve as disinformation agents.

After decades of successfully deploying their "info ops" weapons abroad, the CIA and others turned them on the American people. The Deep State meddles in presidential politics, simultaneously destroying the adversarial media while crushing faith in both political leaders and the process of electing them — democracy has no meaning here.

The tragedy of the people who died on 9/11 was corrupted from the start by those leaders who failed to understand why they died and used their deaths for their own objectives. Twenty years on, the sound of those towers crashing down still echoes through America, and the silence of the dead haunts those still living. The dead deserve to be remembered, honored, and missed — not to be exploited.

The mischaracterization of the killers as if they were "hating our freedom" exploited the dead because September 11 had nothing to do with freedom or a threat to liberty. However, it had everything to do with justice, albeit a distorted sense of justice — similar to the justice envisioned by all other naïve, idealistic, and fanatic do-gooders. The killers were not evil in a Manichean sense: They were not the opposite of good. Instead, they were terrible in the classic Judeo-Christian sense: Twisted in their goodness — just like modern liberals, socialists, communists, and radical leftists. They wanted justice and committed horrific crimes to pursue what they thought was justice.

However, the act of these young Muslim men flying airplanes filled with infidels to die by their suicide was not a failed act of their desire for justice. It was twisted goodness, but not a senseless action by these devout followers of Islam. Theirs was an act of heroism for Allah, justifying their evil deeds of drinking alcohol, having sex with prostitutes, and lying to infidels during the days before commandeering the planes. Their actions were meant to be acts of honor for other young men to follow. Those who believe they have been somehow unjustly injured commit nearly every desperate act and almost every crime. Through their successful killings and heroic suicides, Allah will give them justice; that is their belief.

What makes this tragedy so different? It is not merely that so many people died a horrible death; after all, people die in so many awful ways every day. Perhaps the answer is that this catastrophe was a real tragedy — real but incomprehensible, sudden but uncertain, and avoidable but unexpected. Because 9/11 was not inevitable; it was preventable. Inevitability is comforting and reassuring because it absolves us from responsibility. But this horror was not predestined.

The suffering was in vain — and no lasting good has yet come from it. The threat remains, and the world's discord, injustice, and levels of hate have not abated.

Incidentally, there has never been a period in history when so many people have lived so freely as today, and there has never been a time of such great material and general prosperity as now. Still, thousands each day must risk their lives fighting those whose religious fanaticism threatens us — thousands more work long hours every day to protect the innocent and to lift the downtrodden.

But we find our lives wanting — security and safety are a long way off while living in a broken world at a broken time and coming from broken places. We do not have any purpose in our lives; we live for the day, for the minute, senselessly, irresponsibly, and angrily. We have destroyed our environment, history, identity, culture, and ourselves. And our leaders want to impose all that on other people and cultures. We all know they are wrong and do not trust them, but we feel powerless, defeated, intimidated, and humiliated to fight or do anything — even to live or care.

That is why we secretly admire those young Arabs who were different from us. Yes, they knew what they were doing and why — and our degenerate world had driven them to it. The Western world is soulless, spiritless, enervated, declining, immoral, amoral, nihilistic, hypocritical, without a spark of life worth living for or a flicker of light at the end of the tunnel. Living a primitive lifestyle, being the slaves of Western democracy, and having lost even a semblance of decency, we preach about human rights and equality while being barbaric, unfair, unjust, and unlikable.

The countries of the Western world are all divided and will invade other nations that did not threaten them, did not attack them, and did not want war with them, allegedly to disarm those countries — of weapons they did not even have — or to protect human rights. And then many Americans and Europeans struggle to understand why an enemy would hate them with such zeal.

After September 11, they invaded Afghanistan and Iraq, attacked Libya, and started the Syrian, Yemeni, and Ukrainian civil wars. They killed hundreds of thousands of soldiers and civilians alike and drove hundreds of thousands more from their homes and countries, many of whom did not want the West in their native lands for the same reason Americans wanted the French, British, and Spanish out of theirs — and the entire Western hemisphere — in the 18th and 19th centuries.

Americans and Europeans fear losing their countries to the unwelcome and intrusive millions of the Global South coming to dispossess them of their heritage. They have never been asked or voted for this intrusion but wanted their chosen leaders to stop it.

Unlike previous generations, 21st-century divisions are far broader — not only political and economic but also ideological, social, moral, cultural, and racial.

Abortion, same-sex marriage, transgender rights, socialism, capitalism, affirmative action, Black Lives Matter, urban crime, gun violence, critical race theory, allegations of white privilege and supremacy, and demands that equality of opportunity give way to equity of rewards divide the people, the U.S., Europe, and the entire Western world.

Demands to remove monuments and memorials to those who were, until recently, America's heroes — from Christopher Columbus and George Washington to Thomas Jefferson and Andrew Jackson, from Abraham Lincoln and Robert E. Lee or Stonewall Jackson to Theodore Roosevelt and Woodrow Wilson — divide the American people. They are split today on the most fundamental questions: Has America ever been a country worthy of the loyalty and love of its citizens? And are Americans proceeding toward that "more perfect union" or heading for a reenactment of their previous violent disunion?

American Truth, Myth, Culture, Democracy, and Other Hypocrisies

I am not an inborn pessimist, although I am often mistaken for one, being in that long queue of writers who have observed the decline of Western civilization. The belief that something is amiss, flawed, and wrong with society has recently become widespread, though perhaps in unsure, superficial, and confusing ways. The American people fear that the United States is losing its standing, influence, affluence, and esteem in the world and believe that if they could restore these, they could also rectify everything — a rather reactionary point of view.

While I do not fear the future or long for a return to the past with its genuine and naïve simplicity — I am not a reactionary — I cannot ignore the urgent warnings of ancient and modern thinkers about the pressing issue of societal decline. The urgency of their message prompts me to ask: Isn't it time we paid attention?

Those who maintain that all is well and the world is getting better do not think seriously about serious matters. The "optimists" keep telling people what they want to hear, endorsing current assumptions and prejudices. Their "evidence" is usually statistical, quantifiable, and looks "scientific" to those who would be called sociologists and political scientists or other "experts" in public relations and advertising. However, this evidence and the "detailed analysis" that follows it are almost always superficial, shallow, and manipulated. These methods do not resemble advanced science but are the response to the rise and expansion of democracy. Democracy, in its pursuit of equality, has led to the realization that the opinions of a large number and wide variety of individuals matter and must be "carefully considered" — at least outwardly. Those opinions must also be scrutinized, analyzed, organized, and classified. These requirements have led to dealing with individuals not as singular entities but in the aggregate — individuals become the masses, and those masses must be controlled, managed, satisfied, and pacified.

An even greater irony is that democracy, in its pursuit of equality, spawned the advent of bureaucracy, managed society, and democratic totalitarianism. It is a system where theoretically equal people are restless and indifferent to the welfare of all except themselves. Living in such a world, they are drawn to dull, trivial, facile, and yet beguiling amusements such as mindless TV shows, social media distractions, celebrity gossip, staged political roundtables, and other politically correct indoctrinations. They become pliant and docile instruments of a benevolent but invincible state that manages every aspect of their lives, relieving them of the trouble of thinking and the cares of living.

Questions about human nature, purpose, and destiny are all missing from the optimistic outlook that anticipates continuing progress. However, the objective measure of progress and decline lies in the condition and meaning of life — the trajectory society finds itself on — an evaluation beyond statistical data. Only when we, as critical thinkers, examine the conditions and purposes can we discern whether culture and civilization are progressing, waning, or worth preserving.

The reasoning for optimism is often uninformed by a sense of history; the "good" is hard to identify and achieve; it is not automatically included in the "new." Culture and civilization can be safeguarded only by those capable of such discerning and critical judgments. But we have lost the ability, or even the willingness, to make such distinctions.

Simultaneously, the belief in inevitable decline is as misleading and wrong as the mindless embrace of progress. There must be a third or alternate way between the assurance of inevitable decay and definite improvement. In the United States, not unlike anywhere else in the Western world today, the thinker or observer who seeks that alternative is made an outsider, cast beyond the pale for having the courage and audacity to question ideas, values, and beliefs when society has already given its unanimous evangelical consent. This "with us or against us" attitude is pervasive, intractable, and damaging. It suggests that any critic is an intellectual and moral traitor who must be jeered, mistrusted, and rejected, hindering the healthy exchange of ideas and the progress of society.

But is it not our obligation to refuse to accept assertions without examining the premises, evidence, and underlying motives? Is it not the right of free people, if not their duty, to ask questions? Is it not the responsibility of educated people to ask the right questions, thereby empowering them to engage in intellectual discourse? Objective and unbiased intellectual discourse is not just a luxury of the educated but a necessity for a healthy society to progress and evolve. Through this discourse, we can challenge prevailing ideas, values, and beliefs and foster a culture of critical thinking and skepticism.

Through study, habit, thinking, reflection, and observation, a critic may alienate himself from the other members of his group, network, society, and culture, although he is not a stranger, a foreigner, or an outsider who speaks a different language. He brings knowledge, insight, and a new mindset to understanding the society and culture he belongs to but is perhaps alienated from, with which he is preoccupied. He is a dissident and skeptical about what others take for granted. He may also be a radical, though not a rowdy rebel, emotionally disfigured by his rejection. However, only his intellectual and perhaps even physical isolation grants the critic the freedom, discipline, and perspective needed to look at the world with a cold eye and diagnose the crisis. The critic's role is not necessarily to disrupt or destroy but to question and analyze, providing a necessary initial counterbalance to prevailing attitudes and beliefs and fostering a culture of critical thinking and skepticism that is vital for societal progress.

Nowadays, questions about defending culture and civilization are almost sure to be misunderstood and rejected, and the questioner is likely to be vilified for asking. Yet, these are fair and fundamental inquiries, and the extent of our ignorance of them is further evidence of our decadence. We lack the confidence, integrity, knowledge, and perspective to explore the past, examine our culture and civilization's confused, chaotic, and blurred sources, and investigate its complexities, inconsistencies, contradictions, crimes, and sins. We wish for and go to great lengths to impose a unitary vision that accommodates our present sensibilities.

By contrast, the opposite response is to denounce the past, America, and the West as racist, sexist, xenophobic, oppressive, and evil — another unitary perspective that, while not entirely false, is misleading and one-dimensional in any case. What we need is a more nuanced approach, one that acknowledges the complexities and contradictions of history and culture and allows for a more balanced and comprehensive understanding.

The truth is almost always multidimensional — except when it is not. We must learn to appreciate duality or multiplicity, which amounts to recognizing that no one can monopolize truth in human thought and affairs. Skepticism, correctly understood, breeds neither arrogance nor contempt but humility and, hopefully, a little compassion. This humility and compassion can foster an enlightened and open-minded perspective, allowing us to engage in intellectual discourse with respect and understanding for differing viewpoints.

Why do we commit to a particular idea, belief, or course of action without knowing the basis of that commitment? Trust and conviction, the ultimate answer, provide a reassuring anchor in the face of the inevitable uncertainty we all face. Any promise or effort, however well-conceived and well-intentioned, carries the unintended possibility of error, failure, and even sin. Although the consequences of being wrong are dire, we are all called upon to think, believe, decide, and act.

Based on the best evidence and my complete and honest understanding of the truth, I commit myself and then see what happens. Thinking we change our minds when encountering new evidence that challenges or discredits our original ideas is a mistake. We often stick to what we think, know, and believe, even when faced with damning evidence to the contrary. This habitual adherence to our beliefs can hinder our ability to revise our ideas, beliefs, and conclusions. Instead, we change our minds only when we reexamine and "reconfigure the evidence" that has long been in front of our eyes. It is a lesson in humility to accept that even our best judgments and most nuanced insights are conditional, incidental, and fragmentary; they are only a part of the whole truth and not the complete picture. Nevertheless, these insights are all we have and shall ever have.

Once, I wrote a thesis concerning improvements in the major overhaul of a specific aircraft engine linked to thermodynamics, research and development, manufacturing processes, and cost analysis. I was proud to finish that complex project and thought I had been clever, perhaps even original, in finding the "optimal solution," i.e., the most desirable compromise. My professor and the various industrial, technical, military, and business advisors, all having a vested interest in the outcome of the undertaking, were not as favorably inclined. They thought I had underestimated the difficulty — even impossibility — of discerning a comprehensive answer to a multifaceted problem. Although the conclusion can have many elusive and often fleeting aspects, I needed a truth I could adhere to, comprehend, and believe in during my inexperienced, one-dimensional, overconfident, and self-assured state of mind. My thesis also introduced me to the problem of untruth. In the pursuit of truth, eliminating falsehood is a significant intellectual and moral duty. Untruth, in this context, refers not only to outright lies but also to misconceptions, biases, and incomplete truths. If I have not recognized the complete truth, and perhaps never will, I have tried to convey as much of the truth as I know. And I have at least devoted myself to eliminating as much untruth as possible.

Humans are the only species that ask "Why?" — and not all do so. At best, they have a yearning to know and understand. Some are inherently dissatisfied with themselves, as they ought to be, and wish to be more than what they are. But the more they know, the more disgruntled they become, and the more they want to know; this condition is both apposite and painful. Others wish to interpret and understand the meaning of life and are frustrated when they cannot find the answers they seek — they want to know "why." Nevertheless, continued ignorance and dullness are part of the human tragedy as much as accomplishments are a triumph of mind and spirit.

Life is a constant struggle to know and understand, a pursuit that is more valuable than the mere conquest of power. It is a tragedy to end this noble quest for enlightenment prematurely. Moreover, there is a tyrannical force at the core of human life — it is called culture. This force can influence individuals and societies, shaping their beliefs, values, and behaviors. A culture, with its customs and rituals, is a necessary form of tyranny that binds society together and guides human conduct. Since unlimited freedom is undesirable and impossible, this structure is essential to maintain our humanity and not succumb to our animal instincts and material needs. This assertion is the root of the perpetual struggle between freedom and order, a struggle that culture helps us navigate.

People often need clarification about culture. Although it is quite impossible to trace the origins of any culture, they must have likely begun as efforts to solve problems, then proceeded to preserve the solution in custom and ritual, thereby reminding people who they are and how they came to be. From that moment onward, the intense gravitational force pulls toward the center and moves in the orbit of original intentions. However, when this gravitational force weakens or disappears, cultural decline marked by a loss of values and traditions, known as the "fussing of decadence," presents itself.

People make a mistake thinking their culture is innately superior to others when it is merely different. Pride is understandable and acceptable as long as it does not turn malignant — misunderstanding can lead to dangerous consequences. That is not to say that all cultures are equal or that all customs and practices are worthy of respect and adoption. Nevertheless, the difference does not imply a connection between or relation to superiority and inferiority. If we do not distinguish between "different" and "better," our thinking will be confused, our conclusions flawed, and our actions potentially dangerous.

Cultures are different and not interchangeable. The members of one culture are justified in rejecting another culture that is just as good as theirs merely because it is different. The grounds for this rejection are not rational but cultural. A distinct culture does not have to meet the needs, address the problems, or clarify the collective identity of a particular people. The choices specific people have made over time can preclude other options today. For example, the current Western embrace of plurality may arise from humane motives or a misplaced sense of guilt.

When individuals, nations, societies, or governments make mistakes, carry out misdeeds, or commit atrocities, they should not only feel guilty, express regret and remorse, and make amends, but someone should also punish the guilty accordingly. Nevertheless, we often accept feeling guilty about the wrong things: Instead of examining our souls and repenting our sins, we take pleasure in guilt concerning others' sins, for which we are eager to apologize since it costs us nothing to do so and makes us feel moral and righteous — the cheap apologies for slavery illustrate that.

It goes like this: "Permit me ceremoniously to apologize to you for a wrong I did not commit and a wrong you did not suffer." Oh, wonderful — afterward, we can congratulate each other on being splendid people. Of course, it is better and more manageable to solve a problem that no longer exists — Hypocrisy 2.0, i.e., nothing has changed. Therefore, we need not give much thought to those people, black or white or of any other background, who are today caught in poverty and condemned to a violent existence devoid of purpose and hope — that problem seems intractable. But, like love, genuine apologies ought to be meaningful, directed toward their proper object, and bring recompense to the aggrieved.

Pluralism disregards the need for unity in any culture; it is crucial to make distinctions and not equate unity with uniformity. Cultures may accept and benefit from variations, but no culture can be all things to all people or welcome all customs and practices. Some are, of necessity, set apart because cultures are hierarchical. No democratic or egalitarian culture exists, which is not to suggest that democratic politics is impossible. People commonly make another error in judgment: to say that culture is hierarchical is not to imply that I am speaking about a hierarchy of people. Instead, I mean that cultures present an order of values — they indicate what is essential to a people and what is not. That does not imply a hierarchy among cultures but a scale of values within cultures that discipline elucidates and satisfies.

There should be a productive dialogue between the members of different cultures, emphasizing different values and organizing and making sense of experiences differently. Culture forms ideals toward which to aspire — images of goodness and perfection. Unless, like Western culture today, it has become decadent, i.e., it has lost its purpose; culture is never satisfied with the lowest common denominator but inspires — or it should, since only in that way can it cohere and endure.

In our rush to condemn the tyranny of culture and promote liberation, prove ourselves tolerant of every difference, and deny any hint of cultural bias, we miss the irony that culture is the human protest against uniformity.

Culture is the antithesis of nature, the declaration of independence from determinism, whether material, spiritual, or environmental. Ironically, the tyranny of culture allows human beings the only true freedom they can possess. By acting through preference, selection, and discrimination, culture enables human beings to escape the forces of nature and become active agents in shaping their world. Culture is a spiritual and imaginative creation, an artificial construct that, in dress and cuisine, manners and the arts, political and social institutions, religion, and play, provides a sanctuary for living and erects a defense against chaos. It is culture that empowers us to shape our own destinies.

Americans tend to believe that people enter the public arena as adversaries to press their own interests, often at the expense of others. Such actions, they claim, constitute the essence of democracy, which is the manifestation of "that all men are created equal" and "endowed by their creator with certain unalienable rights" — which they must inevitably assert if they do not wish to have them taken away. However, they are mistaken in their thinking.

In all aspects of life, genuine equality would require that all people be the same. In my time, the advocates of democracy, and I do not count myself among them, have popularized this kind of uniformity with disastrous consequences: they have given rise to envy, hatred, and fear of all differences — emotions that politicians readily exploit. Today, difference suggests an unacceptable inequality or an intolerable advantage that equality must abolish.

Europeans slaughtered each other during much of the sixteenth and seventeenth centuries because they could not tolerate even the slightest religious differences. The same thing is threatening today in the sectarian and political conflicts in the United States and the Western world, and such antagonisms will not fade quickly.

Liberal democracy leads to the conclusion that all differences and distinctions are evil. It increasingly characterizes those philosophically, ideologically, or culturally different as toxins or contagions that must be eliminated lest they destroy social purity and political health. We live in an age of fanaticism, where various absolutisms reign in politics, religion, thought, and opinion. The resurgence and triumph of absolutism have ushered in a period of strife, violence, intolerance, and oppression that will leave a lasting mark on every aspect of life. The uncritical embrace of democracy has inevitably led to an undemocratic world where security and peace are constantly under threat.

A sense of danger dominates our minds — at the exclusion of almost every other concern. We can add the growing disparity between wealth, property, and the influence of the rich and poor to this senseless intellectual and spiritual rigidity and the resulting secular and religious conflicts. Indeed, the privileges of the rich and the division between the rich and poor are hardly new historical phenomena. As in the past, the rich still live so differently from others that they appear to be a different species. Recognition of this development, among many other things, calls the very foundations of democracy into question.

People cannot solely pursue their self-interests or demand equality and rights for themselves and their peers. They also cannot suppress differences, including the right of others to question and protest, i.e., the right to dissent. They must collaborate to serve a higher purpose that is common to all and feel acknowledged for their work and contributions without differentiating or denigrating their status. If such a purpose were to vanish, any community would swiftly deteriorate into competing but inherently unequal individuals and groups fighting over the spoils. This grim prospect has now become a reality and should concern everyone.

Culture provides the identity and purpose that unites society and diminishes the significance of the differences among its members, each with a role to play. Under such circumstances, differences do not provoke resentment, assuming that everyone has the opportunity to live a decent life, care for their family, and perform meaningful work.

Instead of the American myth of "rugged individualism," which glorifies independence and self-reliance, societies thrive on mutual dependence — it cannot be otherwise. Difference can be a source of strength, but only if there is some common purpose for holding the discrete elements together. If any society's cultural foundation is destroyed, the common goal and the emergent differences become intractable — the centrifugal force takes over. We must consider that when we distinguish between patriotism, i.e., the love and devotion to one's country, and nationalism, which can also include the belief in the superiority of one's nation. A patriot is loyal to a particular people, place, history, and specific habits, customs, and cuisine. He may regard these as the best in the world, but he has no desire to export or impose them on others, whom he considers holding their way of life in equally high esteem. Like culture, patriotism is also inward-looking: it can tolerate, even savor, differences because of its common substance and purpose.

Nationalism, by contrast, is outward-looking. The nationalist seeks to exalt his nation's power and perhaps even impose its will on others — becoming an imperialist. This imperialist can then kill other people and wipe out entire generations — but a remnant, however small, of that people will survive to make a fresh start. However, if the imperialist destroys those people's history and culture, or if internal pressures and contradictions bring them to ruin, those same people are finished — as if they never were.

Americans are relatively immature and have become more impatient with time. This impatience, accompanying the haste that governs much of contemporary life, naturally manifests itself more fully in young people than in older persons, but it is not the exclusive attribute of youth. By contrast, culture requires much time, effort, and attention to cultivate, sustain, and understand — however, that perspective is more inimical to Americans nowadays.

But the myths they fervently uphold are even more crucial for Americans than their economic well-being. Myths, devoid of factual basis or historical validity, saturate a culture and resist rational scrutiny; they are not logical but mythological. Because the U.S. is still a relatively young country with a brief past, many Americans have yet to disentangle their identity and history from the national mythology — that they are new people living in the New World. This disoriented state underscores the urgent necessity for critical thinking and the courage to question prevailing narratives.

Myths enable people to reconcile inconsistent and even contradictory ideas and beliefs. People profess that legend describes reality and consider the truth of the tale self-evident. For example, many Americans regard the United States as man's last best hope on earth. Many others do not believe the United States is such a place but continue to wish it were and think it should be. This supposition has given rise to a penchant for exaggerating American misconduct and wrongdoings among critics, detractors, and other faultfinders disappointed in the failure of the U.S. to complete its mission of redeeming the world. They see America as exceptional, not for the goodness it represents but only for the evil it has done.

But, according to the myth, America's very purpose, its sole *raison d'être*, is to confront, not to perpetuate, evil. Therefore, from the Pilgrims' arrival to the Civil War and the abolition of slavery, from entering the world wars of the twentieth century to the fighting in Korea, Vietnam, Iraq, or Afghanistan, every action the United States has undertaken, every venture it has embarked upon throughout its history, has been for the benefit and betterment of humanity. Such big-hearted largesse is the moral obligation America has taken upon itself to bring freedom, independence, and democracy to the world, the fulfillment of which is the American destiny — a concept that embodies the belief in America's unique role in shaping the world and its commitment to spreading its values and principles.

The other equally powerful American myth acting in the negative direction is the persistent apprehension that the United States, as a "uniquely exceptional nation," is under constant pressure, criticism, and attack and that the American creation and liberal values it was founded upon are in danger of collapsing — the denunciation of the past and the misgivings about the future help to stimulate such apprehensions. The often-strident critique of America violates the pristine ideals enshrined in the first and positive myth. For those who occupy this opposing and negative-extremist end of the political spectrum, the ascent of Donald Trump has marked the collapse of liberalism and (though not literally) democracy for which America has allegedly stood since it came into existence. These confrontations of the extremes have been disorienting and will likely continue for a long time.

Can we face reality and cope with our time's complex and stubborn problems? Can we build a more equitable and just world, even if it means giving others some of what we have? Can we acknowledge the part we have played in bringing about inequality and injustice in the first place? Can we at least resolve the issues of guns, abortion, and immigration? Can we better manage our essential resources so that future generations will not be disadvantaged? Can we protect the environment and mend at least some of the damage we have done to it so that future generations may have a future? Can we limit tyranny and prevent oppression, even if it means giving a voice to those with whom we disagree? Or will we continue to rally around our tribal myths, the deeply ingrained beliefs and narratives that shape our identity and worldview, using them to beat our opponents into submission until there is nothing worth saving?

History, with all its wisdom, cannot solve the fundamental problems of human existence. The future, too, cannot promise a utopian state of greater security, happiness, or virtue; in its various forms, evil will persist and may even grow bolder and more widespread. This uncertainty is the inescapable trajectory of individuals and societies as they transition from innocence to sophistication, simplicity to complexity, and vulnerability to security. The illusion of "progress" may veil decadence, corruption, and immorality as human power, arrogance, and self-absorption evolve and mature, shaping the future in ways we may not always anticipate.

The United States is a historical entity and land — not a providential nation uniquely blessed by God. Nothing makes continued American prosperity or even American survival inevitable. A startling array of tensions, conflicts, disparities, and contradictions has marked the history of the United States — just like that of any other country. It is the human condition to live through such tumult.

Far from being a sanctuary from the ambiguities and dangers of historical existence, the future is often a breeding ground for new tyrannies that prove more brutal than the old ones they replaced. Even the hard-won achievement of freedom has brought unforeseen perils as men and women succumb to isolation, fear, anxiety, resentment, and hatred, becoming pawns in the hands of charlatans and demagogues. Without a contrite awareness and a pious acceptance of human limits, there can be no order in society or the soul, and no one can write history without a shudder.

Californian Exodus

A tidal wave of humanity embarked on an invasion of California in what became known as the Gold Rush of 1849. While that deluge continued for years, with its recent surges causing dramatic demographic changes, the flow is retreating in the state.

California's population grew tenfold in one year between 1849 and 1850. Although thousands of broke and dispirited gold diggers, failing to find gold, left the "Golden State" in the 1850s, they were more than replaced by the tens of thousands arriving. According to the 1860 census, the state's population was 380,000, nearly quadruple what it had been ten years earlier (Population of the United States in 1860: California, 1860).

Then, between 1900 and 1920, California's population exploded from 1.5 million to nearly 3.5 million. Though World War II somewhat slowed the growth rate, the state's population exceeded 10 million in 1950, doubling to 20 million by 1970. But during the 1970s, a small number of native Californians began moving to Oregon, Idaho, and Arizona to escape the masses, traffic, and congestion that had characterized their home state (Aisch, Gebeloff, & Quealy, 2014). Other Americans replaced them by moving into California, and Mexicans appeared illegally by the thousands.

When we think of California, a former province of Mexico, we often picture it as always heavily populated by Mexicans. However, when the United States began occupying the area in 1846, there were no more than 7,500 Mexicans in the entire province, providing a stark contrast to the present (U.S. Department of the Interior, National Park Service, 2001). As recently as 1960, the Mexican population percentage was in the single digits. But today, California is 40 percent what is ambiguously called "Hispanic," with 93 percent of those Hispanics being of Mexican birth or descent. The non-Hispanic white population has dropped from 83 percent of California's population in 1960 to 36 percent in sixty years. Moreover, those whites account for only 25 percent of births today, while Hispanic births exceed 50 percent, shaping California's demographic future (U.S. Census, 2020).

If illegal immigration has dramatically transformed the Golden State, so has legal immigration. The Immigration Act of 1965 and various other acts and programs have generated a nearly eight-fold increase in California's Asian population. In the 1950s, Asians, primarily Japanese and Chinese, accounted for 2 percent of the populace. Subsequently, Asians have been the most rapidly growing racial group for the last decade and comprise more than 15 percent of today's population (Budiman & Ruiz, www.pewresearch.org, 2021).

About 1.5 million Californians are Chinese. That means more Chinese live in California than people in New Hampshire, Maine, Montana, or seven other U.S. states. San Francisco's Chinese population has shot up from less than 5 percent in 1960 to 22 percent in 2021, while the city's white population has decreased from 82 percent to 40 percent during the same time. The most striking transformation, however, is in Southern California's San Gabriel Valley, where towns virtually devoid of Chinese residents in the 1950s now boast a Chinese plurality, with some even having a majority. The hometown of Gen. George Patton, San Marino, was 99.7% white in 1970; it is now 28 percent white and 60 percent Chinese (Chowkwanyun & Segall, 2012). The city, among the wealthiest in the United States in terms of household income, has experienced a significant transformation in its real estate landscape as wealthy Chinese from Hong Kong and Taiwan have propelled real estate prices to such levels that the median home price was $2.7 million in 2021.

Equally noteworthy is the growth of the East Indian population. Since it was a small community before 1965, its numbers have now surpassed 600,000, reshaping California's Central Valley. Today, Punjabi is the third most spoken language in the valley, behind English and Spanish, a testament to the scale of this demographic shift (Budiman, https://www.pewresearch.org/fact-tank/2020/08/20, 2020).

There is heated political rhetoric nowadays when anyone mentions the "Great Replacement," referring to nonwhites from abroad, including overseas, replacing the native white populations in European countries or the U.S. But in California, this is not a far-fetched perspective of the future but reality — it has already happened.

California's dramatic demographic change is accompanied by an equally dramatic transition toward the political Left. It is crucial to understand the historical context: Californians elected Ronald Reagan, a Republican, as their governor in 1966 and 1970. However, the current political landscape is vastly different, with Democrats holding the governorship and all other statewide political offices, along with supermajorities in both houses of the California State Legislature. The unsuccessful recall election of Gov. Gavin Newsom in September 2021 serves as a stark reminder of the Democrats' dominance in the state (Myers & Willon, 2021).

The absolute Democratic control in California has led to a dire situation. The Golden State is at the forefront or near the top of the list for public debt, tax rates, failing infrastructure, homelessness, and the number of businesses relocating elsewhere. The state's cost of living is the second highest in the U.S. behind Hawaii — another Democrat-controlled state. California also suffers from excessive gas prices, endless regulations, frequent power outages, and horrendous commuting times. Californians are also dealing with dozens of underperforming public schools with curriculums influenced by politically correct Marxist and other leftist critical cultural theories.

California has the second-highest average home prices in the country, resulting from a population approaching 40 million, while home construction has fallen behind that growth rate. California's near-perfect climate, magnificent geography, and enticing lifestyle continue to lure immigrants and younger people. High home prices are no problem for wealthy newcomers or middle-class people who have owned homes for years, but they are real issues for middle-class families' children and grandchildren and for those businesses that need housing for their employees.

California's increasing and multifaceted problems have led to a net outmigration — primarily of white middle-class residents — that began about a dozen years ago. Even before then, this trend saw friends — white, California-born, conservative, liberal, moderate, and middle-class intellectuals — bidding farewell.

A younger generation has created what might be called the California Exodus. In 2010, 560,000 people left California, and more significant numbers have left yearly since, peaking in 2018 with 691,000. Although people from foreign lands still come into the state, the annual outflow exceeds the inflow, usually by over 100,000 (Beam, 2021). As a result, California lost a congressional seat for the first time in history.

Why did I move out of the state in 1989? My daughter was two years old then, and I did not want to raise her in California. It was a decision that tore at my heart, leaving perhaps the most significant part of my life behind. I moved out with a heavy heart but have never looked back. Why ruin my beautiful memories with the exasperating reality of the present? But I recall looking up at the flagpoles in the '70s. There flew Old Glory, and below it, the Bear Flag. I raised my head and felt both American and Californian. It was a time of pure nostalgia when I felt deeply connected to my chosen home. What could have been better then — and how do I feel today?

Chapter 5

The Rainbow Capitalism of Woke-Globalism

The widely held conservative opinion would have it that the Right's enemy is some variant of Marxism or communism today. However, that notion does not accurately describe people like Facebook's Mark Zuckerberg, Amazon's Jeff Bezos, CNN's Jeff Zucker, or Open Society's George Soros. One can hardly call the tech, media, and finance executives censoring and "de-platforming" the voices of the Right (removing them from online platforms or reducing their reach, as seen in the banning of certain conservative voices from social media platforms) ideological Marxists or Maoists.

Today, the real enemy of the Western world is "rainbow capitalist globalism," a form of corporate, quasi-monopolistic capitalism intricately linked to the central state and its surveillance and control agencies. This system is increasingly aligned with the cultural and political objectives of the Left. The alliance of progressive politics and what was once called "Big Business" has occurred mainly because individuals like Bezos, Zuckerberg, Tim Cook, and many others believe that their long-term interests are best served by entirely deracinating (uprooting from their cultural and national roots), demoralizing, and preferably replacing the hitherto "original," domestic, and thus far relatively homogeneous populations of Western countries.

However, it would be a mistake to think that such goals are pursued exclusively by the Democratic Party of the U.S.

(today dominated by its left-wing factions) or other Western liberal-democratic political parties. Powerful elements within the American Republican Party, the British Conservative Party, and the German Christian Democratic Union (CDU) are also sympathetic to those goals, especially with unrestricted immigration and globalization.

To counter this, the authentic, national-conservative, and populist Right must establish complete independence from the corporate media and the left-liberal intellectual elite donor classes, regardless of their party affiliations. Moreover, the Right must acknowledge that Western culture will continue favoring the leftward movement for the foreseeable future. Therefore, the realistic and conservative Right must rise to the occasion and create a new, effective, intelligent opposition — this is not just a strategy but a necessity in the current political landscape.

The most influential and powerful individuals in all non-populist parties are tools of the corporate donor class. The Democratic Party's political donors with the deepest pockets reside in a handful of elite zip codes in coastal areas.

While elite political donors of the Republican Party are geographically more diverse, living in Dallas, Atlanta, Las Vegas, or Palm Beach, donations from New York City still surpass them.

Regardless of their political leanings, the American ruling elite is the party of Wall Street, Silicon Valley, DC lobbyists, bureaucrats, and leftist intellectuals residing in the affluent suburbs of major cities. The Republican "donor class" mirrors those Sunbelt industries that have been funding the Grand Old Party since the inception of modern "movement conservatism" in the 1950s — and this could be the Right's most significant ideological vulnerability today.

Since World War II, the American Right has steadfastly adhered to fusionism, a blend of military hawkishness, free-market economics, and cultural traditionalism. This ideology, which underpinned the rise of the Goldwater-Reagan paradigm in the 1960s and 1970s, has remained the cornerstone of mainstream conservatism despite its somewhat limited commitment to cultural tradition.

However, Trumpism presented a potent challenge to this model. During his 2016 campaign, Donald Trump proposed an electoral strategy that urged conservatives to take a stand against the establishment's "invade the world, invite the world" policy framework. This strategy, while disruptive, demonstrated the potential for a unified conservative front, instilling a sense of hope for the future of a new conservative Right.

One could argue that President Trump's loss in 2020 was partly due to his failure to fully articulate and aggressively pursue a policy agenda consistent with his 2016 strategy. In the November election, Trump received the highest share of non-white votes won by a Republican candidate in 60 years. His vote share increased across demographics in 2020, except among white men. A more robust effort by President Trump to enact his 2016 policy stances during his term and defend them in his reelection campaign might have improved his performance among white men and secured him a second term.

Not surprisingly, much of the Trump voter base disagrees with the GOP establishment. The American Right was supposed to be, and has traditionally been, an ally of the ostensibly "conservative" business class, an alliance rooted in shared opposition to socialism domestically and abroad. Yet, at best, the business class has frequently been a fair-weather "friend and ally" to conservatives, intending to prioritize the corporate class's objectives even when those conflicted with the values of the broader conservative movement.

One way to achieve this objective is to flood the U.S. with cheap, docile, and willing labor. Consequently, the corporate class has consistently united in its support for illegal immigration through de facto open borders, a situation where immigration laws are not enforced, in direct contradiction to the wishes of most rank-and-file Republican voters and the long-term interests of the American people.

It is also not uncommon to witness the media mouthpieces of the Republican Party railing against "socialism" while remaining indifferent in their defense of, for example, traditional marriage or the heritage of Southern whites.

There is a lengthy list of issues where the interests of conservatives and the corporate class conflict. Trade is another obvious example. Few, if any, of Trump's actions were received with more hostility by corporate elites than his reasonable though moderate efforts to address the worst excesses of trade policies related to globalization. These efforts included renegotiating trade deals to favor American workers and imposing tariffs on Chinese goods to address unfair trade practices.

While the GOP prioritizes tax cuts and deregulation, the intellectual mandarins of "movement conservatism" — the neoconservatives and their allies — prioritize an aggressive foreign policy. If those neoconservatives have grudgingly offered a modicum of praise for Trump, they have done so primarily because of his fealty to the Israeli agenda. The Trump Administration's loyalty was evident in its brokering of an alliance between Israel and the Sunni states of the Persian Gulf and North Africa and its comparative hawkishness toward Iran.

Among other states in the region, Israel, Saudi Arabia, and the United Arab Emirates are guaranteed export markets for American defense contractors, armaments manufacturers, and high-tech companies underwritten by the public sector. With immense holdings in the Middle East and Central Asia, the U.S. petroleum industry is another significant Republican constituency with influential donor-class representatives, such as the Koch family.

The point here is that a prolonged alliance with the ostensibly "conservative" wing of the corporate class is contrary to the interests of the populist Right. Specifically, the latter's adherents typically favor a non-interventionist foreign policy, a more protectionist trade policy, and restrictions on immigration. The main body of an insurgent American Right would necessarily be the "petit-bourgeois proletariat," consisting primarily of working- and middle-class whites. They have experienced an assault on their status, livelihood, and standard of living from the corporate elite, just as they have faced a comparable attack on their moral convictions and cultural interests from the cultural Left.

If the "conservative branch" of the corporate class has been an unreliable friend to the authentic Right, the openly declared enemies include the out-of-the-closet circle of Wall Street financiers, tech oligarchs, and captains of Big Business. The connection between the cultural far Left and tech elites often runs the deepest. Some even believe that the highest government body should be a constitutionally empowered "Department of Anti-racism" (Kendi, 2019). The DOA would be responsible for clearing all local, state, and federal public policies before approval to ensure they do not yield racial inequity. It would monitor these policies, investigate them whenever racial injustice surfaces, and oversee public officials for any expression of racist ideas. The DOA would also apply disciplinary measures against policymakers and public officials who do not voluntarily change their allegedly racist policies and views. The Department of Anti-racism would have absolute power to overrule any other branch, agency, or government official at any level if it found a particular policy "racist."

At one point, some suggested that cutting capital gains tax represented a racist policy because Caucasians were more likely to benefit from such policies than Black individuals. One CEO of one of the world's most influential social media companies (Twitter), who has a significant platform and influence, has already made an eight-digit donation supporting the idea of the "Department of Anti-racism," demonstrating the impact of corporate leaders in shaping social and political issues.

All cultural, racial, demographic, generational, economic, political, and technological trends favor the Left.

To the extent that one can trust opinion polls, public opinion shifts to the left on practically every contentious social issue, particularly among young people. The ongoing American and Western demographic transformation, characterized by the increasing diversity of a multiracial and multicultural society with its radically changing social norms, also favors the Left. Growing economic disparities call for wealth redistribution, an idea embraced by leftist circles. The mainstream media, cable networks, and social media combine to provide the cultural Left with a nearly all-encompassing propaganda apparatus, strengthened by the Left's domination of virtually all "ideas industries," i.e., the intellectual marketplace and professions, from education to advertising, and from law to human resources.

For those seeking to establish a genuine media presence for the Right, the primary challenge lies in avoiding indebtedness to donor interests. This is a significant hurdle that could compromise the integrity of any such project.

An independent conservative media would have to scrupulously avoid dependency on large corporate donors seeking to steer any project toward their own ends or allow ideologues to infiltrate it with conflicting objectives. Institutional mechanisms must prevent such co-optations. Moreover, any independent conservative media must surpass the technical standards, competence, and professionalism demonstrated by mainstream communication channels by employing skilled specialists as managers, technicians, and journalists.

Maintaining high standards of professional ethics, personal competence, and reputability — challenges that destroyed the once-promising "Alternative Right" — is also essential. Either way, such an effort will undoubtedly be a daunting task.

Given the prevailing trends, it is unlikely that the traditional conservative Right will be able to form either a national majority or a national coalition government anywhere in the foreseeable future. Even the American Republican leadership appears to be implicitly aware of this and seeks to serve as an obstructionist opposition force by placing favorable appointees to the Supreme Court and blocking Democratic legislation in the U.S. Senate.

Conservative leaders have pursued this strategy primarily to counter threats to the interests and benefits of the Republican donor class — such as wealth taxes or minimum wage increases — while collaborating with the Democrats on areas of policy agreement, such as interventionist foreign policy and "free trade."

Therefore, a new conservatism with a fresh, unswervingly populist idea must be built based on the working class and small businesses. With its inclusive approach, this movement has the potential to attract support from a wide range of groups, including minority segments and intellectual communities, broadening its base beyond white and Christian populations. It would be beneficial for this new movement to emphasize regional autonomy since it is doubtful that it will gain a significant electoral foothold in metropolitan areas. Nevertheless, conservative strongholds must survive alongside the centralized leftist administrative state.

The most feasible option for the Right is to create an alternative, substitute, or "shadow" infrastructure based in regions and localities where the Right still dominates. This strategic move emphasizes building conservative districts, havens, and enclaves while keeping the centralized state on the defensive. Successful models of such efforts already exist, such as the "Second Amendment sanctuaries" that gun rights supporters have established in many localities or the conservative-leaning states that have implemented their own healthcare systems. They demonstrate how appeals to local authorities and the support of local governments, such as the State of Texas, can counter the efforts of authoritarian central governments. This approach empowers the Right and allows it to maintain its influence.

The Mormon or Amish subcultures, Christian communities, or South Africa's Orania, an Afrikaner community, stand as inspiring examples of how a conservative counterculture can endure and survive even within a context of contrary majority hegemony and broader social deterioration. Their resilience is a beacon of hope, demonstrating that the conservative Right can weather the storm. Meanwhile, the fractious nature of the Left — referring to its tendency to be internally divided and in conflict — will likely prevent a permanently cohesive leftist ruling coalition from forming, allowing some breathing room for the populist Right.

The Marxist Worldview Behind Economic Solutions

The United States has become divided into several population strata: from highly educated and affluent to those left behind; from European extraction to non-Caucasian races; and from ideologically conservative to politically leftist. The economic gaps have once again inflamed cultural and social disparities, creating an atmosphere of intense polarization, cultural hostility, alienation, bitterness, and resentment.

The Left's solution is simple but faulty: turbo-charge the economy with "infrastructure" dollars, green-new-deal pork, and government programs. The money will fill the gap, fire up the economy for everyone, and make polarization and all other evils disappear.

Those promoting this idea see the world primarily through an economic prism; for them, economic inequalities can explain all other problems, with society neatly divided between those who have money and those who do not. The lack of funds necessarily leaves people in poverty, oppression, resentment, and polarization. Therefore, social structures that cause inequality must be uprooted and replaced with those that do not.

The proposed but flawed solution sends a definite message: Money will buy happiness, and "free money" will solve all resentment problems. Money collected through higher taxes on the rich will buy prosperity and smother inequality. Spend boldly, quickly, generously, and uninhibitedly. Do not worry about the details; unlimited spending on "good projects" today will ensure a positive return on investment tomorrow. The Modern Monetary Theory (MMT) will take care of the financial issues; everything will turn out well in the end (Globerman, 2021).

That is the Democrats' worldview, which is also the Marxist worldview. Karl Marx saw everything through the economic prism. His dialectical materialism taught that the class struggle between the wealthy and the poor determines history, and all problems are reducible to economic models that the government must devise, control, and manage to promote equality. By implementing systemic change, the state will take from the rich and give to the poor. However, it is crucial to recognize the fallacy in this approach, as it oversimplifies complex societal issues and fails to account for the diversity of human experience.

As proven in all countries experimenting with socialism worldwide, the Marxist worldview is flawed. Modern Western European countries, Scandinavian countries, and even China became economically successful only when they implemented capitalism to some degree. The success of capitalism in these nations, which supports the social programs that socialists envy, is a reassuring testament to its effectiveness.

While a valuable tool, economics is not the most critical prism — on the contrary. Only after a nation or country determines its philosophical goals, ideological direction, political system, and social programs should it decide on the tool with which it can reach those aims. Marxism, communism, and pure socialism view political philosophy backward. Their dialectical materialism, based on a government-controlled socialist economy, does not determine happiness or solve all social problems. Instead, it reduces humans to animal instincts, as seen in the lack of individual freedom and the suppression of personal ambition within such systems.

The conservative worldview maintains that human nature, with its unique qualities and individual dignity, is the foundation of all political, social, cultural, and religious endeavors as well as the sciences. It values the diversity of human experience and the potential for individual growth and contribution above mere economic sustenance.

When economics dominates, humanity weakens, and history is reduced to the economic endeavors of individuals and classes, with Man seen merely as a wealth-seeking and wealth-consuming animal. Conversely, the conservative worldview addresses societal issues beyond economics, such as cultural preservation, individual rights, and personal development, to ensure a more balanced and holistic approach to governance. When economics alone prevails, a cold, heartless vision of society takes control, leaving no room for the higher ideals that add purpose to life. The lessons of postmodernity have revealed that the most critical problems are not economic but moral. Although money may buy pleasure and possessions, it cannot acquire or determine happiness, which explains why unhappiness exists in every social class, including the extremely wealthy. This realization should prompt us to reflect on the societal impact of such a vision and the importance of moral values in our lives.

Government programs alone cannot restore broken families, shattered communities, and a decaying culture. We can combat these issues only through moral renewal and the advancement of non-economic values. By focusing on filling the spiritual voids that haunt people's lives, we can better fight against the devastations of a lack of culture, absence of refinement, atavistic lifestyles, want of civility, loneliness, boredom, despair, and suicide than by merely issuing government checks.

The socialist solution to socialism's problems is always more socialism, a materialistic, inhuman, and Marxist worldview that distorts reality and harms the soul. The danger of socialism should raise a red flag and prompt us to question the direction of our society.

The latest progressive idea is to transfer wealth from the taxpaying classes of Western countries to their global, transnational, and Third World elites. For the real masters of the universe, establishing justice, equality, and reversed discrimination for the world's fortunate poor are rewarding exercises.

The stated goal of the 2015 Paris Climate Agreement is to save the planet from the ravages of climate change caused by carbon dioxide emissions. Industrial nations produce CO_2 emissions from many of the world's factories, farms, ships, aircraft, and cars. Under the Paris Accords, the wealthier countries of the Western world were to set and meet strict national targets for reducing their carbon emissions. Together, these reductions were supposed to prevent any rise in the planet's temperature of more than 1.5 degrees Celsius over pre-industrial levels and were presented as the world's last hope of avoiding a climate catastrophe this century (United Nations, 2015).

The climate has been sending the public urgent warnings about killer hurricanes, droughts, wildfires, river floods, rising sea levels that swamp coastal towns, cities, and islands, and melting polar ice caps.

With the apocalyptic scenario thus laid out if "we" failed to act, there arose the inevitable question: How much money would the global elites and their Third World clients need from the Western world to grant a conditional absolution for its past sins of carbon emissions? Answer: The rich nations must hand over $100 billion per year to repair the damage done by climate change to the poorer countries and pay them for reorienting their energy reliance away from coal, oil, and gas to greener, sustainable forms like sun, wind, and water, ushering in a brighter, more sustainable future (OECD, 2021).

According to the Paris Accords, the U.S., playing a pivotal role, should reduce carbon emissions annually and contribute the most significant portion of the developing world's $100 billion annual wealth transfer. However, in 2016, an inconceivable event aborted the Paris climate scheme: the American people elected Donald Trump president of the United States. President Trump swiftly pulled the U.S. out of the accords, calling the Paris deal its real name: a rip-off of his country.

Meanwhile, if carbon dioxide is a pollutant, China, the world's number one polluter, was permitted to increase its carbon emissions until 2030 — ditto for India. Thus, China is responsible for 28 percent of the world's carbon emissions, while the U.S. contributes half of that share, with its contribution falling.

Then came President Joe Biden, who immediately reentered the Paris deal. He first pledged to contribute $5.7 billion as a payment on the U.S. share of the $100 billion;

then, he vowed to double that contribution to $11.4 billion. Congress has yet to appropriate either sum.

The coal-fired power plants that the Chinese built in poorer nations contribute to global carbon emissions. But they also enable the peoples of Asia and Africa to enjoy the benefits such plants produce in the 21st century — electricity, heat, and light — just as coal and oil improved the quality of life for 19th and 20th-century Americans.

There is no doubt that Americans will face increasing demands again, both in terms of financial contributions and further reductions in carbon emissions. Critics will likely dismiss President Biden's $11.4 billion pledge as insufficient, calling for more substantial commitments.

The leaders of the world's biggest economies have endorsed a worldwide minimum tax rate of 15 percent on the profits of large businesses (OECD, 2021). The agreement, feeding the voracious appetites of high-tax nations, has since gained momentum and pledges in 136 countries — an irony that a group of rich countries pushes for policies to disadvantage poorer countries.

The deal's objective is to create a tax cartel because high-tax countries believe that this will reduce competition from countries with lower taxes and simpler tax structures. However, it is important to note that the arrangement also benefits wealthier, higher-tax countries by shifting revenues, i.e., siphoning off money from those lower-tax countries where companies are headquartered, for example, Ireland or Luxembourg, to countries where companies make their sales. This change could potentially boost the economies of high-tax countries. On the other hand, the global minimum tax could also bring much-needed revenue to poorer countries (although possibly not more Foreign Direct Investment), leveling the playing field in the global economy. It sounds fair. However, the urgency to feed wealthy nations' enormous and ever-growing budgets is at the core of the matter.

Here is what is really behind the global minimum tax: Most countries, along with the United States since the Tax Cuts and Jobs Act in 2017, use some form of a "territorial" system. This system, a fundamental principle of sound tax policy, means that governments do not tax their taxpayers' foreign-earned incomes — that revenue is taxed by the foreign jurisdiction where it is earned. Companies can choose where to locate their business based on which country has the best tax regime. This procedure pressures governments with harsh tax regimes to become less draconian.

The governments of high-tax countries do not like this competition, which is why they have been anxious for years to undermine it with a global minimum tax. And while the U.S. government will benefit immensely from the new regime, American companies with foreign subsidiaries and income will not, potentially leading to financial strain and reduced competitiveness. This could also have implications for individual taxpayers, as companies may pass on the increased tax burden to consumers in the form of higher prices.

The curious thing is that some advocates do not even bother hiding their goal of extracting more revenue from businesses. For example, former U.S. Treasury Secretary Lawrence Summers greeted the new deal:

"Countries have come together to make sure that the global economy can create widely shared prosperity, rather than lower tax burdens for those at the top. By providing a more durable and robust revenue base, the new minimum tax will help pay for the sorts of public investments that are fundamental to economic success in all countries" (Summers, 2021).

Of course, Mr. Summers believes that higher tax rates necessarily lead to more tax revenue, and politicians will always use the money wisely to stimulate growth. Like his left-liberal handlers, he has much faith in the notion that socialist politicians, using their Modern Monetary Theory, will finance worthy investments instead of introducing economic distortions or buying votes with corporate welfare.

Furthermore, studies by the Tax Foundation, the International Monetary Fund (IMF), the Organisation for Economic Co-operation and Development (OECD), and other institutions show that raising the corporate tax rate is one of the least effective ways of increasing revenue. Such a move could lower the gross domestic product, partly because it lowers investments, a worrying trend for the economy.

Corporations, despite their public image, are a vital part of the economy. If we push them too hard, how many pay raises will they be able to afford for American workers? They also need a responsible government, which means having options if taxes become too burdensome. And what about the prices of their products that we, as consumers, pay?

The irony is that while the United States and its wealthiest friends benefit at the expense of poorer countries, the agreement they sell is to fight inequality at home. Or, as

Mr. Summers says, to avoid "lower tax burdens for those at the top."

Wealthy nations could address their budget burdens by cutting spending, for which most politicians do not have the stomach in a democracy. Moreover, if these high-tax countries have a problem taxing their multinational corporations, they could change other policies like transfer pricing rules. But they should not tell other, allegedly sovereign nations how to tax income within their own borders, much less set up a global tax cartel.

Although the average taxpayer may feel indifferent to this development, they should know that this cartel is only the beginning. Once a system like that is in place, it is only a matter of time before revenue-hungry legislators extend the minimum tax rate to individuals.

American Political Economy, Political Ideology, and Political Philosophy

U.S. policymakers, including those making foreign policy, now face an environment in which power is increasingly measured and exercised in economic terms. State-controlled capitalism challenges a "free-market" economy as the prevailing model; technological disruption, climate change, and various forms of inequality are straining the agreement between the government and its people. In such a world, economics will, at a minimum, be the main deciding factor in the United States' success or failure in domestic politics, foreign policy, and geopolitics.

This is especially true concerning China, the emerging real or imagined adversary already reaching the economic strength, influence, and success that the Soviet Union never enjoyed. While military power will always matter, the growing competition between the United States and China will sooner or later depend on how effectively each attend to its national economy and influences the global economy.

Looking at U.S. history from the early years to the era following World War II, shifts in strategy have sometimes entailed a change in economic philosophy — from mercantilism through *laissez-faire* absolutism and Keynesianism to neoliberalism. National security issues have proved critical to those transitions. That remains the same today as the United States embarks on a new era of multipolar competition among great powers and grapples with powerful constraining forces such as technology, inequality, identity, credibility, morality, and climate change. The need for a new economic philosophy is more urgent than ever.

It is crucial to recognize that today, even domestic policy experts acknowledge that economists have made several missteps and that significant correctives are overdue. However, it is the responsibility of politicians to rectify philosophical, ideological, social, and political errors before providing a new strategy for economists to develop the latest economic development tools — this is a critical role that policymakers must play.

Nevertheless, the United States will have to move beyond the prevailing economic theory of the past few decades (sometimes imperfectly called neoliberalism) and rethink how the economy operates, which new objectives it should serve, and how the government must restructure the economy to achieve those goals. Again, this is a philosophical, ideological, political, social, and geopolitical imperative first, and only then an economic one. Consequently, the national security, legislative, executive, judicial, foreign policy, and other government communities must play a proactive and decisive role in this domestic economic policy debate, proposing and helping to deliver the needed reforms.

The time has come for philosophers, political scientists, and foreign policy professionals to recognize, formulate, and develop those new policies and strategies that should be comprehensive and forward-thinking, addressing immediate economic concerns, long-term sustainability, and global competitiveness. These are the policies and strategies they will provide to economists to change their economic assumptions, both domestic and international. These policymakers have neglected to address the issues that economists have identified as goals over the past thirty-some years.

Economics and foreign policy have never been kept distinct, despite what modern liberal "experts" claim today. In the past, U.S. grand strategy also determined economic theories that matched the moment, and strategists were central to the discussions. For example, the United States fended off established empires built on mercantilism in the country's infancy. Well aware that it could not compete against experienced, developed, and wealthy countries like France and Britain, the U.S. government adopted a high labor-cost model by offering more money to attract European experts for geopolitical reasons. Experts on foreign policy need not and should not be inactive in the emerging economic policy debates.

The post-war era and the Cold War, two pivotal periods in history, ushered in a new economic narrative, albeit with some similarities. The U.S. government found itself adopting a formula proposed by the British economist John Maynard Keynes to bolster the American economy and the broader Western world. This strategy, which involved stimulating industrial production and consumer demand through public investment and favorable monetary policies, was designed to achieve full employment. The growth rate was set to outpace that of the Soviet economy and its satellite countries in the decades following World War II. While history often simplifies the rise of Keynesianism during these years as a necessary response to the Great Depression, World War II, and the looming threat of Soviet-backed communism, it was not immediately clear in the early days of the Cold War that this approach would become the norm in the West.

This shift occurred because the West argued that the key to outperforming the Soviets was to abandon the *laissez-faire* economic policies that had dominated the pre-Depression era. The new adversary had to be confronted and restrained using its own tactics, albeit with modifications. These modifications included state control (without state ownership), social benefits (within a capitalist framework), and investment and industrial development (aligned with Western ideology). Unlike the Eastern Bloc, the Western world constructed its postwar system on the foundation of controlled capitalism, a system that reflected and upheld Western values, doctrines, and polity.

History has reached another milestone today. The growing competition with China and the resulting shifts in the international political and economic order away from liberal democracy and the euphemistically called "rule-based system" founded on present-day Western principles should provoke appropriate responses from the contemporary policy establishment. However, the only prevailing and agreed-upon philosophy is merely reflexive confidence in competitive "free" markets as the surest way to maximize individual liberty and economic growth. Moreover, a corresponding neoliberal belief is still officially present, according to which the function of government is best limited to securing those competitive markets through enforcing property rights and the aforementioned "rule of law," only intervening in the supposedly rare instance of market failure.

Despite the tacit recognition that neither the above philosophy nor the supporting politics and enforcing economics have been working satisfactorily, at least since the end of the Cold War, Western leaders have been unable to come up with a proper response to the relentless and unstoppable development of non-Western, non-liberal, and non-democratic countries. The Western rulers and their policy establishment have not found the answer to what should replace liberal democracy and the "free market" (social democracy and state control?). Any alternative, such as "democratic socialism," centralized administration, i.e., globalization, or state-owned companies, would point in the direction of "illiberal competition," a term used here to describe a system that does not adhere to the much-cherished liberal-democratic Western values, thereby admitting defeat.

Instead, left-liberal Western policymakers have learned that "underinvestment is a bigger threat to national security than the U.S. national debt." To them, it is already beyond question that secular stagnation (whereby only unstable financial conditions can bring about satisfactory growth), not debt, is the more pressing national security concern. They explain that the world has had a 10-year live experiment proving that austerity and lack of investment, notwithstanding low growth, produce "destabilization" and "illiberal autocrats," i.e., Hungary's Viktor Orbán, Brazil's Jair Bolsonaro, Russia's Vladimir Putin, China's Xi Jinping, Turkey's Recep Erdoğan, Poland's Jarosław Kaczyński, Slovenia's Janez Janša, et al. (EDP Network, 2018).

The progressive Western policymakers see these "illiberals" trying to prevent their enlightened, leftist, socialist, liberal, globalist, multicultural, gender-free, critical race theorist, woke, or other radical extremist policies from being implemented. Being, luckily, Western, they can finance any expenditure concerning the ideological, political, social, cultural, identity, and economic wars by using their Modern Monetary Theory (MMT).

Relying on the MMT, the do-gooder Left smartly emphasizes the distinction between "good debt" — which is debt used for productive investments that can generate future income or economic growth — and "bad debt" — which is debt used for non-productive purposes or that does not generate future income or economic growth. According to the Wizards of the West, investments in infrastructure, technology, innovation, and education fall under "good debt" and will secure long-term competitiveness for America *vis-à-*

vis China. There are no worries about moral values, philosophy, culture, tradition, or national identity here — only about limitless investment financed by an unlimited money supply. With inflation and interest rates lagging, policymakers should not be intimidated by arguments that the United States and the Western world cannot afford these investments.

As the fake but self-proclaimed altruistic Wizards argue, bad debt does indeed pose a risk without significantly enhancing medium- and longer-term growth potential. Therefore, they say, the Trump administration's 2018 tax legislation and any trickle-down tax cuts for corporations and the wealthiest people (anything "given" to them is "bad debt") are essentially redistributing trillions of dollars from lower- and middle-income people to the richest — and society must recognize them as "bad debt." A more cautious approach to such policies — just leave it to them — could lead to a more equitable distribution of wealth and a more stable society, say the Wizards.

So, the Wizards' first solution was the discovery of the Permanent Money River springing from its headwaters at the MMT and providing eternal cash flow for creating "good debt."

Second, the Wizards have started advocating their "industrial policy" as deeply American (broadly speaking, government actions aimed at reshaping the economy), in addition to being something close to evident today. Alexander Hamilton's vision for U.S. manufacturing, i.e., protectionism, was the first American industrial policy, a tradition carried forward throughout U.S. history as government interference

— until it lost favor with the neoliberals in the 1980s. However, rather than picking the eventual winners in specific sectors, governments would invest in large-scale projects — like putting a man on the moon, developing nuclear fusion reactors, or achieving net-zero emissions — requiring innovations across many industries. Of course, that would have nothing to do with a socialist planned economy, would it? Instead, it is about "beating the enemy at their own game."

The most significant geopolitical incentive to return to industrial policy this time is climate change. It will require a surge of deliberate and directed public investment that underwrites a shift to a post-carbon U.S. economy through research and development, the deployment of new technologies, and climate-friendly infrastructure. In short, the government must compel businesses to do the right thing since companies do not know what is good for them. Such methods have historically been used only in wartime, the Eastern Bloc, or socialist systems — now the West knows better. Of course, America's competitors have been following the exact blueprint successfully, using their own hard-earned money. Their investments have already paid off in several areas, like artificial intelligence, solar energy, and 5G technology. Without the government providing clear policy guidelines and directions regarding Western and non-Western competition, U.S. firms will continue to lose ground if the country relies heavily on private-sector research and development and short-term profit-making applications. However, a shift in focus to long-term, transformative breakthroughs could inspire a new wave of innovation and set a new standard for Western progress.

Third, it is time for policymakers to abandon outdated and long-obsolete ideas about free trade, terms of trade, and Adam Smith. Instead, let us embrace a more nuanced approach to trade policy that aligns with the complexities of the 21st century. It is almost unbelievable that while finance is tackling Modern Monetary Theory, the government still explains trade in 18th-century terms. Not every trade deal is beneficial, and more trade or free trade is not always the answer; they are merely phrases without much actual content today. U.S. trade policy has suffered many honest and deliberate mistakes over the decades by accepting politically biased, unfair, and pro-deal arguments and trade deals at face value.

Unbiased thinkers and national-conservative economists must look beyond individual agreements to challenge the basic premises of trade theory in today's economy. For example, the notion that trade will invariably benefit all parties and make all participants better off — provided the loser could, in principle, be compensated — is being criticized in economics. This critique is especially well-deserved given the United States' appalling track record of reining in the gains by collecting frivolous corporate taxes in the first place, let alone distributing them broadly.

However, the Left's proposal to aggressively target tax havens and loopholes that undermine many theoretical gains from trade will not simply solve the problems associated with business, commerce, and the economy. Leftists are always concerned about the taxes collected being fairly distributed — to serve their fallacious cause of social justice. They would always punish the wealthy, corporations, and any entity from which there is money to take away, but this is not the solution. While ensuring that the taxes collected are fairly distributed is crucial, creating and investing in high-paying, high-quality jobs and continuously increasing real wages are just as important. Whether free trade, mercantilism, protectionism, or any combination thereof can help attain these goals is a question of detail.

Instead, Western politicians, diplomats, and other experts keep harping on "strategic yield," a term that refers to the long-term benefits or advantages gained from a particular action or policy, "economic dividends," and "currency manipulations" when blaming China for everything. Since their plan of engaging China while keeping it contained went miserably astray, the West could not find its place under the sun. Based on Chinese tradition, culture, and characteristics, Chinese development is the antipode of Western values, desires, and power. For example, the Chinese effort of the Belt and Road Initiative (BRI), along with the Chinese desire and capability to break out of the ideological, political, economic, and military constraints the West has placed around the once-greatest civilization on earth, is construed by the West as a combined set of infrastructure projects designed to ensure and enhance Chinese power across continents. And since China cleverly funds much of the BRI through its hard-earned foreign exchange reserves (paid for by Western greed and unscrupulous irresponsibility), Western propaganda keeps charging that the Chinese have amassed their cache through years of intervening heavily in foreign exchange markets to depress the value of the Chinese currency and make Chinese exports more competitive. And that is against the U.S. dollar, the politically neutral, stable, and reliable reserve currency that never loses its value — does it?

Fourth, leftist foreign-policy experts do not agree that what is suitable for U.S.-based multinational corporations is necessarily advantageous for the United States — and I am afraid I also have to disagree with that. U.S. politicians, diplomats, and other lobbyists travel the world advocating for American companies to win contracts and deals in foreign countries. While the jobs created by these contracts and agreements are not always solely in the United States, and not all the benefits go to U.S. workers or communities, it is the responsibility of the U.S. government to ensure that these companies, which it supports in obtaining business contracts overseas, are held liable to compensate the state and society for the services rendered to them at American taxpayers' expense. If this is not the case, the American system, including its political, financial, and legal frameworks, is faulty.

The leftist "experts" keep raising, with great indignation, the issue of the pharmaceutical industry. The United States is the undisputed leader in drug development, and most U.S. trade negotiators have regarded pharmaceuticals as one of the significant sources of export strength. Indeed, U.S. pharmaceutical companies may own the intellectual property, but the active ingredients, such as COVID-19 vaccines, are manufactured primarily abroad. That might seem like an unsurprising fact of globalization; yet the largest sources of U.S. drug imports by value are not low-wage countries but Ireland, Germany, and Switzerland. Although this is not the case with global capital migrating to low-wage countries, it does not necessarily occur solely because of tax sheltering, as the Left likes to assert immediately. High-tech pharmaceutical products are costly to develop and require highly sophisticated equipment and processes to produce reliably. The more refined, expensive, and complex the high-value product and its manufacturing process, the more likely it is to be produced reliably and safely by developed industries in advanced countries.

That being understood, my judgment is still out on the American system, which does not stand up to big business and government in advocating for the American people and society. That system as a whole must be overhauled from the bottom up, not merely the tax structure, foreign policy, education, legal procedures, antitrust measures, or financial rules, but also growing inequality, stagnant real earnings, lack of social cohesion or patriotism, multiculturalism, or globalism — everything else needs reexamination and renewal, too.

It is crucial to underscore the necessity of a "grand strategy," recognizing that any new economic philosophy for today's world will only be as effective as the "grand strategy" that precedes it. This task is not solely for economists; it requires a collective effort and a clear, well-defined roadmap. Even Marxist materialism acknowledged this, but its failure to deliver a competent strategy and the selection of unreliable fellow travelers based on ideological conformity led to its demise.

The nominee of the Biden Administration for Comptroller of the Currency, Ms. Saule Tarikhovna Omarova, who would oversee most of the banking assets in the United States, has spoken ardently about the idea of a Federal Reserve takeover of consumer bank deposits and bankrupting fossil-fuel companies (Toomey, 2021). If Ms. Omarova's views are implemented, they could significantly transform the financial and energy sectors of the United States. Instead of defending her previous statements, she has clarified that she did not intend to make the controversial remarks about energy firms. She has proposed that a substantial increase in Fed power could stimulate discussions and introduce new ideas to Congress, including the concept of a central bank digital currency.

Each hypothetical scenario involves a significant expansion of the central government's authority to manage resources and regulate banking. They represent a socialist vision for American financial services and provide a roadmap for a comprehensive overhaul of the central bank's balance sheet, a change of monumental scale, to reshape the fundamental structure of modern finance. By focusing on the Fed, a series of suggested reforms would redefine the role of a central bank as the primary public platform for generating, coordinating, and distributing financial resources in a "democratic economy" — a concept referred to as the People's Ledger (Omarova, 2020).

The reforms envision the complete migration of demand deposit accounts to the Fed's balance sheet on the liability side of this ledger. On the asset side, they advocate a comprehensive restructuring of the Fed's investment portfolio, thereby maximizing its capacity to channel credit to "productive uses in the nation's economy." In short, the central government would decide which parts of the economy deserve financing. There has even been a plan for the government to take ownership stakes in large financial firms. So, how does this plan differ from any Soviet or socialist economic system?

To break socialism in the UK, the Thatcher government once had to build a political coalition to privatize inefficient and corrupt state-run industries. Ms. Thatcher became prime minister in 1979 during the Cold War. To alleviate concerns that privatization could allow foreign players to gain control of key sectors, the government would retain, for a time, a stake in the companies it was turning over to private investors. Therefore, Thatcher's government agreed to let the state keep a portion of an asset as payment for getting it out of total state control and into private hands. But now, the Biden Administration's proposed structural reforms are advocating a move in the opposite direction: encouraging new government "participation," i.e., ownership and power in firms that private investors currently own.

As a reminder, a 2006 *Wall Street Journal* editorial titled "Socialism in Reverse" summarized the Thatcher era: "... By the mid-1970s nearly every commercial activity in Britain was operated by the public sector — in most cases poorly and at a high cost to consumers and taxpayers. Mrs. Thatcher acted swiftly as Prime Minister to reverse 30 years of this creeping socialism, privatizing steel plants, coal mines, Rolls Royce, oil companies, the telephone system, and a major airline" (WSJ Opinion, 2006).

As a result, the British economy flourished. By reducing government ownership, Ms. Thatcher not only expanded individual prosperity but also empowered millions of people, transforming them into capitalists.

A property-owning democracy, where the percentage of families owning their homes and businesses rises and the number of individual shareholders increases, is a significant step toward a fair and equal society.

In a socialist system, the state gets involved in either ill-suited activities or beyond its capabilities. The government always desires to concentrate political and economic power in its own hands, believing it knows how to manage businesses. But state control can never be improved merely by "clever" experts managing it who then arrogantly claim they "know best" and are serving the "public interest" — as determined by them. State control is fundamentally flawed because it denies people the power and opportunity to bear responsibility for their actions.

Conversely, privatization shrinks the state's power, and private enterprise, at least theoretically, enlarges the people's capacity.

The policies for honest, impartial, and orderly privatization, controlled capitalism, fair competition, distributism, private property, and ownership are fiercely opposed once again by left-liberal and socialist intellectuals today. Too many prefer to rely on easily accessible subsidies rather than apply the political, economic, and financial discipline necessary to cut costs, increase profits, become more competitive, pay fair taxes, and invest in profitable projects benefiting society. No, they prefer the captive customers commanded by a monopoly or the secure job in a high-overhead industry rather than the strenuous, productive life of a work-based society, discipline-based liberty, and merit-based enterprise.

However, such conditions reveal a universal truth: to create an open and fair market, one must take the state out of the market.

Modern Monetary Theory — The Woke Economic Panacea

In many respects, the U.S. national debt is the foundation of the global financial system. In 1995, the U.S. national debt totaled more than $4 trillion, and in 2021, it stood at $28 trillion and will grow significantly in the coming years. What that debt represents and how it works are intrinsically intertwined — although, in recent years, the interplay has not functioned as it was supposed to, and, allegedly, no one knows precisely why. Even economists are deeply conflicted about the national debt outside the political arena. Specifically, the national debt refers to the level of U.S. federal debt held by the public, in contrast to the debt held by the government.

National Debt vs. Budget Deficit

There is a distinction between the federal government's annual budget deficit — known as the fiscal deficit — and the outstanding federal debt, recognized in official accounting terminology as the national public debt.

When the U.S. federal government spends more than it earns, it generates a budget deficit. To bridge this gap, the U.S. Treasury Department issues and sells Treasury bills, notes, and bonds. These "financial products" or "securities" of the Treasury play a pivotal role in financing the budget deficit by borrowing from domestic and foreign investors.

The government sells these Treasury securities to investors, corporations, financial institutions, and other governments worldwide, effectively borrowing the cash it needs to provide governmental services.

The national debt is the federal government's net accumulated or piled-up annual budget deficits *and* the total amount of money the U.S. federal government owes its creditors. Simply put, fiscal or budget deficits are the individual trees in the vast forest of the national debt. The U.S. federal government can acquire the cash to provide governmental services by issuing different securities, effectively managing its budget deficit, and contributing to the national debt.

During World War II, the national debt ballooned as the United States drastically increased defense spending to finance the war, resulting in the country's debt rising to more than 100% of gross domestic product (GDP). The debt decreased in the postwar years, then rose again, starting with Ronald Reagan, only to taper off in the early 2000s. However, beginning in 2008, the national debt soared without ever falling again. Moreover, simultaneous tax cuts, the financial crisis, ensuing bailouts, and increased social benefits also contributed to the deficit. Today, almost half of government spending is allocated to Social Security, Medicare, and Medicaid, and these outlays are expected to increase with the aging population.

Current estimates show that the U.S. national debt will increase to 117% of GDP by 2025 and that the country is on course to surpass the debt record set after World War II by 2023 (CRFB Budgets & Projections, 2020). Nevertheless, many economists still conclude that more federal spending is preferable to too little. Although it is questionable how to think about the national debt, there is broad agreement today that simply comparing it to household debt, such as credit cards, mortgages, or student loans, for example, is the wrong way to consider it.

The most crucial difference is that you cannot generate new dollars if you run out of dollars at home. However, the government has no such encumbrance, and when it creates new dollars, people still respect their value worldwide. These "new dollars" are not physical currency but represent the government's ability to create money through various mechanisms such as fiscal policy and the Federal Reserve. Many on the progressive side say the national debt is not even "real" but merely part of the money supply that people find necessary, practical, and helpful — the same way one finds money "useful."

The government "manages," i.e., increases its debt by issuing Treasury securities, which come in various forms, such as bills, notes, and bonds. These securities are highly sought after due to their stability, high marketability, and the government's reputation for never defaulting on its promises. They are considered the safest assets issued by a trusted government. Banks are required to hold a certain quantity of these securities as a precaution against market collapses, such as the one experienced in 2008.

Moreover, Treasuries are also very popular abroad because of the U.S. dollar's status as the world's reserve currency — a rank achieved, ironically, in the wake of the U.S. spending binge during World War II. As the world's reserve currency, the U.S. dollar is used for international trade and is held in significant quantities by central banks and other major financial institutions. This status makes Treasury securities a common investment for banks worldwide. About 60% of all foreign bank reserves are in U.S. dollars today. Furthermore, the good news is that foreign investors own about half of the publicly held U.S. debt, chief among them being China, which owns around $1.1 trillion in Treasuries (Seth, 2021).

The bad news lingering somewhere in the background is that there could come a point when the world changes its mind about the dollar and the value it represents. The U.S. national debt could influence this change, or it might be something else. However, when the almighty dollar ceases to be the global reserve currency, the United States will have a more challenging time covering the interest it already owes, not to mention borrowing more. In addition, if investors decided to sell off their U.S. Treasuries *en masse* and there was not enough demand (or trust) from other investors to purchase them, that would inflate interest rates, making Treasuries a more desirable investment and increasing borrowing costs. This could potentially lead to a decrease in government spending, a slowdown in economic growth, and a decrease in the value of the dollar, which in turn could have significant implications for the global economy.

The United States enjoys many benefits simply because of America's role in the global economy. But how would, should, and could the U.S. respond to a mass sell-off? Would the Federal Reserve step in and buy Treasuries itself to keep costs down? There is already precedent for the Fed buying

Treasuries when no one else would. For instance, during the Great Depression, the Fed bought government securities to inject money into the economy and lower interest rates. This is partly how America financed World War II: The Fed agreed to purchase Treasuries to keep interest rates low and keep borrowing costs manageable for the federal government. The public did likewise; war bonds were aggressively marketed to the people (appealing to patriotism) mainly to keep inflation under control while interest rates remained artificially low to finance the war.

However, those interventions could only be effective in the short term. Except for renewed demand for U.S. debt, inflation would spiral out of control sooner or later, leading to an outcome with many cautionary examples: Germany in the 1920s, Yugoslavia in the 1990s, and Zimbabwe in the 2000s. In each case, deficits and increasing national debt, accompanied by low interest rates, resulted in high inflation, which drove up interest rates and borrowing costs, leading to declining employment and increasing desperation. The potential impact of U.S. debt and inflation on the economy cannot be overstated.

Many economists regard inflation fears as a retro problem with known effective remedies. Indeed, concerns about the U.S. government's response to the 2008 financial crisis aroused similar fears, but they never came to pass. Something closer to the opposite is true — the Fed has had to deal with persistently low inflation since 2008 despite low interest rates. Has public borrowing become less harmful than it used to be? Has the world shifted so much since 2008 that inflation is a different concept today from what it was during the financial crisis? Has the economy undergone a massive transformation due to globalization?

The central bank even announced that it would let inflation run a little hot for a while to make up for years of persistently low inflation, suggesting that interventions by the Federal Reserve in the Treasury market would have to be almost excessive to have any impact on inflation.

How long global demand for U.S. Treasury securities will grow or the immediate effects of slowing demand has yet to be determined. But at a turning point, we will see a spike in interest rates, depreciating currency, and inflation. The U.S. government's obligation to service the debt is a significant concern, as the more money that goes to servicing it, the more it will crowd out other national priorities. Roughly a quarter of the publicly held U.S. debt is issued through short-term securities that must be regularly refinanced and are subject to changes in interest rates (Congressional Budget Office, 2020). While those rates are low now, and the Fed will — indeed it must — keep interest rates at or near zero, any increase in rates in the future will also increase the amount of money the U.S. government owes to investors.

Moreover, even a slight increase in interest rates leads to a significant rise in interest payments. Let me point out the fallacy of the optimists and illustrate the gravity of this situation with the analogy of a person jumping out of a tall building. When asked while "passing," or rather falling, by the fifth floor, how it's going, he answers, "So far, so good." Well, does that sound reassuring?

However, advocates of Modern Monetary Theory (MMT) allege that the U.S. cannot run out of money to pay creditors and investors because the U.S. "controls," i.e., makes the world accept its currency. So, unlike countries that cannot, i.e., are unable to, create an unlimited amount of their currency and remain unpunished forever, the U.S. government can "self-finance" itself. Whenever a particular security matures, the U.S. Treasury has to find the money to honor it. However, it can simply "re-auction" or sell a new security to raise the necessary cash (Ponzi scheme). This way, the government can pay back the old debt with a new one and, in a sense, never has to repay the debt, which can grow indefinitely.

Nevertheless, critics claim that the money that could have been used for investment in economic growth must instead be applied to make interest payments to investors. Additionally, higher deficits and debt can impact development and temper growth in the future by causing uncertainty, insecurity, and doubt — in short, higher risk for investors. An immense national debt could eventually increase the cost of capital for businesses, potentially stifling investment and innovation. It is called "private-sector crowd-out" when the government's borrowing reduces the funds available for private investment, leading to a potential slowdown in innovation and economic growth. Those are new kinds of risks and changes.

The national debt also means that the government is buying something on credit. If that something bought with new debt today helps the economy grow tomorrow, that will mean more revenue for the government — and the whole process pays for itself. While that is theoretically true, it is risky. Imagine that you are, for example, the general manager of a company. You must focus on where your expenditures and investments are going and identify your targets very carefully because you certainly do not want to add to the company's debt needlessly — causing other problems.

For the government, debt can often be seen as just a number that keeps growing: the reserves are referred to as *money*, and the Treasuries as *debt* — but what is the real difference? They are both electronic digits in a ledger that earn interest. This perspective can lead to a dangerous belief that there's no limit to how much the government can spend, potentially leading to reckless financial decisions. It is crucial to remember that every dollar spent is a dollar that must be repaid with interest, which should serve as a reminder of the importance of responsible financial decisions and the need to consider the long-term implications of debt. Nevertheless, the government will continue to "fund itself" on credit for the foreseeable future. The question is what the country gets for that debt and how long the world keeps buying it — and that depends mainly on how that debt, i.e., spending power, will be used.

The public usually accepts debt issuance as long as the proceeds stimulate economic growth, leading to the country's long-term prosperity. When debt fuels economic expansion, current and future generations reap the rewards. Supporters of MMT maintain that there are no risks involved with such "well-spent expenditures" — the government and the people will recoup all investments in the future that stimulate the economy today. Therefore, the government should create money not only to service or refinance the debt due but also to keep the economy going, something the government did during the war — but this time, forever. Very convenient indeed.

The future is always built today, and politicians keep saying, "Oh, well, we will worry about this in the future." But no one ever worries about the future — other than the next election.

How Bad Is National Debt?

Despite some common ground, economists and financial analysts have significantly divergent opinions regarding the implications of federal debt. Governments that run fiscal deficits must bridge the gap by borrowing money, which can lead to crowding out or reduced capital investment in private markets. Furthermore, the issuance of debt securities to service these debts impacts interest rates, a critical relationship managed by the Fed's monetary policy tools.

Progressive supporters of Modern Monetary Theory (MMT) hold a unique viewpoint that sets them apart. They argue that a long-term budget deficit is sustainable and preferable to a government surplus. However, most economists do not embrace this perspective.

Keynesian macroeconomists argue that a current account deficit can be advantageous, as it can stimulate aggregate demand in the economy. While the current account reflects a country's foreign transactions, a *current account deficit* measures its trade when the value of the goods and services the country imports exceeds the value of the products it exports.

Most neo-Keynesians promote fiscal policy tools like government deficit spending, but only after monetary policy (the Fed's intervention) has proven ineffective and nominal interest rates have hit zero. On the other hand, traditional economists of the Chicago and Austrian schools argue that government deficits and debt can have a lasting, detrimental impact. They suggest that these factors can permanently harm private investment, manipulate interest rates, influence the capital structure, suppress exports, and unfairly hurt future generations through higher taxes or inflation.

Government Expenditures

The national debt is the net accumulation of budget deficits. The top expenses constitute the most significant factors of the national debt, and they are in the U.S. for 2021 as follows:

- *Medicare/Medicaid and Other Healthcare Programs*
  In 2021, $1.4 trillion will be allocated to healthcare benefit programs, including Medicare and Medicaid (U.S. Department of Health and Human Services, 2021).

- *Social Security Program and Disability Pensions*
  Aiming to provide financial security to retired and disabled people, total Social Security and other expenditures are approximately $1.1 trillion (U.S. Social Security Administration, 2021).

- *Defense Budget Expenses*
  $752 billion is allocated for the U.S. Defense Budget in 2021 (U.S. Department of Defense, 2020).

- *Other Miscellaneous Expenses*

Government expenses include veterans' benefits, transportation, international affairs, and public education.

Methods Used to Reduce Debt (Forms of Government Borrowing)

A country's national debt can only be reduced in five ways: by increasing taxation, reducing spending, restructuring the debt, monetizing the debt, or outright defaulting. The federal budget process directly tackles taxation and spending and can create restructuring or possible default recommendations.

- *Monetization*

  If a country has its own fiat currency, it can always create, i.e., print, as much money as it needs to pay its debts, provided those debts are denominated in its currency. This process is somewhat euphemistically referred to as "debt monetization." There is a limit to how much debt can be monetized before a country starts suffering from inflation or hyperinflation, and desperate efforts to monetize debt have often pushed countries well past that critical point. Monetizing debt can make creditors reluctant to lend to a country if inflation substantially lowers the value of how much creditors are repaid.

- *Interest Rate Manipulation*

  Governments maintain low interest rates to stimulate the economy, promote investment, generate tax revenue, and ultimately reduce the national debt. Low interest rates facilitate borrowing for individuals and businesses. Borrowers then spend that fresh money on goods and services, creating jobs and tax revenues. The United States, the European Union, the United Kingdom, and several other nations have utilized low interest rates with some degree of success. Nevertheless, interest rates kept at or near zero for extended periods have yet to prove to be a long-term solution for debt-ridden governments.

- *Spending Cuts*
One way to cut debt is to reduce spending, which can be difficult for two reasons. First and foremost, each government expenditure has its constituency advocating for it — and that faction will fight efforts to cut that expenditure, making spending cuts politically challenging. Second, spending cuts can damage the economy through a negative multiplier effect during a severe economic downturn. The resulting downturn can reduce revenue enough to impair the ability to repay debts, so governments must carry out spending cuts carefully.

- *Raise Taxes*
On the other side of the equation are tax increases. In the U.S., federal government revenues have been below their 50-year average of 17.4% of Gross Domestic Product (GDP) for 14 of the last 20 years because, just like cutting spending, raising taxes can be politically painful as various interest groups defend their tax exemptions (Tax Policy Center, 2019). Moreover, raising taxes can also have a negative multiplier effect, complicating efforts to reduce debt.

- *Bailout*

  Several countries have received debt bailouts, either from
  the International Monetary Fund (IMF) over several
  decades or from the European Union (EU), as was most
  prominently demonstrated in Greece during the European
  debt crisis beginning in 2009. These bailouts impose
  harsh requirements to reform a country's economy, and
  there is serious debate about whether the structural
  adjustments the IMF or EU imposed on bailed-out
  countries had an overall positive or negative effect.

- *Default*

  Defaulting on debt, including going bankrupt and
  restructuring payments to creditors, is a common and
  often successful strategy for debt reduction.

Politicians and the media are distracting people from the
fact that debt and inflation are pressing issues in the Western
world today.

Since 1971, when the United States refused to continue
exchanging U.S. dollars for gold, destroying the Bretton
Woods system, countries have been free to print as much
money as they want — paper money without any backing
whatsoever. This proved too tempting and soon led to severe
inflation, particularly in the U.S.

In the 1970s, the U.S. dollar became so unpopular in the
financial markets due to uncontrolled inflation that President
Jimmy Carter had to issue "Carter bonds" denominated not in
U.S. dollars but in West German marks and Swiss francs in
1978.

Federal Reserve Chairman Paul Volcker, appointed in mid-1979, dared to fight inflation. In 1980, he raised the prime interest rate to over 20 percent to keep inflation under control. This drastic measure worked, and inflation in the U.S. was back at around 3 percent in 1983.

Nevertheless, even after that, states kept spending more money than they had — they just printed it. The same act that would land an ordinary citizen a few years in jail does not seem to bother central banks: they print money if the earnings are insufficient to pay the bills. Imagine having a credit card whose monthly statements you never have to pay; you simply throw the bill in the wastebasket and keep shopping. The interest will be carried over to the following month's account statement — a dream for every shopping queen but a reality for every government.

The years 1987, 2001, and 2008 were marked by severe financial crises: Alan Greenspan, who was Chairman of the U.S. Federal Reserve under four presidents (Reagan, Bush Sr., Clinton, Bush Jr.) between 1987 and 2006, invented the panacea against financial market crises: lowering interest rates opened the floodgates of money. In 2008, the so-called Quantitative Easing (QE) was introduced, whereby a central bank purchases government securities or other securities from the market to expand the money supply and stimulate lending and investment. QE is an elegant term for increasing the money supply via the printing press.

The difference between the crises of 1987, 2001, and 2008 was that the floodgates have remained open since 2008 — and have never closed again. Interest rates stayed at zero, and the major central banks engaged in unprecedented actions, such as buying bonds and stocks — just about anything the "normal market" would not do. This caused the size of Western central banks' balance sheets to multiply.

Since 2008, the balance sheet statements of the major central banks (USA, ECB, Japan, China) have increased from $7 trillion to $31 trillion. In other words, $24 trillion was printed. Since March 2009, the S&P 500 stock market index has continued to rise after the crisis. Although all central bankers spoke of a strong economy, they did not raise interest rates while continuing to print money — until today, almost fourteen years after the crisis.

You can buy more with less of your funds when interest rates are virtually zero. A simple example of this is from the real estate market of Switzerland, one of the most financially stable countries with its own "safe haven" currency (although the Swiss franc, or CHF, has also been fiat money since 2000). A well-off family can spend CHF 5,000 per month to finance their home, equating to CHF 60,000 annually. Twenty years ago, in Switzerland, this family paid about 5 percent interest for a five-year mortgage; therefore, it could finance a house for 1.2 million francs (60,000/5 percent). With a mortgage interest rate of 1 percent, a family with the same budget can finance a home worth 6 million Swiss francs. So, the real estate booms in the West have nothing to do with merit; they are just inflated by free money.

Since 2008, key interest rates, such as the prime lending rate, in the West have practically remained the same. The reason given by the central banks is that inflation is still too low, which is nonsense. As the example above shows, the printed money did not leave the financial market, so price inflation did not occur in consumer goods but in real estate, stock, and bond prices. This development led to the current situation: stocks, bonds, and real estate have never been valued so highly in economic history. All of this took place on the back of savers receiving no interest on their accounts; on the contrary, they are even being charged negative interest rates, which means they are effectively paying the bank to hold their money. Most people do not have access to the financial markets, as they lack the means to buy real or financial assets. While the wealthiest 10 percent of the population benefited immensely from this situation, the rest have been left out in the cold.

Beginning in 2016, the U.S. Federal Reserve increased the key interest rate slightly, which led to a crisis in the so-called repo market as early as September 2019. In the repo market, institutional investors can "finance themselves," i.e., borrow money at short notice by depositing securities and settling on the repurchase agreement. However, this crisis went unnoticed by most market participants as the U.S. Federal Reserve pumped vast amounts of money into the repo market to calm the situation.

Nevertheless, COVID-19 masked this looming financial crisis: central banks had another excellent reason to bring interest rates back to zero — if they were not already there — and open the floodgates on an unprecedented scale. After losing 31 percent of its value by March 23, 2021, the S&P 500 recovered to pre-COVID-19 levels within six months.

But even after the COVID-19 crisis, the money floodgates were not closed; interest rates remained at zero, and central banks continued to buy bonds and shares. In contrast to previous crises, which resulted in the financial market as the sole beneficiary of funds, trillions were distributed directly to the people during the COVID-19 pandemic, leading to a glut of money in the consumer goods market — and the inflation genie finally found its way out of the bottle.

The case of Switzerland and its money printing deserves particular explanation. In contrast to the U.S. and the EU, Switzerland did not spend more money than it took in — thanks to its debt limit law, which sets a cap on the amount of debt the government can incur. However, the Swiss National Bank (SNB) started printing money to buy euros and U.S. dollars to stop the Swiss franc from strengthening, thereby indirectly weakening the Swiss export industry. Switzerland now has the largest balance sheet total in the world in relative terms because it printed money when there was no immediate domestic need for it and used it to buy foreign currencies to keep the exchange rates stable *vis-à-vis* the Swiss franc. However, this is an incomprehensible strategy because the Swiss franc accounts for around 0.2 percent of the world's reserve currencies — the U.S. dollar is around 59 percent; this corresponds to a factor of almost 300. The total assets on the balance sheets of the SNB in December 2021 were around 1,000 billion CHF, while those of the Fed were 9,000 billion CHF. This mismatch is beyond compare. The equity of the SNB was about 20 percent at the end of 2021. If Switzerland's foreign currency reserves, mainly held in U.S. dollars and euros, lose 20 percent of their value, the SNB will be, at least theoretically, bankrupt.

The great injustice of inflation is that it affects the poor disproportionately more than the rich. Wealthy individuals do not feel that their filet is 20 percent more expensive. Inflation is painful for the middle class, who stand indignantly at the gas pump. However, it is a disaster for the poorest, who already had their backs against the wall before inflation. Unlike income tax, which demands more from the rich than the poor, inflation is the most unfair tax because the effects are the opposite. I am surprised that the Left does not prioritize fighting inflation with the urgency needed to help the people it allegedly represents.

Why not raise interest rates to above-inflation levels when central banks know that, as Paul Volcker demonstrated in 1980, that is the only effective anti-inflation policy?

The reason is the debt: if the central bank raises the prime interest rate, states will also have to pay higher interest on their mountains of debt, which they cannot afford. Furthermore, the financial and real estate markets are so highly valued and bolstered with free money that a significant interest rate hike will lead to a collapse.

To divert attention from their unsustainable financial practices, Western central banks, in collaboration with their governments and "international institutions," continually fabricate new global crises — a pandemic here, a war there, a refugee disaster here, or a food emergency there. This strategy is akin to a "Ponzi scheme," a fraudulent investment design that pays returns to its investors from their own invested money or the money paid by other, subsequent investors, rather than from profit earned by the operation.

However, as the saying goes, "the pitcher will go to the well once too often" — and we are nearing that point.

To control inflation, the interest rates of 10-year treasury bills should be about 1 percent higher than the inflation rate. Official inflation figures, if one can believe them at all, are regularly manipulated by the states to look favorable and save money on pensions and other expenses. For instance, a successful fight against inflation would necessitate a key interest rate of 3.5 percent for the Swiss real estate market, as mentioned earlier. This rate is 4.25 percent higher than the current -0.75 percent rate. As a result, the 10-year mortgage rate would be around 5 percent. However, what was considered normal twenty years ago would now trigger a collapse in the Swiss real estate market, given its current inflated state.

So, it seems that the West financially has its back against the wall — a better term than "broke." I always assumed that a government had to represent the interests of its own people. This principle should forbid imposing sanctions, for example, on other countries, which, on the one hand, yield little benefit and, on the other hand, plunge the sanctioning country into the abyss. Unfortunately, the West does not seem to see the danger or does not want to acknowledge it. Indeed, why should it? Its progressive managers can print all the money they need — with the help of their Modern Monetary Theory (MMT).

Chapter 6

Europe — A Subsidiary of the Global Empire

A civilizational struggle is unfolding before us, a battle for the very essence and future of Europe.

Emigration is an ontologically detrimental phenomenon. It is terrible if a person cannot stay and live in his native country, find happiness and vocation there, and has to leave, especially under duress. Occasionally, a person has to leave his homeland because his life is in danger, or the regime wants to coerce him or imprison him, or he would starve to death. These are all valid reasons. However, even if someone were to leave his homeland, ideally, the goal should be to return later. Therefore, if we want to help someone forced to leave his country, we should not encourage him to stay outside.

Thus, I urge the European Union to live up to its name and invest in, build up, and develop Central and Eastern Europe to bring it to the level of Western Europe. The goal must be to create the same standard of everyday living and working conditions for everyone in the EU. After all, what is the purpose of a so-called "European Union" if not to level the playing field and ensure equality and prosperity for all its member nations and peoples?

However, the Western world makes "Easterners" desire to go elsewhere because conditions are better and maintained more effectively in another place — particularly in the West — undermining people's commitment to their own countries.

After the communist era, the inexperienced Eastern Europeans made many mistakes and quickly lost control over their vital national resources — including their future. The energy sector, the banking sector, the prime of local industry, the media, arable land, and labor all passed into the hands of foreigners — transferred to them by the old socialist rulers looking for a smooth and reckoning-free transition (for themselves) into the "capitalist system" and its hierarchy.

Westerners live in a globalizing, post-national, liberal-democratic society with leftist tendencies and want even more. They also demand that Central and Eastern Europe and the rest of the world conform to this model. However, any regional desire to protect national identities, cultures, traditions, or history immediately encounters Western ideological attacks. These left-liberal assaults, originating from Brussels but linked to American liberal and economic powers, reveal a more profound truth. The West does not want the East to be free; they want Eastern Europe to be "free" only on Western terms — and that does not include parity, fairness, impartiality, or tolerance. It includes what they call "Western values," the "rule of law," and other Western narratives aimed at keeping Central and Eastern Europe in a state of colonial dependency forever.

Central and Eastern Europeans prefer preserving their nation-states because they believe they can attain democracy only within national frameworks. Having endured and resisted many empires, they do not want to become members of yet another empire — be it global, European, or any other.

On the other hand, the West desires a global empire based in Washington and a subsidiary empire, a European superstate based in Brussels. This European superstate, which is already being called the United States of Europe, would further erode the sovereignty and independence of Central and Eastern European nations, a prospect that many in these regions find deeply troubling.

Now then, despite the allegedly "mutual good intentions," there must be an ongoing communication problem between East and West, mustn't there? Or is there something more than that?

Nation-states vs. the European Union

European Member States must unite to confront the looming threat of a superstate, a force that could strip nations of their sovereignty. They must demand more respect for sovereign countries and form a new resistance against the creation of the United States of Europe. The individual nation-states must retain control over their own destinies.

Attempts to transform European institutions into supranational establishments that take precedence over national constitutional organizations create confusion, undermine the sense of the Treaties, and call into question the fundamental role of the Member States' constitutions. The brutal imposition of the will and command of politically stronger entities on weaker ones, as seen in Hungary and Poland, settles the disputes over competencies.

Using political structures and law to create a European superstate and new forms of social networks manifests the past's dangerous and invasive social engineering, which must prompt legitimate resistance. The supranational activities of European institutions also concern issues that should remain within the competencies of the member states. For example, the attempt by the Court of Justice of the European Union (CJEU) to preclude or overrule the decision of the Constitutional Tribunal of Poland regarding the interpretation of the Polish constitution must be denounced. The moralistic overactivity seen in recent years within the European Union has resulted in a dangerous tendency to impose an ideological monopoly, undermining the basis for the functioning of the European community as a willing group of free nations.

Although consensus should remain the primary means of reaching a common position in the Union, recent attempts to change, abolish, or circumvent this procedure threaten to exclude some countries from influencing the decision-making process and transform the Union into a particular oligarchy. That could lead to the *de facto* incapacitation of national constitutional institutions, including governments and parliaments, reducing them to merely approving decisions already made by others.

Despite the challenges, there is a prevailing desire for cooperation among the member countries, and a spirit of community, friendship, and solidarity permeates the nations and societies of the European continent. A reformed Union, built on this goodwill, interest, and enthusiasm, promises a brighter future, while a Union that rejects reform risks squandering these opportunities.

Many misfortunes have marked European history, especially in the last century. Nations and states have suffered terribly in defense of their sovereignty and territorial integrity against aggressive governments. After World War II, some European countries still had to contend with Soviet totalitarian repression for decades before gaining independence. Their freedom and peace among cooperating nations are significant achievements for many Europeans, providing a sense of permanent security and ideal conditions for development. The integration process has significantly contributed to establishing lasting structures of collaboration, maintaining order, and developing understanding and good relations between countries, thereby ensuring a sense of security and reassurance within the European community.

Unfortunately, over the last ten years, a series of crises, including ideological disputes, political disagreements, migration issues, and economic downturns, have shaken European cooperation, leading to a standstill, mainly because some nations feel deprived of their sovereign rights in the decision-making process.

The European Union urgently needs a profound transformation. Instead of safeguarding Europe and its heritage and ensuring the free development of European nations, the EU has become a source of problems, concerns, and uncertainty. Sadly, it is increasingly becoming an instrument of radical leftist forces that want to alter the Union ideologically, demographically, culturally, and religiously, ultimately creating a nation-free continent. These forces strive to establish a superstate, eradicate European traditions, and modify fundamental social institutions and moral principles.

There is legitimate resistance against using political structures and laws that aim to create a European superstate and a new social order through dangerous and violent social engineering that has been encountered in the past. In recent years, the moral overzealousness of the EU institutions has led to an alarming trend of enforcing an ideological monopoly.

Any cooperation among the nations of Europe must be built on a foundation of respect, not destruction — respect for the history and culture of European states, respect for Europe's Judeo-Christian heritage, and respect for the shared values that unite these nations. When Europe grapples with a severe demographic crisis, low birth rates, and an aging population, the solution lies in family-friendly policies, not mass migration — the family, the basic unit of all nations, must be respected and preserved.

Nations created the European Union to empower themselves to act more effectively and attain specific goals they could not achieve as individual states — their sovereignty must be protected, now and in the future. To be sure, the principle of delegation determines the competencies of the Union: all competencies not delegated to the Union belong to the Member States based on subsidiarity.

However, the European Union's institutions have consistently reinterpreted the European Treaties in recent decades. The result is that these institutions' power limits have shifted to the significant detriment of the Member States. This outcome is incompatible with the Union's fundamental values and undermines the confidence of European nations and citizens in the EU institutions.

To stop and reverse this process, we need to go beyond the existing principle of transferring competencies. Establishing the definite scope and inviolable purview of the EU Member States and creating an appropriate mechanism to protect their competencies by involving national constitutional courts or equivalent institutions is vital.

Consensus is the cornerstone of a strong Union. Recent attempts to circumvent this procedure threaten to exclude certain countries from reaching decisions, making the Union a special oligarchy. All this leads to de facto obstruction of national constitutional bodies, such as governments and parliaments, thus limiting the national decision-making process to the mere approval of decisions already taken by others.

In response to Hungary's law banning the "promoting or portraying" of homosexuality or gender reassignment "as an end in itself" to minors and restricting sexual education in schools, the European Union and Western media's discourse have indulged its worst nature. While touting the virtues of federalism, i.e., centralization, tolerance, and diversity in pursuit of union, the EU abuses the idea of "a just union" by dogmatically blackmailing and punishing a sovereign nation for not being diverse enough relative to "European norms," arrogantly making that country a pariah and trying to force it to adapt its independent domestic policy. In doing so, the EU risks bringing about the conflicts it was supposed to avoid, as it undermines the sovereignty and self-determination it was founded to protect.

The Hungarian law is well within the boundaries of Hungary's sovereignty. It is not an outlier in European practice and does not warrant an extreme reaction. Despite this, Ursula von der Leyen, President of the European Commission, has claimed that the law violates "all the fundamental values of the EU" (Eder & von der Burchard,

2021). Dutch Prime Minister Mark Rutte stated, "Hungary has to repeal the law and be brought down to its knees" (Stares, 2021). Moreover, he would even have Hungary leave the EU if necessary. The wisdom, good taste, and tact of a leader from an allied and wealthy Western European country arrogantly threatening to bring a newly free but still-exploited ex-Eastern-bloc state to its knees for not agreeing with him are outrageous. But even more troublesome is a draft of a European Parliament resolution punishing Hungary by withholding EU funds through the application of EU rules unrelated to Hungary's LGBTQ law. This could lead to a significant loss of financial support for Hungary and potentially strain its relationship with the EU, impacting the union's stability and future.

Ms. von der Leyen announced legal steps against the Hungarian law — actions that are likely to succeed only if the charges do not pertain to the actual content of the LGBTQ law, as that topic falls outside Brussels' purview. To get around this, Ms. von der Leyen wants to exploit how the Hungarian law might violate EU regulations concerning the free movement of goods. However, with her legal attacks on Hungary, she is undermining the fundamental values of the EU, for which she had initially charged Hungary. It is not true, as Ms. von der Leyen would have us believe, that Hungary's LGBTQ law goes "against the fundamental values of the EU" that have existed thus far.

In any case, coercing others to conform to a single view of rights has a troubling history on the diverse continent of Europe. The realist politics of international coalition-building requires a "rainbow alliance" vs. a "traditionalist alliance" of wildly different states. The EU was supposed to facilitate that goal by making issues of national particularity off-limits. However, the Union seems dangerously intent on violating national sovereignty and political independence in a targeted fashion based on a homogenizing agenda. Even if the EU succeeds in maximizing expressive individualism and LGBTQ rights, success through these means will spell the death knell of the European project.

History suggests that a diverse polity like the EU can only survive as a democratic federal arrangement or an autocracy. Tremendous diversity leads to irreconcilable political differences. When a disagreement arises, the options are either the suppression of the opposition (dictatorship), allowing national governments to set their own policies (federalism), or dismantling the federation (disunion). Peaceful political and economic cohabitation within the European Union requires a genuinely federal approach that limits Brussels' authority to act. That is why subsidiarity is the core principle of Europe's union, and the EU should behave politically like a *de facto* federation.

Ultimately, Europe has considerable strength in its diversity. The issue is not about pitting Western Europe against Eastern Europe or progressive Europe against traditionalist Europe. It is about preserving this rich political and cultural diversity and finding a balanced, tolerant, and neutral approach that respects the unique identities of each member state while fostering unity and cooperation within the EU.

Commission President von der Leyen's conduct should worry every member state or EU citizen since it shows that the EU can aggressively and arrogantly intervene in the domestic policies of any country on any subject matter at any moment if a large enough bloc demands it.

The majority of Europeans would resent the treatment Hungary is currently receiving since they want considerable autonomy to determine how their country is governed. Indeed, that autonomy has initially been a vital part of the original bargain — one of the elements that made the EU different from the ever-more-centralized federal USA, particularly on topics for which the EU does not have explicit authority, such as education, media, and child protection. If allowed to continue, Mr. Rutte's and Ms. von der Leyen's actions will set a precedent that could undermine the subsidiarity principle and any meaningful claim of national autonomy. This will exacerbate Euroscepticism even further, with the possibility that more member states will eventually follow the British precedent and leave the EU.

While federal politics is, by nature, fragile, maintaining a stable federal union is historically rare. Federations are apt to give way to *de facto* unitary states, as is arguably the case in Switzerland or Austria, or disintegrate into component states, as did Czechoslovakia and Yugoslavia, and as nearly happened to Canada and Belgium. The EU has few elements necessary for a stable federal union since, compared with national governments, it is relatively weak — it has comparatively little tax revenue and, among other things, no army or police. Furthermore, national-level politics in Europe attract far more attention than EU politics. Combining these realities with the flexibility of the EU's secession clause (Article 25), in the struggle between national and European elites, national interests still stand a better chance of being prioritized — à la Brexit.

The political elites are playing to domestic constituencies in Europe. No structure in the EU incentivizes national politicians to work for long-term European stability. Without an enforcement system that requires elites to follow the principle of toleration, the European project of political unification could quickly become the cause of the very conflict it is supposed to avoid.

Prime Minister Orbán hopes the EU's response to Hungary's law will ignite the populist and national-conservative flames in his country and beyond. By eliciting this strongly anti-national EU response, Mr. Orbán aims to shift the debate from issues like corruption, realignment toward China and Russia, or the promotion of Christianity in a generally secular country back to his role as a defender of Hungarian society against wokeness and atomization. This role of national preserver is not new to Mr. Orbán; his proven track record in opposing communism before 1990 positions him as a freedom fighter against a new form of authoritarianism. His approach is likely to resonate with many EU citizens.

How would the Netherlands, one of the Hungarian law's loudest and most aggressive critics, react to being treated like Hungary? The Dutch also have cultural norms and rules that differ from those of the rest of Europe. When the Netherlands introduced gay marriage in 2001, the EU did not revoke this Dutch law (O'Neill, 2004). Dutch abortion and euthanasia legislation also differ from the European norm, focusing on the quality of life instead of the length of life regarding elderly care (Library of Congress, 2016). Then there is the Dutch practice of being a tax haven and voting against multiple European referenda (Oxfam International, 2016). Lastly, many people in the Netherlands enjoy dressing up as Black Pete, a practice that has been called racist. When members of the UN criticized this cultural norm, Prime Minister Rutte stood by it, saying: "Guys. Folk traditions, come on. What Christmas songs you should sing, how you celebrate Christmas and Easter — this isn't what politics is about" (Bahceli, 2015).

Many Dutch citizens would be upset if others attacked the Netherlands as they did Hungary over these topics. They would recognize that these issues fall under Dutch sovereignty, protest against the interference, and respond angrily to the EU's use of political, legal, and financial means to bring the Dutch government and polity to its knees.

Therefore, the political dynamite with which EU elites are toying is very dangerous. EU treaties include the subsidiarity principle for a good reason. This principle, which emphasizes decision-making at the most local level possible, is a cornerstone of the EU's structure. There are immense differences in political opinions among the populations of the EU member countries, as could be expected from a political constellation containing 27 states and spanning the width and breadth of a continent. There are only two options to avoid significant conflicts while maintaining a political union — which should not transpire in any case. The first option is to suppress all opposition, as the Soviet Union, China, and other totalitarian states have done. When Mikhail Gorbachev implemented his democratic reforms, he quickly found precious little holding the USSR's many ethnicities together other than Moscow's strong arm. The second option is the federation, as the United States and the European Union used to do, and Switzerland is still doing. That requires significant autonomy for the state governments.

Discussing divisive political topics at the federal level can be dangerous and lead to political factions. Federations dissolve when irreconcilable differences arise. Every major political crisis in the United States has emerged from the federal government's sudden centralization of authority — including the American Civil War. The major conflicts in the U.S. today revolve around various social and cultural changes that divide the country. EU members are luckier; they can invoke Article 25 to leave the union at any moment, so significant federal-level disagreements within the EU could drive member states away. But, as Brexit showed, the economic, social, and political costs would be enormous — possibly fatal to the EU.

In their heated response to Hungary's law, Mr. Rutte and Ms. von der Leyen are playing with fire. They appear to be advocating for any means, short of violence, to punish Hungary for policies that are not substantially different from the European norm ten, fifteen, or twenty years ago — before the EU started turning ever more sharply to the left — or even today. This aggressive stance goes against the central tenet of the European project: the subsidiarity principle. If this becomes the norm for addressing intra-European disagreements, it will jeopardize the survival of the European Union and raise serious questions about its future in the political sphere.

Although European conservatives today tend to hold a negative view of the European project, European unity was a Christian Democratic idea born from the dreams of not Enlightenment nationalists but anti-Jacobin politicians. There is a strong conservative case for a robust, highly pluralistic but not politically consolidated "European Union," which should not even be called "Union" but rather a "European Business Alliance," a term that reflects a more conservative, less politically integrated vision of European unity.

However, there is a compelling conservative case against the European Union's current trajectory. Europhiles have consistently argued against a uniform and undemocratically liable superstate, and it is on these grounds that they initially supported the European project. A scenario without the EU is preferable to a homogenizing, unaccountable, imperious superstate. Yet, progressive pro-EU parties are now doing what Eurosceptics have consistently warned against — subordinating national interests to the specific values of dominant Western nations. This misuse underscores the need for a more conservative approach to EU governance and highlights the potential negative consequences of the EU's current trajectory.

Ironically, those most fervent about the European experiment are also the ones most willing to jeopardize it by doggedly pursuing their own ideology-based goals. The EU's readiness to penalize Hungary for its LGBTQ law poses a significant threat to the interests of all Europeans, regardless of their stance on the EU. The imposition of progressive political homogeneity is not a sustainable path to unity.

347

Europe urgently needs politicians who are ready to defend the rules and norms that underpin its functioning. Any attempts to penalize member states for making decisions that are not uniformly popular must be denounced. If Brussels continues to erode the authority and independence of member states, the EU's diverse and unique character will be at risk, potentially leading to its demise.

Eurosceptic conservatives and populists have a crucial role to play. They are responsible for ensuring the EU remains true to its core values or for bringing about its end before a departure from these values inflicts lasting harm on all Europeans. Their influence is significant, and even the most ardent Europhiles would agree that a tyrannical, leftist, and globalist EU dictatorship is a worse outcome than no EU at all.

A Tale of Two Europes

April 18, 2021, marked the 70th anniversary of the signing of the Treaty of Paris, which established the European Coal and Steel Community (ECSC). This community, formed by France, West Germany, Italy, and the three Benelux countries, laid the foundation for European integration. Its primary aim was to facilitate economic recovery and help transcend old animosities, particularly by encouraging Franco-German reconciliation. The community's focus on these key industries was a strategic move to ensure that war between these nations, especially France and Germany, would become unthinkable and materially impossible.

The Treaty of Rome, a significant milestone in the evolution of European integration, further solidified this arrangement; in 1957, it gave birth to the European Economic Community (EEC). As envisioned by French President Charles de Gaulle, the EEC was a platform for nation-states to cooperate closely without sacrificing their sovereignty. This EEC was the Europe that de Gaulle and his immediate successor, Georges Pompidou, sought to build, where each state retained its unique essence and identity, regardless of the institutional framework.

However, in 1984, François Mitterrand, France's socialist president, stated: "We have to rid Europe of the Ten of its differences and lead it resolutely along the path to the future" (Mitterrand, 1984). The approval of the Single European Act (SEA) solidified that pathway in 1987. The SEA's provisions significantly increased the power of the bureaucratic apparatus in Brussels and paved the way for further political and economic integration with a series of agreements, treaties, acts, and regulations limiting member states' national sovereignty.

Thus, the eventually evolved European Union became a concoction of left-liberal and socialist "community of values" run mainly by unelected fellow travelers. The European Commission Against Racism and Intolerance (ECRI) illustrates this transmutation. This ECRI is the Council of Europe's "independent human rights monitoring body," founded in 1993. It is one of many examples of how the EU apparatus actively promotes contemporary ideological, political, and cultural orthodoxy while dismissing the Old Continent's authentic heritage. It is particularly obsessive about promoting unlimited, uncontrolled, and primarily Muslim immigration, resulting in massive demographic shifts throughout much of Europe. In a left-liberal democracy, a political system that combines liberal democratic elements with left-wing political ideologies, one has to do everything he does not want to do, but one cannot do anything he should.

Former Soviet Bloc countries, particularly Hungary and Poland, have taken a firm and resolute stand against the Brussels-based EU bureaucracy. Despite their hasty and reckless entry into the EU in 2004, they have adamantly rejected mandatory migrant quotas. Since the migrant flood reached Europe in late 2015, Hungary has even gone so far as to construct a barbed-wire fence along its border with Serbia and Croatia, effectively halting the influx of migrants via the Balkans. This bold action has garnered support from those who believe in preserving national identity and sovereignty. Moreover, Hungarian authorities brusquely deport all illegals managing to enter, despite the European Court of Justice ordering the country to stop doing so ("Hungary has failed to fulfil its obligations under EU law in the area of procedures for granting international protection and returning illegally staying third-country nationals," 2020).

Furthermore, following his fourth general election triumph in 2018, Hungarian Prime Minister Viktor Orbán boldly intensified his confrontation with the EU establishment, proclaiming the end of the era of liberal democracy. His position, starkly contrasting with the EU-promoted leftist liberal democracy, unmistakably underscores the tension in European politics. "We have replaced a shipwrecked liberal democracy with a 21st-century Christian democracy, which guarantees people's freedom and security.

It supports the traditional family model of one man and one woman," he told deputies in his latest acceptance speech (Reuters Staff, 2018).

Mr. Orbán did not just reject liberal democracy; he vehemently asserted that a "liberal non-democracy" had supplanted it, underscoring his resolute rejection of the former. He also highlighted that Brussels, in its current form, cannot address people's issues.

Poland's ruling Law and Justice Party follows much of Viktor Orbán's rhetoric. Its leader and former Prime Minister, Jarosław Kaczyński, supports new European integration based on greater cooperation between sovereign nations in a Christian Europe. Most Poles still support lifestyle choices compatible with the teachings of the Catholic Church, thereby rejecting Brussels' influence. The government of Mateusz Morawiecki remains unwavering in its rejection of migrant quotas.

The experiences of Hungary, Poland, and other former Soviet Bloc countries provide compelling evidence that the one-party communist regimes were less corrosive to a nation's soul than Western-style liberalism. These regimes controlled the state, but their ability to penetrate society was limited. East Germans, Poles, and Hungarians share a more steadfast spirit of national identity, family, and communal values than their fellow Europeans west of the Iron Curtain, underscoring the depth of their cultural values.

The most painful European divide is between the heart and the mind, as the increasing abandonment of spiritual values and moral considerations by Western European residents demonstrates. Man has already lost a sense of place and history, making resistance to rationalistic humanism difficult. That confusion also facilitates the spread of quasi-religious cults such as climate change, transgenderism, and multiculturalism.

America once thought it was in its interest that a united Europe rejoin — those two continents used to share the same civilizational genes. However, today, the corrosive effects of liberalism and socialism have already left multiple permanent scars, debilitating sickness, and the shadow of death on both continents — the game is almost up. The embers of resistance in the East may smolder for a while, desperately trying to rekindle the flame that will torch the Beast of Brussels. I wish them Godspeed and will rejoice if they succeed and mourn if they fail — because the stakes are high. Only they remain the future, the nations composed of those who are still themselves by blood and heritage, proudly and enthusiastically taking up the fight. These are real men — no LGBTQ+ types here — and brothers who cherish the same native soil that has produced the thousand-year-old civilization of their ancestors.

Millions of Eastern Europeans are well aware that the true strength of their nation lies in its monolithic monoculturalism, which is unashamedly monoethnic, masculine in its behavior, and viscerally patriotic. If "diversity is strength," then the United States, the United Kingdom, or France are the future of the Western world, and one can only look at them to understand what that means.

What is wrong with a nation retaining its identity and characteristics as a distinct people? The Eastern European nations' loyalties are not global or "European" *à la Bruxelles* using the European Union. Those nations are not guilt-ridden; they cannot be bothered by microaggressions, systemic racism, or safe spaces. Indeed, they will not destroy the monuments of their historic national heroes and will not be impressed by the new Leader of All Progressive Humanity, either in the Kremlin on the Potomac or the Imperial Chancellery in Brussels.

Those "other peoples" toward the sunset adequately represent the West's civilizational decrepitude and self-hate virus, which now emanates from the global occidental sphere. As things stand during this writing, the occidental team is the allegorical and literal enemy of truth, value, and virtue. Its defeat and others' victory will be a great and glorious event.

Germanism, Merkelism, Wokeism

It is 2021, and a 96-year-old resident of a special-care facility in Germany, a woman of advanced age, found herself in a harrowing situation. Accused of being a Nazi war criminal, she attempted to escape from her accusers. She was apprehended and spent time in jail, pending the outcome of the court proceedings (D'Agata, 2021).

In 1954 and 1962, she testified concerning a concentration camp near Gdansk (then Danzig), where she had to work as a stenographer during World War II. She has never been charged since she was not involved in the deaths of the 65,000 inmates who perished in that camp. She merely belonged to those clerical workers, primarily young girls, whom the German government had ordered to that location but was never associated with the facility's SS units nor set or carried out their procedures. Yet, the politically charged and government-controlled German judicial system treats this elderly lady as a war criminal today, a stark and unwarranted injustice.

This case is a mind-boggling example of German pride and enthusiasm in confessing sins. That means the strange combination of zealous self-debasement and righteousness characterizing the German reputation in recent years for ostentatiously and overeagerly parading their forefathers' iniquities before the world, particularly before the leftist and woke media in other Western countries.

During the 1950s and 1960s, the pro-Western and anti-Soviet West German government — with the connivance of the Western allies — went somewhat grudgingly and halfheartedly after murderous Nazis who had committed real atrocities. However, the German state of today seems motivated by a radically changed leftist disposition affecting the entire justice system, leading to cases like the one involving the 96-year-old woman. Once that system is through with the old lady, it will investigate a 100-year-old invalid suspected of possibly collaborating remotely with some Nazi malefactor (Schulze, 2021).

As these peculiar investigations unfold, it is ironic to note that contemporary German political parties are filled with officials who were once informers for the former East German communist secret police, the notorious Stasi. The Stasi, with its pervasive surveillance and control, had a significant influence on the political landscape of East Germany. Germany's post-communist party, Die Linke ("Left Party"), now parading as "democratic socialist," has openly promoted individuals to leadership positions who, like

Gregor Gysi, held influential roles in the East German communist regime.

Gysi's father, Klaus Gysi, was Minister of Culture in East Germany from 1966 to 1973 and State Secretary for Church Affairs from 1979 to 1988. Of course, he was a member of the East German Communist Party, euphemistically called the Socialist Unity Party (abbreviated SED in German), and after German reunification, the Party of Democratic Socialism (PDS). His son, Gregor Gysi, was the last chairman of the East German Communist Party and controversially rebranded the SED as a "democratic socialist" organization. The SED was first renamed the awkward-sounding Socialist Unity Party of Germany/Party of Democratic Socialism (SED/PDS) and later the Party of Democratic Socialism (PDS). Gregor Gysi remained as party chairman until German reunification in October 1990. In the first all-German elections, he was elected to the Bundestag and is still a member of the German Parliament. In 1998, the Bundestag's investigation committee decided that Gysi had been a Stasi collaborator from 1978 to 1989 and fined him 8,000 German Marks, or about $4,700. However, the Free Democratic Party (FDP) and the PDS disputed the verdict, and Gysi appealed the finding. In any case, he retained his seat in the Bundestag in the 1998 elections. In June 2007, the PDS and WASG (Labour and Social Justice) formally merged to form a united party called Die Linke (The Left).

Individuals like Gregor Gysi have rarely faced the consequences that have befallen the, by comparison, blameless 96-year-old lady. Germany's former foreign minister Joschka Fischer even began his career as a bomb-throwing leftist terrorist — but that inconveniently embarrassing fact hardly ever comes up in the leftist German mainstream media. The German Left has not become a model of tolerance either since Fischer's stunning success as a media star 20 years ago. Accordingly, Die Linke discussed how to eliminate the "influence of old white men" at a recent party meeting.

And who am I to complain about all that? Princeton University's Woodrow Wilson School of Public and International Affairs invited Joschka Fischer to join the school's faculty for one year beginning in September 2006 (Princeton University, 2006).

Mr. Fischer, a high-school dropout who never attended college or university, nor did compulsory military service or any alternatives, became a left-wing militant. As a reward, he was elected to the West German parliament to represent the Green Party in 1983. That started his spectacular political career culminating at a U.S. Ivy League university — where else?

One can compare how the Germans are hounding elderly stenographers of the Third Reich with the "punishing" of their communist East German leaders, or how post-Soviet Russia handles its communist mass murderers. In 1991, Lazar Kaganovich, a Soviet deputy premier under Stalin, died peacefully in bed in Moscow at the age of 97. No attempt was ever made after the collapse of the Soviet Union to prosecute Kaganovich, who ranked as one of the most villainous mass killers. Among his numerous evil deeds, Kaganovich was in charge of carrying out Stalin's collectivization of agriculture in Ukraine, a task that resulted in millions of deaths through starvation during the famine of 1932–33. Later, during the Great Purge, starting in 1936, Kaganovich was instrumental in bringing about hundreds of thousands more deaths. His heinous crimes were comparable to those of any Nazi mass murderer, yet no international call was made for his prosecution or imprisonment.

Thus, the actual mass killers and secret police collaborators who caused untold suffering but belonged to the Left seem to avoid the fate of the poor old lady. The former lackeys of totalitarian communist regimes can do well in today's woke versions of democracy.

Federal elections rearranged Germany's new 736-seat *Bundestag* in September 2021, which the mainstream media declared the end of an era. The new governing coalition of social democratic, green, and nominally liberal parties will change little in Germany's foreign and security policy. This newest leftist team will remain staunchly opposed to any form of a sovereign, i.e., nation-state-like decision-making, and the migratory onslaught from the Third World is sure to continue unabated. Thus, after the German elections, there is a continuation of what has become the standard among liberal-democratic Western nations, including the United States: a relentless line of concessions to the "woke" progressive Left. Yes, there is an end to the Merkel era in Germany — and most people should see this as good news — but nothing of substance has changed.

Six elected political parties have seats in the 20th *Bundestag*, the German federal parliament. Four of the six belong to the reigning political establishment, which is solidly multiculturalist, leftist, and globalist, regardless of party name or color. This establishment, the German Deep State, firmly controls the government bureaucracy, media, money, culture, and most aspects of ordinary Germans' everyday lives.

Merkel's Union coalition (the Christian Democratic Union, CDU, and its Bavarian counterpart, the Christian Social Union, CSU) is the big loser of the German election, having scored just over 24 percent, their worst showing since 1949. The Union is usually falsely described as "center-right," but that designation is misleading: they are more leftist than the Social Democrats were 30 years ago. There is no real "center-right" political party in Germany today.

The Social Democratic Party of Germany (SPD) won the 2021 elections. With 25.7 percent of the vote, the SPD attained its best result since 2005. Because it emerged as the largest party for the first time since 2002, it will be the dominant party in the new red-green-yellow coalition with the Greens and Free Democrats.

The SPD's major coalition partner will be the Green Party, the "wokest" of all leading European political parties, known for its progressive stance. A bizarre group that relentlessly advocates population replacement and sexual deviancy, the Greens took 15 percent of the vote. The failure of the Greens to do even better is a disappointment for their leftist corporate media machine.

The third coalition partner in the SPD-led government will be the "business-friendly" Free Democratic Party (FDP, or "the Liberals"), which gained just above 10 percent of the votes. Best described as embodying the German version of the milquetoast, i.e., timid, unassertive, and spineless, propagating ostensibly classical liberalism with a touch of neoconservative Russophobia, the Liberals are supposed to keep some of the Greens' lunacies in check and maintain a not-too-leftist political aura, thus preserving the mirage of a functional Western political system.

With the CDU/CSU Union playing the role of ever-so-loyal opposition, this sham quadropoly will keep controlling every aspect of Germany's political, economic, and cultural factors more solidly than its equivalents in any other major Western country. The scene is bleak, with the single political party on the right, Alternative for Germany (AfD), reduced through state-organized demonization, government manipulation, internal treason, and police surveillance to about one-tenth of the electorate. For each of the four "regime parties," it is an act of duty to solemnly declare that the AfD will not participate in any coalition discussions under any circumstances. Likewise, the Left party (Die Linke) is also not considered a suitable coalition partner by the four establishment parties in any scenario — at the moment. The Left, the sixth party in the Bundestag, won the required minimum of five percent of the vote, which is still remarkable for the successor, or replacement, of the former East German Communist Party — euphemistically called the Socialist Unity Party of Germany (SED).

Chancellor Angela Merkel's 16-year tenure has been marked by massive violations of the law — especially during the colossal migrant crisis and the euro bailouts — and a "progressive," i.e., self-destructive, energy policy that moved away from using nuclear power plants and coal in the name of climate change based on dubious science. Merkel's claims of "no alternatives" for her dictatorial fiats have further destabilized and undermined an already fragile society — including her own party, the CDU. Nevertheless, her successors stand for the same policies, provenly disastrous though they are.

In reality, the phony quadropoly, i.e., the four-party Deep State Dictatorship, sings in unison on migration, COVID-19 restrictions, climate change, and denying debate or tolerating opposition. Merkel's legacy is her remarkable doggedness and calamitous consistency in every respect. Of course, the dark premonitions were already present following the collapse of the Soviet Union and the reunification of Germany. Merkel merely perpetuated the fashionable Zeitgeist of the end of 20th-century Europe: the collective death wish of a tired civilization. She embodied most of the German electorate: philosophically idealistic, ideologically supine, politically leftist, socially oversensitive, physically comfortable, intellectually lazy, and morally bankrupt — ideal material for any totalitarian dictatorship. It is a tragedy of world-historical proportions.

Having managed to maintain Germany's "clientelist" system, a political strategy that relies on the distribution of benefits to individuals or groups in return for their political support, Angela Merkel will finally disappear from the political scene — just as the first cracks in the German structure are beginning to show.

In December 2021, many years too late, Angela Merkel's reign finally ended. Her tenure lasted sixteen interminable years, from which Europe would soon reap dire consequences, such as economic challenges, social unrest, and political instability, profoundly affecting Germany.

The increasing leftist transformation of Angela Merkel's political party, the CDU, is starkly evident in its present state. Initially rooted in Christian values — and the social market economy developed from those values — the CDU, under Merkel's leadership, has systematically replaced conservative principles with leftist activism. This shift has abandoned the middle class and favored clientelism for influential social target groups and a few large lobbies, leaving a void where conservative principles once stood.

Let me list just a few points that come to mind when looking back over the 16 Merkel years, beginning with the immigration of one to two million "refugees" into Germany. Then, there was the deadly wave of terrorism and the devastation of the Greek economy during the euro crisis. Next came the censorship laws that limited freedom of expression on social networks, followed by direct interference in the outcome of the elections in Thuringia. The disorganized exit from nuclear and coal power and the criminalization of any criticism concerning COVID-19 measures. The politicization of the German Constitutional Court and the undermining of the Dublin Regulation concerning the reception of asylum seekers. The severe energy shortages and the political instrumentalization of the Office for the Protection of the Constitution (the German version of the FBI). The ever-increasing dependence on the Russian energy market and the legalization of same-sex marriage and child adoption by same-sex couples. The trivialization of euthanasia and the incapacitation of the

German defense forces. The failure to keep up with digital transformation and to build a modern internet network. The explosion of the crime rate and the denial of constitutional rights to the unvaccinated. The social polarization of the German population, the refusal to pay adequate and promised NATO contributions, the soaring prices, including real estate and rent, and the dangerously aging infrastructure. Increasing crimes committed against conservative intellectuals and politicians. The endangerment of the car industry. The rise of (Muslim) anti-Semitism. The trivialization of the crimes committed in communist East Germany. The manipulation of the once-free media through a systematic subsidy policy. The blatant interference and propagandistic meddling in the internal affairs of European neighbors and alleged "allies." The introduction of a legal system that limits fundamental rights to combat "global warming." Higher taxes for increased spending. The worsening of ambiguous international relations with the UK, Russia, Turkey, Brazil, Poland, and Hungary, among many others — including the United States.

Admittedly, some of these points are not entirely due to Angela Merkel's actions or solely her responsibility, and their development would have been unthinkable without the leftist radicalization of public opinion seen throughout the Western world. However, Merkel's own party consented to the outcome and the leftward slide, abandoning almost everything that defined Christian democracy three generations ago. Moreover, one should remember the central motivating theme of contemporary German society, built on its historical guilt for the Third Reich's crimes and the moral arrogance arising from the belief that Germany has "learned from her mistakes." Germany has always been a breeding ground for a left-wing philosophy that blended ideological naivety, socialist politics, communist messianism, Western masochism, economic superiority, and the self-satisfaction of being on the "right side of history."

Thus, Merkel, socialized by the East German communist dictatorship, is a product of her time and a catalyst for the increasingly harmful trends of Western civilization. Such trends include the devaluation of human life through policies that promote abortion, euthanasia, and transhumanism. For instance, her support for abortion rights and her stance on euthanasia have been controversial. Additionally, there is the relativization of the family through the absurdities of gender theory and LGBTQ ideology. There is also the destruction of the middle class through anti-capitalist activism that, however, cowardly refrained from confronting big corporations. Furthermore, there is the ousting of "democracy" by the influence of international institutions, politicized courts of law, clientelism, and bureaucracy. The deliberate and unashamed deindustrialization of Europe and the Western world has occurred through transferring assets, capital, and knowledge to Asia and the rantings of global warming theorists. The legal instrumentalization of "human rights" by a European elite intent on imposing ideological choices on the entire continent is also notable. Additionally, there has been the systematic demonization and persecution of conservatism in the name of the "anti-fascist" struggle, and the precipitous demographic decline of indigenous Europeans. The appalling deterioration of schools through the politicization of education and the "democratization" of universities has also taken place. Merkel alone has not caused these developments, but she has supported them and accelerated their growth. Leveraging Germany's political and economic power, influence, and prestige, she has done everything to impose these trends throughout the European Union, alienating many vital partners. For instance, her policies on immigration and multiculturalism have accelerated the growth of parallel societies of immigrants who refuse cultural integration and impose their customs.

It is a question that often arises: What is it about Angela Merkel that fascinates so many people, especially those abroad and on the left? What about the undeniable fact that her power system has consistently prevailed in elections still considered free?

Angela Merkel's ability to maintain power is a testament to her political acumen. She has skillfully utilized her two significant personal assets: being a woman and her ability to conceal any form of personality behind a facade of boring solidity. These traits have earned her the support of feminists and a reputation for competence. Despite a political program more aligned with the Left and the Greens than with conservatism, she has managed to win over middle-class voters. By positioning herself as a bulwark against "populism" and the antithesis of Donald Trump, she has garnered sympathy on the international scene and among the politically correct German electorate.

Ultimately, Merkel's self-destructive long-term policy has enabled Germany to benefit from the consequences of the euro crisis in the short term. Given the instability of markets and the economic and social decline of the European periphery, weakened and troubled by a German-imposed austerity policy, many investors rushed to the German business and financial markets, which are renowned for their "solidity." They flooded these markets with money while accepting meager interest rates, which may have boosted Germany's consumption and production amid a generalized economic crisis. In Germany's interest, this money could and should have been used to create a solid financial reserve, renew the aging infrastructure, and improve the poor state of the German education system, but none of that happened. Instead, the Merkel system immediately turned all this money into various politicized subsidies to sustain its popularity and buy the support of its power base — the media, immigrants, left-wing NGOs, the bureaucracy, environmental initiatives, Big Business, and the Brussels elite — without raising taxes. Thus, today, there is not much left, as evidenced by the state of the German education system, the aging infrastructure, and the lack of a solid financial reserve.

Merkel is stepping away from Germany, which is in crisis and on the brink of economic disaster. The CDU is reeling from a loss of confidence, while the political, media, and educational systems are predominantly influenced by leftist movements. Society is polarized and marked by censorship, denunciations, and ostracism. Merkel's decision not to seek another term as chancellor and to stay out of the election campaign has disrupted the status quo. The CDU suffered a significant blow in the September 2021 elections, paving the way for the socialists and ecologists to take control of the next government. This is the logical outcome of a 16-year-long ideological shift away from Christian democracy toward the Left, with potentially far-reaching consequences.

After running the country to keep her handlers happy and herself in power for as long as possible, Angela Merkel slowly disappears from the scene just as the first cracks begin to show. Bled dry but flooded with migrants, Germany is teetering on the brink of destabilizing an entire continent of which it is the main economic and political engine. Ironically, today's generation will probably not remember the Merkel era as the real reason for the impending crisis that will engulf it, but rather as the "good old days" before the last façades of the post-war social, economic, and political paradigm crumbled for good. However, those "good old days" were characterized by a strong economy, a united West German society, and a respected political system.

Solving the "German Problem" — A Long-Overdue Wish

The new German governing parties have laid out a plan that could ruin Germany and Europe in four to five years. The Social Democrats, the Greens, and the Free Democrats have agreed on a government program that will define the future of Germany if personal ambition does not interfere. Based on historical experience, the "German future" will spread throughout Europe — leaving behind a trail of destruction, as it usually does.

In Germany today, apart from a few minor parties, no political force stands on the ground of reality, and the entire political landscape needs a rational and balanced approach. The political parties, whether winning or losing elections, are ideologically driven to the extreme. The single opposition party, the Alternative for Germany (or "AfD," as it is known in German), facing the united (socialist, green, and liberal) Left, is also an irrational German formation. It is devoid of a coherent, rational system of viewpoints and is not based on the Right or conservatism but instead on a set of ideological and emotional fragments.

The Germans have retained their worst qualities from under the post-World War II ruins, namely fanatic idealism, naive voluntarism, attraction to the irrational, and blind faith in the forced transformation of society. They still want to perform a miracle by using sheer will and brutal force to save the "climate" — regardless of space, time, or the laws of physics. They do not want to deport people any longer but to import them. For the sake of variety, they do not wish to persecute homosexuals this time but persuade heterosexuals to embrace all the sexual perversions that the public has attributed to the SA (*Sturmabteilung*) leadership in happier times.

This whole nonsense would not occur to the average German. But after reading, listening to, and watching it in the mainstream media, which distribute the uniformly same propaganda typical of the "complete freedom" apparent in all liberal democracies, he can no longer think or believe in anything else. The state, party leaders, and cultural and scientific elites parrot the same message — voluntarily, naturally, "freely," and "spontaneously."

In this sense, the Germans voted "freely" for the madness that would now befall them. The average German stubbornly believes the state and politicians — more than other people in Central and Eastern Europe. Germans generally believe, admire, and follow the powerful: The Emperor, the *Führer*, or the Chancellor knows what he is doing. Nor does it shake their faith how often this unconditional trust has not produced much success in the last hundred-plus years of history.

In Germany, establishing *climate communism* is currently the primary political goal of the new governing parties. For them, the government program is Scripture because it is officially written, signed, and approved (it must have a seal); therefore, they will execute it even if it turns out they have to demolish villages and towns, evict people, or the wind does not blow, and the sun does not shine. The idea of designating two percent of Germany's territory for installing wind turbines is proof that someone can have a mental health condition without any visible signs. Of course, wind turbines are those massive, ugly structures made from nonreusable material and are not recyclable when their warranty expires, so they will be buried somewhere in the greenest way possible.

Germany is one of the most densely populated areas in Europe, and from now on, one of its attractions will be the ability to see at least one "windmill" from any point in the country and even hear it in a "lucky" case. Moreover, one will also have an excellent chance to stand above a dead and buried windmill. It is also likely that the Greens' demand will become a real threat, and all building owners will be required to install solar panels on their roofs. The costs are, of course, to be borne by the owners.

It is also natural that the new governing coalition will be much more pro-immigration than the previous one because German ingenuity can make things that are already going badly even more catastrophic than if they had been left alone. Thus, it is also clear that gender ideology will be introduced and enforced with the determination of the Nuremberg Laws.

And who cares about the costs? Not the Germans; they are not worried about it, as rising energy prices are not a tax increase but merely the "passing on of the cost to the consumer" — because the liberal Free Democrats are very much opposed to an open and direct tax increase. On the other hand, passing on the costs is "natural." The tens of millions of wage-earners who maintain their standard of living in the German middle class will slide down into the lower middle class, but that is, after all, their problem; they voted for it.

This shock will hardly affect migrants, who will benefit from some aid and receive even increased support, just as it will not impact the wealthiest people. However, the cost increases will burden small businesses and energy-intensive medium-sized enterprises and quickly put the entire German economy on a downward slope, with its competitive advantages already challenged by high energy prices.

All this is the natural consequence of the regime's energy transition concept to shut down most of the stably producing nuclear power plants next year — there seems to be a government program to eradicate energy stability in Germany. There is no discussion about what genuinely existing and non-imaginary technologies could achieve the "climate goals," or what can be done with the "New

Germans," with two-thirds of Syrian refugees still living on welfare (MacGregor, 2021).

Incidentally, German power outages could also cause disruptions in Central Europe's electric grid. And since the Germans will always prefer having darkness somewhere other than in Germany, they will certainly not tolerate others having electricity while they do not.

The real bad news is that the Germans, through the EU, want to extend three of their projects to all reluctant Member States. The first retaliatory weapon is the resettlement of migrants, the second is gender violence, and the third is total climate neutrality based on non-existent technologies and technical possibilities.

In comparison, the plan to occupy Moscow six weeks after the beginning of the German attack on the Soviet Union in 1941 was a reality itself. However, the irrational and arrogant acts of today's Germany were not typical before 1933, and after 1945, the new and "democratic" West German governments directly avoided them.

But the fanatic, insolent, contemptuous politicians of the Left are not even lying to the German people today. They are not telling them the usual political deceptions or making promises they do not intend to keep — they honestly take the final victory entirely seriously. And the Europeans will be sacrificed for it just as easily and nonchalantly as in World War II. Germany is merely a few "green steps" away from failing to secure the energy supply for its population and industry, even at very high energy prices. And no one is even bombing them today; it is just simple suicide, which they want to extend to the rest of Europe, too.

The European version of wokeness is unfolding under the watchful eyes of Germany's new leftist government. Europe's leftists are elated about this; Germany will advocate for Europeanism with its social, equality, environmental, fiscal, and digital policies. Furthermore, the dominant German government is set to develop the EU into a central federal state, paving the way for a new superstate.

Moreover, if Germany's political, economic, and long-term civilizational interests were to ignore the shackles of moralistic rhetoric, it could be argued that the Federal Republic of Germany has a more natural community of long-term geopolitical interests with Russia than with the U.S.

A "neo-Bismarckian" German policy toward Russia would make sense from the German perspective and could be a game-changer. Under Chancellor Bismarck, the towering genius of Europe's 19th-century diplomacy, Germany and Russia last had a genuine strategic partnership rooted in the compatibility of interests and the absence of insurmountable obstacles. One could renew such a partnership, and the Germans would undoubtedly continue it if it were only up to them. Germany and Russia's fundamental compatibility rests on the fact that they are both traditional European nation-states pursuing limited objectives by limited means — in contrast to the leaders of the United States, who follow the special interests of lobbies and the Deep State. It is not solely due to American insight or discernment that this German-Russian strategic option has been rejected by Berlin — so far. The potential impact of any German-Russian strategic option, if accepted, could lead to significant geopolitical shifts.

From a realist perspective, it is in the national interest of the United States to develop a close partnership with Russia and a strategy of equal proximity *vis-à-vis* the German-dominated European Union and China. An alliance between the European Union and its continental neighbor, Russia, would create a gigantic Eurasian and most likely anti-American empire with virtually unlimited human, natural, and economic resources. Such development could significantly shift the balance of power in Europe and, at least indirectly, the world.

The only way out of this predicament, and a long-ignored alternative in the national interest of the American people, is a direct American-Russian association, if not an alliance. With such an accord, the world's two most significant military powers would peacefully come together, becoming friends and business partners. This alliance could be a beacon of hope for global peace and stability while preventing, i.e., short-circuiting, the EU from a strategic linkup with Russia and Asia. As the United States' strategic interests are already in Asia, committing Russia to an American ally would secure U.S. control over the Asian continent and dominance over the Northern Hemisphere while denying another German-Russian Pact, an EU-Russian partnership, and any possible direct Sino-European Axis in the future. By tying Russia's strategic position and interests to the U.S., America could easily position itself worldwide, assuring peace, business, and resources.

Given the potential advantages to America, one might wonder why U.S. political leadership seems to ignore, prevent, and reject mutually beneficial arrangements between the American and Russian peoples. What could be the reasons behind this stance?

Bibliography

TIME Essay. (1970, January 12). Convergence: The Uncertain Meeting of East and West. *TIME*, p. Vol. 95 No. 2.

Spengler, O. (2021). *Decline of the West.* London: Arktos Media Ltd.

Talbott, S. (1992, July 20). America Abroad: The Birth of the Global Nation. *TIME*, p. Vol. 140 No. 3.

Talbott, S. (2008). *The Great Experiment.* New York: Simon & Schuster.

Burnham, J. (1941). *The Managerial Revolution: What is Happening in the World.* New York: John Day Company.

Kirk, M., & Madsen, H. (1989). *After the Ball: How America Will Conquer Its Fear and Hatred of Gays in the 90's.* Doubleday: New York.

Beauvoir, S. d. (1953). *The Second Sex.* New York: Knopf.

Beauvoir, S. d. (1976). *The Ethics of Ambiguity.* New York: Citadel Press.

Huxley, A. (2004). *Brave New World.* London: Vintage Classics.

Huxley, A. (2006). *Brave New World Revisited.* New York: Harper Perennial Modern Classics.

Douglass, F. (2016). *Narrative of the Life of Frederick Douglass.* Mineola, New York: Dover Publications, Incorporated.

Powell, J. (2012, February 2022). The Economic Leadership Secrets of Benito Mussolini. *Forbes.*

Coudenhove-Kalergi, R. N. (2019). *Pan-Europa*. Independently published.

Marx, K., & Engels, F. (2014). *The Communist Manifesto*. New York: International Publishers Co.

Marx, K. (1843). *A Contribution to the Critique of Hegel's Philosophy of Right — Introduction*. Retrieved from https://www.marxists.org: https://www.marxists.org/archive/marx/works/1843/critique-hpr/intro.htm

Fukuyama, F. (1992). *The End of History and the Last Man*. New York: Free Press.

Life Magazine. (1939, March 6). Fascism in America. *Life Magazine*.

Tocqueville, A. d. (2018). *The Old Regime and the Revolution*. Lagos, Nigeria: Origami Books of Parrésia Publishers Ltd.

Mussolini, B. (1933). *The Political and Social Doctrine of Fascism*. London: Hogarth Press.

Berdyaev, N. (2015). *The Russian Idea*. Warsaw, Poland: Andesite Press.

Chernyshevsky, N. (1989). *What Is to Be Done?* Ithaca, New York: Cornell University Press.

Solzhenitsyn, A. I. (1974). *Letter to the Soviet Leaders*. New York: Harper & Row.

Dostoevsky, F. (2015). *The Possessed*. Scotts Valley, California: CreateSpace Independent Publishing Platform.

Solzhenitsyn, A. I. (2003). *The Gulag Archipelago*. London: The Harwill Press.

Solzhenitsyn, A. I. (1980). *The Oak and the Calf: Memoirs of a Literary Life*. Philadelphia: Franklin Library.

Solzhenitsyn, A. I. (1978, June 8). *A World Split Apart: Solzhenitsyn's Commencement Address Harvard University.* Retrieved from https://www.solzhenitsyncenter.org: https://www.solzhenitsyncenter.org/a-world-split-apart

Solzhenitsyn, A. I. (2017). *March 1917: The Red Wheel, Node III, Book 1.* Notre Dame, Indiana: University of Notre Dame Press.

Berdyaev, N. A. (1918). *Spirits of the Russian Revolution.* Retrieved from http://www.berdyaev.com: http://www.berdyaev.com/berdiaev/berd_lib/1918_299.html

Solzhenitsyn, A. I. (1993, September 25). *A Reflection on the Vendée Uprising.* Retrieved from https://www.solzhenitsyncenter.org: https://www.solzhenitsyncenter.org/reflection-vendee-uprising

Lievens, M. (2011). Singularity and Repetition in Carl Schmitt's Vision of History. *Journal of the Philosophy of History*, 105–129, Volume 5: Issue 1.

European Community. (1987, July 1). *https://eur-lex.europa.eu/EN/legal-content/summary/.* Retrieved from https://eur-lex.europa.eu: https://eur-lex.europa.eu/EN/legal-content/summary/the-single-european-act.html

Smith, M. S. (1992). The Méline Tariff as Social Protection: Rhetoric or Reality? *International Review of Social History*, Volume 37 , Issue 2 , August 1992 , pp. 230 - 243.

List, F. (2013). *The National System of Political Economy.* Wilmington, Delaware: Vernon Press.

Le Monde. (2003, September 12). Jean-Claude Trichet critique Paris : "I'm not a French man". *Le Monde.*

Kiska, R. (2019, December 12). *https://www.acton.org/religion-liberty/volume-29-number-3*. Retrieved from https://www.acton.org: https://www.acton.org/religion-liberty/volume-29-number-3/antonio-gramscis-long-march-through-history

Forbes, R. P. (2007). *The Missouri Compromise and Its Aftermath: Slavery and the Meaning of America*. Chapel Hill: The University of North Carolina Press.

Mowry, G. E. (1966). Sober Second Thoughts on Van Buren, The Albany Regency, & Wall Street Conspiracy. *The Journal of American History*, Volume 53, Number 1, June 1966.

U.S. Congress. (1883, January 16). *Milestone Documents, Pendleton Act (1883)*. Retrieved from U.S. National Archives Web site: https://www.archives.gov/milestone-documents/pendleton-act#

Darrah, D. (1939, October 2). All Britons 20 to 22 Called. *Chicago Daily Tribune*, p. 1.

Engdahl, F. W. (2011). *Full Spectrum Dominance: Totalitarian Democracy in the New World Order*. Palm Desert, California: Progressive Press.

TIME Foreign News. (1956, November 26). "We Will Bury You!". *TIME*, p. Vol. LXVIII No. 22.

Tocqueville, A. d. (1969). Democracy in America. In A. d. Tocqueville, *Democracy in America* (p. p. 703). New York: Harper & Row Publishers.

Provencher-Gravel, A. (2008). *The Ambiguities of Rousseau's Conception of Happiness (dissertation)*. Boston: Boston College.

Rawls, J. (1999). *A Theory of Justice.* Cambridge, Massachusetts: Belknap Press.

Hobbes, T. (2017). *Leviathan.* London: Penguin Classics.

Jasso, C. (2019). The Life of Julia: A Failed Progressive Political Campaign. *Pepperdine Policy Review*, Vol. 11, Article 1.

Locke, J. (1980). *Second Treatise of Government.* Indianapolis, Indiana: Hackett Publishing Company, Inc.

Hamilton, A., Jay, J., & Madison, J. (2014). *The Federalist Papers.* Mineola, New York: Dover Publications, Inc.

Arendt, H. (1973). *The Origins of Totalitarianism.* San Diego, California: Harcourt, Inc.

Au-Yeung, A. (2020, July 8). Jeff Bezos' Net Worth Hits All-Time High Of More Than $180 Billion. *Forbes.*

Horch, A. (2020, May 4). *www.cnbc.com/2020/05/04/.* Retrieved from CNBC LLC: https://www.cnbc.com/2020/05/04/almost-half-of-america-now-carrying-credit-card-debt-and-more-of-it.html

Simons, B. (2015, November 4). *www.afrikanblackcoalition.org/2015/09/.* Retrieved from www.afrikanblackcoalition.org: https://www.afrikanblackcoalition.org/2015/09/a-new-constitution-or-the-bullet/

Abraham, V. (2021, June 3). *www.teenvogue.com/story.* Retrieved from www.teenvogue.com: https://www.teenvogue.com/story/united-states-needs-new-constitution

Stasio, M. (2019, March 31). *https://variety.com/2019/legit/reviews*. Retrieved from https://variety.com: https://variety.com/2019/legit/reviews/what-the-constitution-means-to-me-review-1203177085/

Benner, K. (2021, November 16). F.B.I. Set Plan to Track Threats Against School Boards and Teachers. *The New York Times.*

Wulfsohn, J. A. (2021, November 6). *www.foxnews.com/media/*. Retrieved from www.foxnews.com: https://www.foxnews.com/media/fbi-raids-home-james-okeefe-ashley-biden-diary-project-veritas

Cohen, M. (2021, November 18). *https://edition.cnn.com/2021/11/18/politics/*. Retrieved from www.cnn.com: https://edition.cnn.com/2021/11/18/politics/steele-dossier-reckoning/index.html

Reuters Staff. (2021, July 14). *www.reuters.com/article/*. Retrieved from www.reuters.com: https://www.reuters.com/article/us-usa-racism-un-idCAKBN2EK05Z

Murica, L. (2021, July 12). *www.lawenforcementtoday.com*. Retrieved from www.lawenforcementtoday.com: https://www.lawenforcementtoday.com/fbi-encourages-people-to-snitch-on-family-and-friends-for-suspicious-behaviors/

Chu, J. (2021, June 8). *www.congress.gov/bill/*. Retrieved from www.congress.gov: https://www.congress.gov/bill/117th-congress/house-bill/3755

Davidson, D. J. (2003). *The Wisdom of Theodore Roosevelt.* New York: Kensington Publishing Corp.

Lincoln, A. (1859, April 6). *https://www.abrahamlincolnonline.org/lincoln/speeches/*. Retrieved

from https://www.abrahamlincolnonline.org: https://
www.abrahamlincolnonline.org/lincoln/speeches/pierce.htm

Adams, J., Franklin, B., Jefferson, T., Sherman, R., &
Livingston, R. (1776, July 4). *https://www.archives.gov/
founding-docs/*. Retrieved from https://www.archives.gov/
founding-docs/declaration-transcript

Lynch, A. (2002). Woodrow Wilson and the Principle of
'National Self-Determination': A Reconsideration. *Review of
International Studies*, Vol. 28, No. 2 (Apr., 2002), pp.
419-436 (18 pages).

Bigart, H. (1970, May 9). War Foes Here Attacked By
Construction Workers. *The New York Times*.

Melchiondo, K. R. (2021, October 29). *https://
www.bilzin.com/we-think-big/insights/publications/2021/10/*.
Retrieved from www.bilzin.com: https://www.bilzin.com/we-
think-big/insights/publications/2021/10/privacy-portal-30

Adams, J. (1798, October 11). *https://
founders.archives.gov/documents/*. Retrieved from https://
founders.archives.gov: https://founders.archives.gov/
documents/Adams/99-02-02-3102

Goldsmith, J. (2020, October 28). *https://www.project-
syndicate.org/commentary/*. Retrieved from https://
www.project-syndicate.org/: https://www.project-
syndicate.org/commentary/does-united-states-still-interfere-
in-foreign-elections-by-jack-goldsmith-2020-10

Hadley, D. P. (2019). *The Rising Clamor: The American
Press, the Central Intelligence Agency, and the Cold War*.
Lexington: The University Press of Kentucky.

Fredericks, B. (2020, June 26). Russia secretly offered
bounties on US troops to Taliban, report says. *New York Post*.

Population of the United States in 1860: California. (1860). *https://www2.census.gov/library/publications/ decennial/1860/.* Retrieved from https://www2.census.gov/: https://www2.census.gov/library/publications/decennial/ 1860/population/1860a-06.pdf

Aisch, G., Gebeloff, R., & Quealy, K. (2014, August 19). Where We Came From and Where We Went, State by State. *The New York Times.*

U.S. Department of the Interior, National Park Service. (2001). *National Historic Trail Feasibility Study and Environmental Assessment.* U.S. Department of the Interior, National Park Service, 2001.

U.S. Census. (2020). *https://www.census.gov/library/ stories/state-by-state.* Retrieved from https:// www.census.gov: https://www.census.gov/library/stories/ state-by-state/california-population-change-between-census- decade.html

Budiman, A., & Ruiz, N. G. (2021, April 29). *www.pewresearch.org.* Retrieved from www.pewresearch.org: https://www.pewresearch.org/fact- tank/2021/04/29/key-facts-about-asian-americans/

Chowkwanyun, M., & Segall, J. (2012, August 27). *https://www.bloomberg.com/news/articles/2012-08-27/.* Retrieved from https://www.bloomberg.com: https:// www.bloomberg.com/news/articles/2012-08-27/how-an- exclusive-los-angeles-suburb-lost-its-whiteness

Budiman, A. (2020, August 20). *https:// www.pewresearch.org/fact-tank/2020/08/20.* Retrieved from https://www.pewresearch.org/: https://www.pewresearch.org/ fact-tank/2020/08/20/key-findings-about-u-s-immigrants/

Myers, J., & Willon, P. (2021, October 22). California's recall election officially ends as Newsom prepares for 2022. *Los Angeles Times*.

Beam, A. (2021, May 8). *https://apnews.com/article*. Retrieved from https://apnews.com: https://apnews.com/article/california-health-immigration-coronavirus-pandemic-d4df0f6a2eef7a3dc4a6d27c65df7b84

Kendi, I. X. (2019, October 3). Pass an Anti-Racist Constitutional Amendment. *Politico*.

Globerman, S. (2021, May 18). *https://www.fraserinstitute.org/studies/*. Retrieved from https://www.fraserinstitute.org: https://www.fraserinstitute.org/studies/primer-on-modern-monetary-theory

United Nations. (2015). Paris Agreement. *Paris Agreement*. Paris: United Nations.

OECD. (2021). *Climate Finance and the USD 100 Billion Goal Forward-looking Scenarios of Climate Finance Provided and Mobilised by Developed Countries in 2021-2025 Technical Note*. Washington DC: OECD Publishing.

OECD. (2021, October 21). *https://www.oecd.org/tax/*. Retrieved from https://www.oecd.org: https://www.oecd.org/tax/international-community-strikes-a-ground-breaking-tax-deal-for-the-digital-age.htm

Summers, L. H. (2021, October 31). A triumph for Detroit over Davos. *The Washington Post*.

EDP Network. (2018). *Democracy Promotion in Times of Uncertainty: Trends and Challenges*. Frankfurt a.M.: Peace Research Institute Frankfurt.

Toomey, P. J. (2021, November 18). *https:// www.banking.senate.gov/newsroom/minority/*. Retrieved from https://www.banking.senate.gov/newsroom: https:// www.banking.senate.gov/newsroom/minority/toomey-ive- never-seen-a-nominee-with-more-radical-ideas

Omarova, S. T. (2020, October 20). *https:// papers.ssrn.com/sol3/*. Retrieved from https:// papers.ssrn.com: https://papers.ssrn.com/sol3/papers.cfm? abstract_id=3715735

WSJ Opinion. (2006, July 29). Socialism in Reverse. *The Wall Street Journal.*

CRFB Budgets & Projections. (2020, April 13). *https:// www.crfb.org/blogs*. Retrieved from https://www.crfb.org: https://www.crfb.org/blogs/budget-projections-debt-will- exceed-size-economy-year

Seth, S. (2021, December 30). *https:// www.investopedia.com/articles/investing/040115/*. Retrieved from https://www.investopedia.com: https:// www.investopedia.com/articles/investing/040115/reasons- why-china-buys-us-treasury-bonds.asp

Congressional Budget Office. (2020, March). *Federal Debt: A Primer.* Washington DC: Congressional Budget Office. Retrieved from https://www.cbo.gov/publication/ 56309

U.S. Department of Health and Human Services. (2021). *https://www.hhs.gov/sites/default/files/*. Retrieved from https://www.hhs.gov: https://www.hhs.gov/sites/default/files/ fy-2021-budget-in-brief.pdf

U.S. Social Security Administration. (2021). *https:// www.ssa.gov/policy/docs/statcomps/supplement/2021/.*

Retrieved from https://www.ssa.gov: https://www.ssa.gov/policy/docs/statcomps/supplement/2021/oasdi.html

U.S. Department of Defense. (2020, February 10). *https://www.defense.gov/News/Releases/Release/Article/2079489/*. Retrieved from https://www.defense.gov: https://www.defense.gov/News/Releases/Release/Article/2079489/dod-releases-fiscal-year-2021-budget-proposal/

Tax Policy Center. (2019). *https://www.taxpolicycenter.org/briefing-book/*. Retrieved from https://www.taxpolicycenter.org: https://www.taxpolicycenter.org/briefing-book/what-are-sources-revenue-federal-government

Eder, F., & von der Burchard, H. (2021, June 23). *https://www.politico.eu/article/*. Retrieved from https://www.politico.eu: https://www.politico.eu/article/european-commission-legal-steps-hungarys-anti-lgbtq-law/

Stares, J. (2021, June 24). *https://www.telegraph.co.uk/world-news/2021/06/24/*. Retrieved from https://www.telegraph.co.uk: https://www.telegraph.co.uk/world-news/2021/06/24/eu-leaders-vow-fight-discrimination-bitter-row-hungary-anti/

O'Neill, A. R. (2004). Recognition of Same-Sex Marriage in the European Community: The European Court of Justice' s Ability to Dictate Social Policy. *Cornell International Law Journal*, Volume 37, Issue 1, Article 6.

Library of Congress. (2016, January 15). *https://www.loc.gov/item/global-legal-monitor/2016-01-15/*. Retrieved from https://www.loc.gov: https://www.loc.gov/item/global-legal-monitor/2016-01-15/netherlands-new-

regulation-on-late-term-abortions-and-terminations-of-lives-
of-neonates/

Oxfam International. (2016, May 23). *https://
www.oxfam.org/en/press-releases/*. Retrieved from https://
www.oxfam.org: https://www.oxfam.org/en/press-releases/
netherlands-top-eu-tax-haven-commission-data-shows

Bahceli, Y. (2015, August 28). *https://www.reuters.com/
article/*. Retrieved from https://www.reuters.com: https://
www.reuters.com/article/uk-dutch-un-tradition-
idUKKCN0QX1O420150828

Mitterrand, F. (1984, May 24). *https://www.cvce.eu/
content/publication/2001/10/19/*. Retrieved from https://
www.cvce.eu: https://www.cvce.eu/content/publication/
2001/10/19/cdd42d22-fe8e-41bb-bfb7-9b655113ebcf/
publishable_en.pdf

"Hungary has failed to fulfil its obligations under EU
law in the area of procedures for granting international
protection and returning illegally staying third-country
nationals", Case C-808/18 (Court of Justice of the European
Union December 17, 2020).

Reuters Staff. (2018, May 10). *https://www.reuters.com/
article/*. Retrieved from https://www.reuters.com: https://
www.reuters.com/article/us-hungary-orban-vision-
idUSKBN1IB206

D'Agata, C. (2021). *96-year-old woman on trial in
Germany for suspected Nazi war crimes.* New York: CBS
News.

Schulze, R. (2021, October 12). *Justiceinfo.net.*
Retrieved from https://www.justiceinfo.net: https://

www.justiceinfo.net/en/83153-why-try-a-100-year-old-nazi.html

Princeton University. (2006, June 17). *https://www.princeton.edu/news/2006/06/17/*. Retrieved from https://www.princeton.edu: https://www.princeton.edu/news/2006/06/17/wilson-school-names-germanys-joschka-fischer-visiting-lecturer

MacGregor, M. (2021, July 14). *https://www.infomigrants.net/en/post/33597/*. Retrieved from https://www.infomigrants.net: https://www.infomigrants.net/en/post/33597/germany-twothirds-of-syrian-refugees-unable-to-support-themselves

www.ingramcontent.com/pod-product-compliance
Lightning Source LLC
Chambersburg PA
CBHW070327090426
42733CB00012B/2388